Contents

Foreword by the Publisher ... **i**
The Philosophy of Ṣalāt al-Jumuʿah ... ii
Forty Ḥadīth on Ṣalāt al-Jumuʿah and Ṣalāt al Jamāʿah ... iv
Comprehensive Rulings on Ṣalāt al-Jumuʿah ... vii
Scholarly Analysis on Ṣalāt al-Jumuʿah ... viii
Prayers and Supplications ... ix
Supplication (Duʿāʾ) after Ṣalāt al-ʿAṣr ... x
Supplication (Duʿāʾ) for Friday ... x
Prostration (Sajdah) of Thanks ... xi
Supplication (Duʿāʾ) for Muslim Unity ... xi
Visitation (Ziyārah) for Friday ... xii
Ziyārat Āle Yāsīn ... xii
Visitation of the Immaculates ... xiii
Supplication (Duʿāʾ) for the 12th Imam ... xiii
Supplication (Duʿāʾ) from Imam al-Mahdī ... xiii
Importance of This Work ... xv
A Word on the Translation ... xvi
Conclusion ... xvii

Philosophy of Ṣalāt al-Jumuʿah ... **19**
The Main Reason for the Gathering on Friday ... 23
Contents of the Jumuʿah Sermons ... 27
A Ḥadīth in Relation to the Sermons of Ṣalāt al-Jumuʿah ... 33

Forty Ḥadīth: Ṣalāt al-Jumuʿah and Ṣalāt al-Jamāʿah ... **41**
Ṣalāt al-Jumuʿah: In the Quran ... 45

1. Merits of Participating in Ṣalāt al-Jumuʿah ... **45**
1. Ḥajj of the Deprived ... 45
2. Performing Ḥajj and ʿUmrah Every Friday ... 46
3. Recommended Times for Hastening ... 46
4. Steps that Protect an Individual ... 47
5. Measure of One's Spiritual Proximity to Allah ... 47
6. Insurance Policy to Enter Paradise ... 47
7. The Traveller ... 48

2. Necessity of Participation in Ṣalāt al-Jumuʿah ... **49**
8. Minimal Amount of Participants ... 49

9. Radius for Participation 50
10. Who is Excused from Attending? 50
11. Consequences for Intentionally Abandoning 51
12. Outcome of Spiritual Negligence (Ghaflah) 52
13. Demolition of a Community 52
14. A Way to Identify a Hypocrite 52
15. Working During Prayer Time 53
16. Incarcerated Muslims 53
17. How to Prepare 54

3. Etiquettes to Observe 54
18. Manners to Observe 54
19. Recompense for Sins of the Previous Week 55
20. The Angels are Obligated to Record 56
21. Greeting the Individuals Attending 56
22. The Political and Ethical Program for a Believer 57
23. Remaining Silent During Time of Sermons 58
24. The Sermon is Equivalent to Two-Rakaʿāt of Ṣalāt 59
25. Acceptance of One's Supplications 59

4. Merits of Participation in Ṣalāt al-Jamāʿah 60
26. The Greatness of Congregational Prayers 60
27. Wisdom behind Congregational Prayers 61
28. Two Pages of Liberation 62
29. Lines of Those in Jihād (Sacred Struggle) 62
30. The First Rows of the Prayers 63

5. The Necessity of Ṣalāt al-Jamāʿah 63
31. Being Present in the Community 63
32. Severing Relations with Some People 64
33. Not Giving Importance 65
34. Penalty for Intentionally being Absent 66
35. The Scale of Recognition 66

6. Manners of Ṣalāt al-Jamāʿah 67
36. Rushing to be Present 67
37. The Prayer Leader 67
38. Unification of the Hearts 67
39. The Prayer Leader is Not Accountable 68
40. Being Swift in Completing the Prayers 68

Practical Rulings of Ṣalāt al-Jumuʿah 71

1.1 Introduction 71

1.2 Jurisprudential Rulings 73
1.2.1 Method of Performing Ṣalāt al-Jumuʿah 75
1.2.2 Conditions for its Obligation 76
1.2.3 Condition One: Time 76
1.2.4 Condition Two: Participants 78
1.2.5 Condition Three: Prayer Leader (Imam) 78
1.2.5.1 Conditions of the Prayer Leader (Imam) 79
1.2.5.2 One: Age of Maturity (Bāligh) 81
1.2.5.3 Two and Three: Sane (ʿĀqil) and Legitimate Birth 81
1.2.5.4 Four: Shīʿa Ithnā-ʿAsherī 82
1.2.5.5 Five: Just (ʿĀdil) 83
1.2.5.6 Six: Quality of Recitation (Qirāʾat) 84
1.2.5.7 Seven: Gender 87
1.2.5.8 Eight: Never a Recipient of the Islamic Penal Code 88
1.2.5.9 Nine: Method of Performing the Prayers 88
1.2.5.10 Ten: Direction of Prayers (Qiblah) 89
1.2.5.11 Eleven: Prayers Must be Correct 89

1.3 Conditions for a Correct Ṣalāt al-Jumuʿah 93
1.3.1 Condition One: Congregation 93
1.3.2 Condition Two: Two Sermons 94
1.3.3 Condition Three: Physical Distance 95
1.3.4 Condition Four: General Conditions 97

1.4 Participation in Ṣalāt al-Jumuʿah 97
1.4.1 Women and Ṣalāt al-Jumuʿah 99
1.4.2 Travellers Taking Part 99
1.4.3 Ṣalāt al-Jumuʿah of Travellers 99
1.4.4 Speaking During the Sermons 100
1.4.5 Listening to the Sermons 101
1.4.6 Missing the Two Sermons 101

1.5 Those Who Do Not Attend Ṣalāt al-Jumuʿah 101

1.6 Business Dealings During the Time of Adhān 102

1.7 Step by Step Method of the Ṣalāt 102

1.8 Conclusion 139

Ṣalāt al-Jumuʿah During the Occultation (Ghaybah)........141

Abstract........141

The Primary Discussion........144

Mālikī School of Jurisprudence........148
Shāfiʿī School of Jurisprudence........150
Ḥanbalī School of Jurisprudence........151
Ḥanafī School of Jurisprudence........152
Shīʿa Imāmīyyah Jurisprudence........157
Non-Legitimacy of Ṣalāt al-Jumuʿah in the Occultation........159
Second Argument: Established Practice........161
Third Argument: Opposition to Consensus (Ijmāʿ)........166
Fourth Argument: The Dilemma Between Obligation... 167
Fifth Argument: Likelihood of Corruption in the Texts........170
Sixth Argument: The Narrations........173

Last Word: Reviving the Spirit of Ṣalāt al-Jumuʿah........181

1. Reflecting on the Importance of Ṣalāt al-Jumuʿah........181
2. The Spiritual Impact of Ṣalāt al-Jumuʿah........182
3. Ṣalāt al-Jumuʿah as a Social Catalyst........183
4. Addressing Contemporary Challenges........184
5. The Role of Youth and Future Generations........185
6. A Call to Action........186

The Soul's Journey on Fridays........189

1. Duas and Ziyārat: Anchoring the Soul in Devotion........190
2. The Mental Health Benefits of Spiritual Connection........190
3. Importance of Connection to the Ahlul Bayt ﷺ........191
4. Friday as a Gateway to the Mercy of Allah ﷻ........192
5. A Call to Action: Reclaiming the Blessings of Friday........193

Duʿāʾ after Ṣalāt al-ʿAṣr........195

Supplication (Duʿāʾ) for Friday........199

Prostration (Sajdah) of Thanks........205

Prostration of Gratitude (Sajdah al-Shukr)........207

Supplication (Duʿāʾ) for Muslim Unity........209

Special Visitation (Ziyārah) for the Day of Friday........213

Supplication (Duʿāʾ) for the 12th Imam........219

Transliteration Table

The method of transliteration of Islamic terminology from the ʿArabic language has been carried out according to the standard transliteration table mentioned below.

ء	ʾ	س	s	م	m
ا	a	ش	sh	ن	n
ب	b	ص	ṣ	و	w
ت	t	ض	ḍ	ه	h
ث	th	ط	ṭ	ي	y
ج	j	ظ	ḍ		
ح	ḥ	ع	ʿ		
خ	kh	غ	gh		
د	d	ف	f		
ذ	dh	ق	q		
ر	r	ك	k		
ز	z	ل	l		

Short Vowels		Long Vowels	
ـَ	a	ا	ā
ـِ	i	ي	ī
ـُ	u	و	ū

Honourific Symbols Table

The following icons are used extensively in this book when referencing notable personalities.

عزّ وجلّ	*ʿAzza wa Jalla* Mighty and Majestic Used for Allah عزّ وجلّ
ﷺ	*Ṣallallahu ʿalayhi wa ālihi wa sallam* May Allah bless him and his family and grant them peace Used for Prophet Muḥammad ﷺ
عليه السلام	*ʿAlayhis Salām* Peace be upon him (singular) Used for male Prophets or Imams عليه السلام
عليهم السلام	*ʿAlayhimus Salām* Peace be upon them (plural) Used for three or more Prophets or Imams عليهم السلام
عجّل الله تعالى فرجه الشريف	*ʿAjjAllahu Taʿalā Farajahul Sharīf* May Allah, the Exalted, hasten his noble relief (reappearance) Used specifically for Imam al-Mahdī عجّل الله تعالى فرجه الشريف

In the Name of Allah,

the All-Compassionate,

the All-Merciful.

Foreword by the Publisher

The importance of prayer *(ṣalāt)* in Islam cannot be overstated. It is one of the branches of faith *(Furūʿ al-Dīn)*, a daily spiritual sojourn that connects a believer to the Creator – Allah ﷻ, and a transcendent oasis during worldly anxieties. Among the obligatory prayers, *Ṣalāt al-Jumuʿah* – the Friday Prayer, holds a special place of significance.

It is not merely a prayer, but rather, a weekly gathering of Muslim communities, a time for spiritual renewal, and a reminder of the unity and fraternity that Islam highly encourages.

It is a time to not only pray to Allah ﷻ, but a moment to connect to community members that one may not have seen for an entire week, as we all navigate through the busy rat race of life.

It is a uniquely afforded opportunity to be able to leave work and school in the middle of what is perhaps the busiest day of the week, Friday, at least in the secular "West" where people are busy wrapping up work of that week and getting ready to enjoy the weekend – to spend an hour or so exclusively in the worship of Allah ﷻ on an entirely different level.

This book which you hold in your hands, is a comprehensive exploration of *Ṣalāt al-Jumuʿah* – delving into its philosophy, the review of a collection of relevant *aḥādīth* about *Ṣalāt al-Jumuʿah* (the Friday Prayer) and *Ṣalāt al-Jamāʿah* (the Congregational Prayer), as well as offering the practical rulings based on the guidance of His Eminence, Āyatullāh Sayyid ʿAlī al-Ḥusaynī Sīstānī (may Allah protect him and all of the righteous scholars).

This work also features a unique research piece which analyzes the various opinions of Muslim jurists over the ages, and the status of *Ṣalāt al-Jumuʿah* – from it being an obligation to establish, to its being impermissible to establish and take part in during the major occultation of the 12th Imam عجل الله تعالى فرجه الشريف.

The work concludes with several *ziyārāt* and *duʿās* that we are encouraged to recite on Friday.

In short, this is a book which bridges the gap between theoretical understanding and practical application – providing readers with both the "why" and the "how" of this important Islamic observance, as well as how to make the most of this sacred day.

The Philosophy of Ṣalāt al-Jumuʿah

The first section of this book explores the Philosophy behind *Ṣalāt al-Jumuʿah*. This is not merely an academic exercise, but a crucial endeavour to understand the deeper wisdom and objectives of this Divine prescription. By comprehending the underlying philosophy of this weekly gathering, we can approach this prayer with greater consciousness and derive maximum benefits from it.

As you will see, *Ṣalāt al-Jumuʿah* is intended to be more than just a congregational prayer; it is a weekly convention of Muslims that serves multiple purposes, some of which include the following:

1. First, it reinforces the concept of unity among believers. The gathering of Muslims from all walks of life, standing shoulder to shoulder in prayer, is a powerful reminder of the equality and fraternity that Islam promotes. It breaks down social barriers and fosters a sense of community that extends beyond the confines of the masjid.

2. Secondly, *Ṣalāt al-Jumuʿah* serves as a weekly spiritual rejuvenation. In the hustle and bustle of daily life, it is easy to become disconnected from our spiritual essence. The Friday prayer provides an opportunity to step back from worldly concerns and refocus our relationship with Allah ﷻ. The sermons delivered during this prayer address moral themes, as well as current issues facing the community, providing guidance and perspective through the lens of Islamic teachings.

3. Thirdly, this Congregational Prayer is a means of the dissemination of knowledge. The two sermons *(khutbah)* delivered before the prayer is an opportunity to gain Islamic education. It allows for the discussion of religious, social, and moral issues – keeping the community informed and guided. This aspect of *Ṣalāt al-Jumuʿah* highlights the integration of worship and learning in Islam.

4. Fourthly, *Ṣalāt al-Jumuʿah* emphasizes the importance of time management in a Muslim's life. It teaches punctuality,

and the significance of setting aside time for worship amidst our busy worldly responsibilities. This weekly appointment with Allah ﷻ helps structure our lives around our religious duties. It is true that in the absence of the 12th Imam عجل الله تعالى فرجه الشريف, the Fridy prayers are recommended *(mustaḥabb)* and are not obligatory *(wājib)*, however, this becomes an important time for us to actively remember and pray for our deliverance through the return of our 12th Imam عجل الله تعالى فرجه الشريف. It also becomes an opportunity to 'practice' coming to the Friday prayers, realizing that when Imam al-Mahdī عجل الله تعالى فرجه الشريف makes his advent and establishes *Ṣalāt al-Jumuʿah*, it will be an obligation for all Muslims to attend – based on certain criteria which we will mention later in this book in the section of religious rulings.

5. Lastly, *Ṣalāt al-Jumuʿah* serves as a reminder of the Day of Judgement. Just as Muslims gather on Friday, they will gather on the Day of Resurrection in the presence of Allah ﷻ. This weekly gathering keeps the reality of the afterlife present in our conscious, encouraging continuous righteous deeds and moral behaviour.

Understanding these philosophical underpinnings allows us to approach *Ṣalāt al-Jumuʿah* not simply as a mere ritual, but as a multifaceted act of worship with profound individual and societal implications.

Forty Ḥadīth on Ṣalāt al-Jumuʿah and Ṣalāt al Jamāʿah

The second section of this book presents a compilation of forty *ḥadīth* related to *Ṣalāt al-Jumuʿah* (the Friday Prayer) and *Ṣalāt al-Jamāʿah* (the Congregational Prayer). This collection serves as a valuable resource for understanding the importance and virtues of these prayers as emphasized by Prophet Muḥammad ﷺ and the immaculate Imams of the Ahlul Bayt ﷺ.

The long-held custom which Muslim scholars adhere to regarding compiling forty *ḥadīth* on a particular subject has a lengthy history in Islamic scholarship. It stems from a *ḥadīth* attributed to Prophet Muḥammad ﷺ which states: "Whoever from my community memorizes forty traditions that they are in need of concerning their religion, Allah, Mighty and Majestic, will raise him on the Day of Resurrection as a jurist and a scholar."[1]

This *ḥadīth* has led to the creation of numerous beneficial compilations of the sayings of Prophet Muḥammad ﷺ, as well as the immaculate members of the Ahlul Bayt ﷺ, throughout Islamic history.[2]

The *aḥādīth* presented in this section of the book cover various aspects of *Ṣalāt al-Jumuʿah* and *Ṣalāt al-Jamāʿah*. They highlight the virtues of attending these prayers, the rewards promised for those who participate in them, the etiquettes to be observed, and the spiritual benefits to be gained. Some of the *ḥadīth* discuss the importance of early arrival, others speak about the significance of listening

---

[1] Shaykh Ṣadūq ؒ, *Thawāb al-Aʿmāl wa ʿIqāb al-Aʿmāl*, Pg. 134. The Arabic text of this is as follows:

مَنْ حَفِظَ مِنْ أُمَّتِي أَرْبَعِينَ حَدِيثًا مِمَّا يَحْتَاجُونَ إِلَيْهِ مِنْ أَمْرِ دِينِهِمْ بَعَثَهُ اللَّهُ عَزَّ وَجَلَّ يَوْمَ الْقِيَامَةِ فَقِيهًا عَالِمًا.

[2] For example: The famous book, *Forty Ḥadith*, by the late Āyatullāh Khomeinī found online at: www.al-islam.org/forty-hadith-exposition-second-revised-edition-sayyid-ruhullah-musawi-khomeini

attentively to the sermons, while others emphasize the unity and fraternity fostered through congregational prayers.

These narrations serve multiple purposes:

1. They provide motivation for believers to attend and value both *Ṣalāt al-Jumuʿah,* as well as *Ṣalāt al-Jamāʿah.* By understanding the immense rewards and benefits associated with both *Ṣalāt,* believers are encouraged to prioritize these acts of worship in their lives.

2. The collection of *aḥādīth* offer practical guidance on how to maximize the benefits when attending these prayers. They provide instructions on preparation, etiquette to be observed during prayers, and actions that enhance the spiritual experience.

3. This collection of *aḥādīth* serves as a reminder of the central place that these prayers hold in Islam. They reinforce the idea that Islam is not just a personal faith, but a communal religion that emphasizes collective worship and mutual support among believers.

It is important to note that while this compilation includes forty *ḥadīth* on the topics of *Ṣalāt al-Jamāʿah* and *Ṣalāt al-Jumuʿah,* it is by no means exhaustive. There are numerous other narrations on this subject. However, this collection provides a solid foundation for understanding the significance of these two *Ṣalāt,* as seen in the teachings of Prophet Muḥammad ﷺ and the 12 immaculate Imams ﷷ. Readers are encouraged to reflect deeply on these *ḥadīth,* understand their context, and strive to implement the teachings in their own lives. The true value of knowledge lies not in mere acquisition, but in application, and these forty *ḥadīth* provide ample opportunities for practical implementation in our daily lives.

Comprehensive Rulings on Ṣalāt al-Jumuʿah

The third section of this book presents a comprehensive set of rulings regarding the practical aspects of *Ṣalāt al-Jumuʿah*, based on the guidance of His Eminence, Āyatullāh Sayyid ʿAlī al-Ḥusaynī Sīstānī. This section bridges the gap between theoretical understanding and practical application, providing readers with clear guidelines on how to correctly perform this important prayer.

The rulings covered in this section address various aspects of *Ṣalāt al-Jumuʿah*, including, but not limited to:

1. Conditions needed for *Ṣalāt al-Jumuʿah* to become obligatory.
2. The correct time for performing this prayer.
3. The required number of attendees for this prayer to be valid.
4. The qualifications of the *imam* leading the prayer.
5. Conditions for the validity of the sermons *(khutbah)*.
6. The correct method of performing this prayer.
7. Guidelines for travellers regarding *Ṣalāt al-Jumuʿah.*
8. The relationship between *Ṣalāt al-Jumuʿah* and *Ṣalāt al-Ẓuhr* (noon prayer).

Seeing as how there is no other comprehensive manual in English that highlights these rulings, this section provides clarity on issues that may arise in the practice of *Ṣalāt al-Jumuʿah.* They address common questions and potential areas of confusion, allowing believers to perform this prayer with confidence and correctness.

It is important to note that these rulings are based on the verdicts of Āyatullāh Sīstānī, and as such, they may differ from the views of other Shīʿa scholars. This diversity of opinion is a natural part of Islamic Jurisprudence and reflects the depth and flexibility of Islamic Law in addressing various contexts and situations. It is always best to check the rulings of the *Marjaʿ Taqlīd* whom you follow.

Scholarly Analysis on Ṣalāt al-Jumuʿah

Ṣalāt al-Jumuʿah has been the subject of considerable debate, particularly regarding its status during the Era of Occultation *(ʿAṣr al-Ghaybah)* of the 12th Imam, al-Ḥujjah ibn al-Ḥasan عجّل الله تعالى فرجه الشريف.

In the presence of the Noble Prophet ﷺ or the immaculate Imam عليه السلام, all Muslims unanimously agree that it is an Individual Obligation *(Wājib al-ʿAynī)*, meaning every believer must personally attend this prayer. The question arises, however, in his absence.

Within Sunnī thought, the obligation of Friday Prayer continues regardless, since they do not recognize the need for an infallible Imam appointed by Divine authority for its validity.

Among the Shīʿa Imāmīyyah *(Ithnā-ʿAsharī)*, however, scholarly opinions are more diverse:

1. Some Shīʿa jurists maintain that Friday Prayer remains a Definite Obligation *(Wājib al-Taʿyīnī)* and must be performed without any alternative.
2. Others hold that it is an Optional Obligation *(Wājib al-Taʾkhyīrī)*, giving believers the choice between performing Friday Prayer or the regular *Ẓuhr* Prayer, provided all necessary conditions are in place.
3. Still another group of scholars consider it forbidden *(ḥarām)* to establish Friday Prayer during the

occultation, since no explicit authorization has been given by the Imam ﷺ to appoint a legitimate prayer leader.

At the heart of this disagreement is the question of whether the Imam's ﷺ presence or his direct permission is an essential condition for the validity of Friday Prayer. This issue is deeply tied to Shīʿa theological principles regarding the Imam's ﷺ unique role as the Divinely-appointed leader and guide.

This section of the book analyzes these divergent legal and theological views by examining related Quranic texts, *aḥādīth* of the immaculates ﷺ, and Juristic arguments. It also considers Sunnī perspectives for comparison but gives particular attention to the diversity of Shīʿa scholarly opinion.

Through this discussion, the broader implications of religious authority and leadership during the Imam's عجل الله تعالى فرجه الشريف occultation become evident, shaping contemporary understandings of the status of *Ṣalāt al-Jumuʿah.*

Prayers and Supplications

In the rich tapestry of Islamic spiritual practices, Friday holds a position of paramount importance. It is not merely a day of the week like Monday, Wednesday, or Sunday; rather, it is a period which should be dedicated to one's weekly spiritual rejuvenation. For this reason, the inclusion of specific prayers and supplications in a book about *Ṣalāt al-Jumuʿah* reflects a realization for the believer to have a deep understanding of the spiritual, social, and personal dimensions of this sacred day. Each of these prayers serves a unique purpose, contributing to the holistic spiritual experience of a believer.

Supplication (Duʿāʾ) after Ṣalāt al-ʿAṣr

The time after the *ʿAṣr* prayer on Friday is considered especially blessed. Some of the *aḥādīth* direct us that there is a specific hour on Friday when supplications are answered. Thus, believers are encouraged to continually call out to Allah ﷻ throughout the day of Friday.

The inclusion of a specific supplication for that time of the day emphasizes the importance of seizing this blessed moment. It encourages believers to engage in deep, heartfelt communication with Allah ﷻ, fostering a sense of closeness and dependency on the Divine. This practice also serves as a reminder about the special status of Friday in the Islamic week, urging believers to make the most of its blessings.

Supplication (Duʿāʾ) for Friday

A dedicated supplication for Friday underscores the day's significance in the Islamic tradition. Friday is often referred to as the "the leader of days" *(sayyid al-ayyām)* in Islamic teachings. This supplication encompasses requests for personal and communal well-being, forgiveness, and spiritual growth. By including this supplication, this book emphasizes the importance of starting the blessed day with the right mindset, setting intentions, and seeking blessings from Allah ﷻ for oneself and the broader Muslim community.

Prostration (Sajdah) of Thanks

Although this is something we are recommended to perform daily after each prayer as well as other times of the day, the prostration of thanks is a powerful expression of gratitude to Allah ﷻ. Its inclusion in relation to Friday Prayer highlights the importance of thankfulness in Islamic Spirituality. This prostration serves as a reminder that every blessing, including the opportunity to participate in the Friday prayer, is a gift from Allah ﷻ. It encourages believers to cultivate a heart of gratitude, which is crucial for spiritual growth and contentment. Moreover, it reinforces the idea that true submission to Allah ﷻ involves not just obligatory acts of worship, but also voluntary expressions of devotion and thankfulness.

Supplication (Duʿāʾ) for Muslim Unity

Although it is not 'named' as the supplication for Muslim unity in our textual sources, however, this short, yet poignant supplication has taken on this name in many of our communities in "The West." The inclusion of this supplication is particularly significant in the context of Friday prayer, which is inherently a communal act of worship. This prayer reflects the Islamic ideal of unity and fraternity among believers. It serves as a reminder that despite differences in culture or language, we are united in our faith and submission to Allah ﷻ. By encouraging believers to hold hands and pray to One God – Allah ﷻ, on the Friday afternoon, it fosters a sense of mutual care within the Muslim community, aligning with the broader objectives of *Ṣalāt al-Jumuʿah* as a unifying weekly gathering.

Visitation (Ziyārah) for Friday

The concept of *ziyārah*, often associated with visiting the graves or shrines of revered figures in Islam, takes on a spiritual dimension when included in the context of the Friday Prayer. The concept of visitation involves sending salutations and prayers upon Prophet Muḥammad ﷺ and the 12 immaculate Imams عليهم السلام, as well as Lady Fāṭima al-Zahrā᾽ عليها السلام. It serves to strengthen a believer's connection with the spiritual legacy of Islam, reminding them about the exemplary lives and teachings of those who came before. This practice can inspire us to emulate the virtues of these noble personalities, and by remembering them, they in turn will make mention of us in their prayers.

Ziyārat Āle Yāsīn

Ziyārat Āle Yāsīn is a highly esteemed salutation in Shīʿa Islam, uniquely originating from the 12th Imam, al-Mahdī عجل الله تعالى فرجه الشريف. It serves as a spiritual visitation and a profound affirmation of faith during his Major Occultation.

This *ziyārat* is an act of renewing allegiance *(bayʿah)* and a covenant of love with the living Proof of Allah عزّ وجلّ – Imam al-Ḥujjah عجل الله تعالى فرجه الشريف. It acts as an intricate confession of core Shīʿa doctrines, where a believer confirms one's faith in the Oneness of Allah عزّ وجلّ, the Prophethood of Prophet Muḥammad ﷺ, the Divinely-mandated leadership of the 12 Imams عليهم السلام, and other teachings.

Visitation of the Immaculates عليهم السلام

This comprehensive visitation encompasses salutations and prayers upon Prophet Muḥammad ﷺ and the 12 Imams عليهم السلام. Its inclusion in this book underscores the importance of maintaining a strong spiritual connection with all these revered figures. This practice serves to reinforce our understanding of, and commitment to the teachings and examples set by these personalities.

Supplication (Duʿāʾ) for the 12th Imam عجل الله تعالى فرجه الشريف

The inclusion of a supplication for the 12th Imam عجل الله تعالى فرجه الشريف reflects the love and commitment believers have to Imam al-Mahdī عجل الله تعالى فرجه الشريف, the awaited saviour, who will bring justice and peace to the world. This supplication serves multiple purposes: It reinforces the belief in Divine Justice, and the ultimate triumph of good over evil. It also nurtures hope in the hearts of believers, encouraging us to persevere in righteousness – even in challenging times. Moreover, it serves as a reminder of our responsibility to work towards creating a just and harmonious society – in preparation for, and anticipation of the Imam's عجل الله تعالى فرجه الشريف advent.

Supplication (Duʿāʾ) from Imam al-Mahdī عجل الله تعالى فرجه الشريف

The inclusion of a supplication attributed to Imam al-Mahdī عجل الله تعالى فرجه الشريف also holds profound significance. This supplication contains deep spiritual insights and guidance for believers – enumerating traits which each believer must strive to implement in their lives, while also focusing on areas of life that we need to stay away from if we wish to gain greater spiritual proximity to Allah ﷻ. By engaging with this prayer, believers feel a connection with the Imam of their time, may Allah hasten his advent. It serves as a source of spiritual guidance and inspiration, helping believers navigate the challenges of contemporary life, while maintaining their faith and spiritual focus.

The inclusion of these diverse prayers and supplications in a book about *Ṣalāt al-Jumuʿah* reflects a holistic approach to spiritual practice. It recognizes that the Friday Prayer is not an isolated ritual, but part of a broader spiritual framework that encompasses personal devotion, communal unity, historical consciousness, and eschatological hope. These prayers and supplications serve to deepen the spiritual experience of Friday, transforming it from a mere weekly observance into a comprehensive spiritual journey. They encourage believers to engage in the remembrance of Allah ﷻ, express gratitude, seek forgiveness, pray for the community, connect with the immaculate spiritual leaders عليهم السلام, and hope for a better future. This multifaceted approach helps make the Friday Prayer a truly transformative experience, one that nourishes the soul, strengthens community bonds, and reinvigorates faith.

Moreover, the variety of these prayers caters to different spiritual needs and inclinations: Some focus on personal spiritual growth, others on communal welfare, and a few on broader, eschatological themes. This diversity ensures that every believer can find something that resonates with their current spiritual state and needs.

In summary, the inclusion of these unique prayers and supplications in a book about *Ṣalāt al-Jumuʿah* demonstrates a deep understanding of the multifaceted nature of Islamic

Spirituality. It recognizes that true spiritual growth involves not just the performance of rituals, but also the cultivation of inner states, the strengthening of community bonds, and the maintenance of a historical and future-oriented perspective. By engaging with these prayers, believers are better equipped to make their Friday Prayer experience a cornerstone of their spiritual life – one that reverberates through their actions and consciousness throughout the week – until the next Friday.

Importance of This Work

The compilation and translation of this book represent a significant contribution to Islamic literature, particularly in the English language. By bringing together the philosophy, narrations *(aḥādīth)*, and practical rulings *(aḥkām)* related to *Ṣalāt al-Jumuʿah*, this work provides a comprehensive resource for both religious guides and lay Muslims seeking to understand and correctly implement this important aspect of Islamic worship.

In an era where many Muslims – especially those living in non-Muslim majority countries – may struggle to maintain their religious practices, such comprehensive guides are invaluable. They serve not only as references for correct practice, but also as reminders of the significance and benefits of these acts of worship.

Moreover, this book serves an important role in preserving and transmitting Islamic knowledge. By presenting the rulings of Āyatullāh Sīstānī in English, it makes this valuable guidance accessible to a wider audience, especially those who may not be fluent in Arabic or Persian.

The inclusion of the philosophical aspects of *Ṣalāt al-Jumuʿah* is particularly noteworthy. In a time when many may perform religious duties out of habit or obligation, understanding the wisdom behind these practices can reinvigorate our worship, and deepen our connection to our faith, and to Almighty Allah ﷻ.

A Word on the Translation

Translating religious texts is a task of great responsibility. It requires not only linguistic proficiency, but also a deep understanding of the subject matter, and the ability to convey complex concepts accurately across languages and cultures. We have undertaken this challenging task with diligence and care, striving to maintain the integrity of the original text, while making it easily understandable to English-speaking readers. However, it is important to note that no translation can fully capture all the nuances of the original text. Arabic, the language of the Quran and much of Islamic literature; as well as Persian, which the bulk of this book was taken from, has depths of meaning that are often difficult to convey fully in other languages. Therefore, readers are encouraged, where possible, to seek clarification from knowledgeable scholars when needed.

We acknowledge the support provided by several scholars in helping us understand some of the rulings of Āyatullāh Sīstānī, which were particularly challenging – may Allah ﷻ reward them for their assistance.

Conclusion

This book, with its exploration of the philosophy of *Ṣalāt al-Jumuʿah*, its compilation of relevant *aḥādīth*, and its presentation of practical rulings, serves as a comprehensive guide to this important Islamic observance. It is a testament to the depth and richness of Islamic traditions, and the continued relevance of classical knowledge to contemporary practices. As readers engage with this text, it is hoped that they will gain not only knowledge, but also a deeper appreciation for the wisdom inherent in Islamic practices. May this book serve as a means of enhancing our understanding, improving our practice, and ultimately drawing us closer to Allah ﷻ.

I would like to extend my appreciation to my wife and editor of this book, Sr. Arifa Hudda. Her continued support in life, as well as her 25 years of dedication to the review and editing of hundreds of Islamic texts, in addition to the books which I have been fortunate to write and/or translate is a testament to her love and concern for the propagation of the faith of Islam, as taught by the Ahlul Bayt ﷺ. I ask Allah ﷻ to continue to bless her, keep her healthy, and grant her lots of blessings *(barakah)* in her time and energy to serve the cause of Islam.

We would also like to thank the donors who financially assisted in the publication of this book. We ask you to recite a Sūrah al-Fātiḥa for them and their beloved family members – both alive and those who have passed away.

In closing, above all, we thank Allah ﷻ for the blessing of knowledge, and the opportunity to obtain it. May He accept this work as a means of serving His religion and guide us all to that which pleases Him.

As you read and benefit from this book, please keep all of those who had a role in the publication of this work in your sincere prayers – on Friday and every day of the week.

Saleem Bhimji
Director *of the* Islamic Publishing House
10th Rabīʿ al-Thānī, 1447 AH ♦ 3rd October, 2025 CE
Birth anniversary of Imam Ḥasan ibn ʿAlī al-ʿAskarī عليه السلام

Richmond, B.C., Canada

Philosophy of Ṣalāt al-Jumuʿah[3]

By the Late Āyatullāh Murtaḍā Muṭahharī رحمه الله

Within its teachings, Islam has implemented a weekly prayer service referred to as *Ṣalāt al-Jumuʿah* [literally 'the Friday Prayer'].[4] This prayer has been mentioned in the Quran in the chapter which bears its name, Sūrah al-Jumuʿah (62), in which Allah عز وجل says:

---

[3] This is a translation from the Farsi book entitled, *Khiṭāba wa Mimbar,* which was based on a series of lectures delivered by the late Āyatullāh Murtaḍā Muṭahharī, and is from the fourth section concerning *Ṣalāt al-Jumuʿah.* This work can be found in Farsi at: **shorturl.at/abH57.** The theme of this book is about the *Concept of Lecturing in Islam,* and its various uses within the religion – *Ṣalāt al-Jumuʿah* being one example that the late scholar discussed.

[4] Literally, this term is translated as 'the Friday Prayer,' and as you will see, it is a unique prayer service in Islam, which sets it apart from the five daily prayers – as it is not just a 'prayer,' but it has the unique added component of two lectures which must also be delivered before the two *rakaʿāt* prayer.

﴿يَٰٓأَيُّهَا ٱلَّذِينَ ءَامَنُوٓاْ إِذَا نُودِيَ لِلصَّلَوٰةِ مِن يَوۡمِ ٱلۡجُمُعَةِ فَٱسۡعَوۡاْ إِلَىٰ
ذِكۡرِ ٱللَّهِ وَذَرُواْ ٱلۡبَيۡعَۚ ذَٰلِكُمۡ خَيۡرٞ لَّكُمۡ إِن كُنتُمۡ تَعۡلَمُونَ ٩﴾

> O you who have faith! When the call is proclaimed to prayer on the Day of *Jumuʿah* (Friday – the day of assembly) then hasten to the remembrance of Allah and leave aside all business. That is best for you if you only knew![5]

What is *Ṣalāt al-Jumuʿah*?

Ṣalāt al-Jumuʿah – on Fridays – takes the place of *Ṣalāt al-Ẓuhr*[6] which is prayed daily; however, it differs in several ways from the regular prayers of *Ṣalāt al-Ẓuhr* which we perform.

First off, *Ṣalāt al-Ẓuhr* which Muslims perform is four *rakaʿāt*, however, the *ṣalāt* which is prayed on Friday – whose name is *Ṣalāt al-Jumuʿah* – is only two *rakaʿāt*. So how did it happen that this *ṣalāt* was 'changed' into a two *rakaʿāt ṣalāt*? [We will discuss this later.]

The second difference is that it is obligatory *(wājib)* that *Ṣalāt al-Jumuʿah* be performed in congregation *(jamāʿat)*. As we know, it is **not** obligatory to perform any of the other daily prayers – *Fajr*, *Ẓuhr*, *ʿAṣr*, *Maghrib*, and *ʿIshā* in congregation – although it is highly recommended to perform in congregation with other believers.

The third difference is that in which ever locality *Ṣalāt al-Jumuʿah* is held, it is obligatory upon the people who live

[5] Quran, Sūrah al-Jumuʿah (62), Verse 9.

[6] The prayers which Muslims perform daily at mid-day.

within a two *farsakh*[7] radius of the area of *Ṣalāt al-Jumuʿah* to attend the prayer unless they have a valid excuse [which prevents them from attending].[8]

The fourth difference is that it is not permissible for another *Ṣalāt al-Jumuʿah* to be held within the radius of one *sāʿa* (6 km) in whichever area *Ṣalāt al-Jumuʿah* is established with all the requisite conditions, thus, only that one *Ṣalāt al-Jumuʿah* service can be held.[9]

Just imagine if such a prayer were to be held in certain populated cities keeping these conditions in mind – what kind of enormity and magnitude it would hold!

For example, in the city of Tehran, if there was to be one *Ṣalāt al-Jumuʿah* held here,[10] then we would see that for the distance of two *farsakh* (11.52 km) – from the point of the north area of Shimrān,[11] to the south point near the city of

---

[7] A traditional unit of measure – one *farsakh* is approximately 5.76 km (or 3.58 miles) – thus, two *farsakh* is approximately 11.52 km (or 7.16 miles).

[8] We will expand on the obligation of *Ṣalāt al-Jumuʿah* in the section on Jurisprudence as per the rulings of His Eminence, Āyatullāh Sayyid ʿAlī al-Ḥusaynī al-Sīstānī. (Tr.)

[9] This is limited to *Ṣalāt al-Jumuʿah* being held by other Shīʿa groups – meaning that if there is *Ṣalāt al-Jumuʿah* being established by another group of Muslims, then this has no bearing on the *Ṣalāt al-Jumuʿah* of the Shīʿa community and its validity. (Tr.)

[10] This lecture was given prior to the victory of the Islamic Revolution of Iran in 1979, thus, *Ṣalāt al-Jumuʿah* was not actively taking place across Iran.

[11] A locality in the north of Tehran.

Ray,[12] and from all points stretching 11.52 km to the east and the west of that city – everyone would gather in one area to perform this prayer [in congregation]!

In addition, for 12 kilometers, people from all around would join for *Ṣalāt al-Jumuʿah;* and for 6 kilometers, no other *Ṣalāt al-Jumuʿah* would be permitted to take place – thus, people would be restricted to attending one massive gathering. Just imagine the magnitude of such a gathering that would take place!

Moving on, another difference is that this prayer must be performed as two *rakaʿāt* – not four *rakaʿāt* like *Ṣalāt al-Ẓuhr.*

Why is this?

It has been related quite frequently in the *aḥādīth,* and is also one of the established beliefs of our faith as found in the books of Islamic Jurisprudence that:

وَإِنَّمَا جُعِلَتِ الْجُمْعَةُ رَكْعَتَيْنِ لِمَكَانِ الْخُطْبَتَيْنِ.

> Indeed, *Ṣalāt al-Jumuʿah* was instituted as being two *rakaʿāt* as the two sermons take the place [of the other two *rakaʿāt* which are normally performed for *Ṣalāt al-Ẓuhr*].

This means that this general prayer which all people gather to perform is not like other congregational prayers we sometimes see taking place in the *masājid* where people are scattered about with small groups of people performing their own little congregational prayers separate from one another.

Ṣalāt al-Jumuʿah is also unique because before the commencement of the two *rakaʿāt* prayer, it is obligatory that two speeches be given – thus, the prayer must be preceded

---

[12] A city in the southern area of Tehran.

by two sermons which take the place of the two *rakaʿāt* of *Ṣalāt al-Ẓuhr.*

A point to bring forward is that within our sacred religion of Islam, we have a belief that lectures are a part of the religion – and in the case of *Ṣalāt al-Jumuʿah* (and *Ṣalāt al-ʿEid),* they form a part of the *ṣalāt.* In this regard, the Commander of the Faithful, Imam ʿAlī ibn Abī Ṭālib ﷺ said: "The sermon (delivered during the Friday Prayers) **is** *ṣalāt.*"

During the time that the prayer leader *(imam)* of the Friday Prayer is delivering the two sermons, people must listen to what he is saying – thus, everyone must remain quiet and not say a word – they must be attentively listening to the two sermons.

If the speaker has not come down from the platform or place on which he was standing to deliver the lecture, then all in attendance must remain sitting as if they were in a state of prayers.

There is one exception here that the prayer leader of the Friday Prayer who is delivering the sermons does not sit or stand facing the *qiblah;* rather, he sits and stands facing the people with his back to the *qiblah.*

Therefore, the two sermons which are obligatory in this prayer take the place of the two *rakaʿāt* of *Ṣalāt al-Ẓuhr.*

The Main Reason for the Gathering on Friday

A person may be surprised by learning these Islamic commandments, and may even ask oneself: "What is the reason for all of these formalities in this gathering, and why all of the specific etiquettes to follow on Friday in the prayer service?"

Even more surprising is the fact that the main purpose of gathering in this fashion is to 'simply listen' to the sermon. Thus, how important must these two speeches be, and what life-giving power do they possess?

To sum it up, they are so important that at the time when the one who is performing the *adhān (muadhdhin)* gives out the call and says:

أَللّٰهُ أَكْبَرُ

Allah is the Greatest!

everyone – regardless of where they are, and what they are doing – must drop everything and rush to *Ṣalāt al-Jumuʿah.* They must sit attentively, patiently, and carefully listen to the two sermons.

Following this, they must then perform two *rakaʿāt* of Prayers in Congregation *(Jamāʿat),* and only after performing this, are they free to go back to work, school, or whatever they were previously engaged in.

In the blessed Quran, within Sūrah al-Jumuʿah (Chapter 62), these commandments have been mentioned as follows:

﴿يَٰٓأَيُّهَا ٱلَّذِينَ ءَامَنُوٓاْ إِذَا نُودِىَ لِلصَّلَوٰةِ مِن يَوْمِ ٱلْجُمُعَةِ فَٱسْعَوْاْ إِلَىٰ ذِكْرِ ٱللَّهِ وَذَرُواْ ٱلْبَيْعَ ذَٰلِكُمْ خَيْرٌ لَّكُمْ إِن كُنتُمْ تَعْلَمُونَ ۝٩ فَإِذَا قُضِيَتِ ٱلصَّلَوٰةُ فَٱنتَشِرُواْ فِى ٱلْأَرْضِ وَٱبْتَغُواْ مِن فَضْلِ ٱللَّهِ وَٱذْكُرُواْ ٱللَّهَ كَثِيرًا لَّعَلَّكُمْ تُفْلِحُونَ ۝١٠﴾

O you who believe! When the call is made for the Prayer on Friday, then hasten to the remembrance of Allah (by listening to the sermon and performing the prayer), and leave off business (and whatever else you

> may be preoccupied with). This is better for you if you only knew. And when the prayer is done, then disperse in the land and seek (your portion) of the bounty of Allah, and mention Allah much (both by doing this prayer, and on other occasions), so that you may prosper (in both worlds).[13]

We should also mention a point that usually during the afternoon time (other than on Friday), after the *adhān* is given, the *ṣalāt* should be performed immediately thereafter; however, there is an exception to this rule, which is that on Friday, if it is confirmed that *Ṣalāt al-Jumuʿah* will be performed and all the conditions are met, then it is permissible for the *adhān* to be given **before** the time of *ẓuhr* sets in. Thus, it is allowed that the *adhān* is given and the speeches are then started such that when the time for mid-day *(ẓuhr)* arrives, the two speeches have come to an end.[14]

Once the sound of the *muadhdhin* has been raised for *Ṣalāt al-Jumuʿah*, any kind of business transaction is forbidden *(ḥarām)* – as the Quran highlights:[15]

﴿وَذَرُوا۟ ٱلْبَيْعَ...﴾

---

[13] Quran, Sūrah al-Jumuʿah (62), Verses 9-10.

[14] There is a difference of opinion amongst the *Marājiʿ Taqlīd* in this issue as some permit the *adhān* and two sermons to start before the time of *ẓuhr,* whereas others say that it is not permissible. Refer to the rules of *Ṣalāt al-Jumuʿah* of the *Marjaʿ* whom you follow.

[15] Scholars differ on the interpretation of this ruling. Please refer to the rules of the *Marjaʿ* you follow for further clarification.

And leave aside all business dealings...[16]

This commandment is directly from the Quran and is part of the confirmed rulings of Islam.

Both the Shīʿa and Sunnī scholars have no difference of opinion on this issue that if a valid *Ṣalāt al-Jumuʿah* is taking place, and the *adhān* is being given, then for example, if the store owner is sitting behind the counter and a customer comes to his store and wants to purchase something, cheese for instance, and the store owner has a knife in his hand ready to cut the fresh cheese that the customer wants, if the sound of the *muadhdhin* is heard proclaiming:

أَللّٰهُ أَكْبَرُ

Allah is the Greatest.

then it becomes obligatory *(wājib)* upon both the store owner and the shopper to drop everything they are doing, and as the Quran states:

﴿...فَٱسْعَوْاْ إِلَىٰ ذِكْرِ ٱللَّهِ وَذَرُواْ ٱلْبَيْعَ...﴾

...Then hasten towards the remembrance of Allah and leave aside all business...[17]

They must rush to *Ṣalāt al-Jumuʿah* and leave aside their business transaction for the time being. It is forbidden *(ḥarām)* to indulge in business transactions at that time (according to some scholars), so they must rush towards the prayers, listen to the two sermons, perform the prayers, then go back to their business dealings.

---

16 Quran, Sūrah al-Jumuʿah (62), Verse 9.
17 Quran, Sūrah al-Jumuʿah (62), Verse 9.

Again, so that we can understand how important the issue of this gathering is, it is mentioned in the *aḥādīth* that it is even obligatory upon those who work in the prison system, the management of the prison, and even the police and guards of the prisons to not only be present at *Ṣalāt al-Jumuʿah*, but in fact, they are even obliged to bring the inmates to *Ṣalāt al-Jumuʿah!*

The prisoners must be taken out of their jail cell so that they too can participate in *Ṣalāt al-Jumuʿah* – this great gathering. They too should be allowed to listen to the sermons and partake in the *Ṣalāt*, and when the prayers are complete, they are returned to their prison cells.

Contents of the Jumuʿah Sermons

Now that we have understood the importance of the sermons at the time of *Ṣalāt al-Jumuʿah*, and have better appreciated the main purpose of this gathering, which is to hear the sermons, a question comes up: What must be said or recited in these two sermons?[18]

In *Ṣalāt al-Jumuʿah*, it is obligatory to give two sermons – not one. Thus, the *imam* must give the first sermon, sit down for a short period of time remaining quiet, then once again stand up and deliver the second sermon.

The sermons of Friday are made up of the following components:

1. The praise and glorification of Allah ﷻ.

[18] Further details will be discussed in the section of the Jurisprudence of *Ṣalāt al-Jumuʿah* in this book.

2. Sending of prayers and blessings upon the final Messenger, Prophet Muḥammad ﷺ and the 12 immaculate Imams ☾.
3. The people must be advised on a series of important commandments – which we will explain shortly.
4. A short chapter from the Quran must be recited.

All these elements are a part of the faith of Islam, and nothing has come from outside our teachings!

The *imam* who leads *Ṣalāt al-Jumuʿah* must also follow certain etiquette:[19] some of these include that he should wear a turban *(ʿamāmah)* on his head – just as Prophet Muḥammad ﷺ used to wear one.

May Allah ﷻ have mercy on Ḥājj Aqā Raḥīm Arbāb who was from the city of Iṣfahān – perhaps you have heard about him. He was one of the high-ranking scholars in the fields of Islamic Jurisprudence *(Fiqh)*, the Science of Jurisprudence *(Uṣūl al-Fiqh)*, Philosophy *(Falsafeh)* and Arabic Grammar, and was even versed in the traditional Sciences. He was a student of the late sage, Jahāngīr Khān Qashqāʿī, and just like his teacher, he only wore a simple hat made of animal skin – as opposed to the cloth turban which Muslim scholars are known for wearing.

Otherwise, he looked just like other scholars from the point of view of his daily wardrobe – the outer cloak *(ʿabā)*, the inner cloak *(qabā)*, and his physiognomy. What set him as unique was that he passionately believed in the institution of *Ṣalāt al-Jumuʿah* – and incidentally, he used to lead the Friday Prayers in Iṣfahān.

---

[19] Further details will be discussed in the section of the Jurisprudence of *Ṣalāt al-Jumuʿah* of this book.

Since the people who would come to *Ṣalāt al-Jumuʿah* (back in the days) did not really acknowledge or give importance to *Ṣalāt al-Jumuʿah*, the Friday Prayer that was taking place in Iṣfahān was not that distinguished of a prayer service that Islam envisioned it to be – not only in Iṣfahān, but elsewhere [in Iran] as well. However, whenever Aqā Raḥīm Arbāb came for *Ṣalāt al-Jumuʿah*, he would always have a small cloth turban *(ʿamāmah)* on his head.

I still remember in the month of Farwardīn in the year 1339[20] [according to the Iranian Islamic Lunar Hijri calendar] when I was with him in Iṣfahān, and the topic of *Ṣalāt al-Jumuʿah* came up, he said to me: "I do not know when the Shīʿa will remove the shame and disgrace of abandoning *Ṣalāt al-Jumuʿah* from their necks, at which time the other divisions within Islam who constantly refer to us as those people who have abandoned the *Ṣalāt al-Jumuʿah*, will also be removed from us."

He even expressed a wish and said: "I wish that in Masjid al-Aʿẓam in Qum – which has been built through spending millions of *tumāns*[21] – that one magnificent *Ṣalāt al-Jumuʿah* will take place there."

Going back to the issue of the sermons, when the prayer leader arrives to deliver these, he must do so while in a standing position. In the blessed verse of the Quran, it is mentioned:

[20] This corresponds to April 1960.

[21] The unit of currency used in the Islamic Republic of Iran.

﴿وَإِذَا رَأَوۡاْ تِجَٰرَةً أَوۡ لَهۡوًا ٱنفَضُّوٓاْ إِلَيۡهَا وَتَرَكُوكَ قَآئِمٗاۚ قُلۡ مَا عِندَ ٱللَّهِ
خَيۡرٞ مِّنَ ٱللَّهۡوِ وَمِنَ ٱلتِّجَٰرَةِۚ وَٱللَّهُ خَيۡرُ ٱلرَّٰزِقِينَ ١١﴾

> And (it happened that) when they (some of the companions of the Prophet) saw (an opportunity for) business or pastime, they broke away from it *(Ṣalāt al-Jumuʿah)*, and left you, (O Muḥammad) standing (all alone – while delivering the sermon). Say (to them): 'What is with Allah is better (for you) than pastimes and business, and Allah is the Best Provider (with the ultimate rank of providing).'[22]

This verse conveys multiple points of reflection; however, the prime point is that it refers to those companions of Prophet Muḥammad ﷺ who had no sense of spiritual nurturing and had clung onto the traits and qualities of the people of the Days of Ignorance *(Jāhiliyyah)*. When they spotted some merchandise [the trade caravans entering Madina], or heard the drums, or other instruments being played,[23] they would leave Prophet Muḥammad ﷺ standing alone, and ran after the goods and merchandise which were being sold.

The history of revelation of this portion of the chapter speaks about an event which transpired when once, Prophet

---

[22] Quran, Sūrah al-Jumuʿah (62), Verse 11.

[23] In those days, when trade caravans would approach the city, they would begin to play their musical instruments, letting the people of that region know the traders were approaching town. This is like today where commercials for products are most often accompanied by a jingle or tune to catch the attention of the consumer. (Tr.)

Muḥammad ﷺ was standing, delivering the Friday sermon in the city of Madina. Suddenly, the sound of drums could be heard – this was a sign that a trade caravan was making its way into the city of Madina with goods to sell. As the companions feared that everything would sell out fast, they left the Friday Prayer gathering and ran to see what was on sale so they could buy what was being offered – leaving the final Messenger ﷺ standing (alone).

Our point in bringing this up is with respect to the portion of the verse which reads:

﴿...وَتَرَكُوكَ قَآئِمًا...﴾

...They leave you (Muḥammad) standing (alone)...[24]

is that it is an integral part of the Friday Prayer service that the *imam* must be standing when delivering the two sermons.

Religious scholars note that it is impermissible, and an illegitimate invention *(bidʿah)*[25] in the religion which has no basis in the Quran or Prophetic teachings to sit and deliver the two sermons. Historians note that this is something which Muʿāwiyah ibn Abū Sufyān brought into Islam [in his continued attempts to corrupt and destroy the religion of Islam].

The following issue comes up that: Does the leader of the Friday Prayer and the one delivering the sermons need to be

---

[24] Quran, Sūrah al-Jumuʿah (62), Verse 11.

[25] *Bidʿah* (literally means innovation) is adding something to, or omitting something from, the religion of Islam. *Bidʿah* stands in contrast to *Sunnah* (i.e., a practice or belief that is mentioned in the Quran or *aḥādīth*). In the Islamic tradition, *bidʿah* is an instance of disbelief or polytheism. (Tr.)

the same person – or is it possible that one person gives the two sermons, while another person leads the actual [two *rakaʿāt*] of *Ṣalāt al-Jumuʿah*?

This is a separate ruling which needs to be discussed at length, however, what we can say is that all Shīʿa scholars believe that the person who delivers the lecture and leads the actual Friday Prayer must be one and the same person – two people **cannot** share in this responsibility!

Some scholars note that one of the primary conditions of the *imam* of *Ṣalāt al-Jumuʿah* is that he must be able to deliver a speech, so a person who is mute and cannot speak is not permitted to lead the Friday Prayer. In many *aḥādīth*, it has been mentioned that:

إِمَامٌ يَخْطِبُ.

> The *imam* of *Ṣalāt al-Jumuʿah* (the one who leads the prayer) must be the same one who gives the two sermons.

Another condition is that the *imam*, while standing and delivering the speech, must be leaning on, or holding a sword, a spear, or a stick in his hand, and he must deliver the speech in this fashion.[26]

---

[26] The scholars differ whether the *imam* must be physically holding the item, or if it is sufficient for it to be in his vicinity. Refer to the *Marjaʿ Taqlīd* you follow for further details. (Tr.)

A Ḥadīth in Relation to the Sermons of Ṣalāt al-Jumuʿah

In the sermons of *Ṣalāt al-Jumuʿah*, in addition to the praise and glorification of Allah ﷻ, the mention of the Noble Prophet ﷺ and the 12 immaculate Imams ؑ, and the recitation of one short chapter being obligatory *(wājib)*, it is also obligatory on the *imam* to advise the listeners of their duty to Allah ﷻ – that is, to have *taqwā* – God-consciousness. As much as is possible, the prayer leader must also advise the listeners about various issues relevant to the Muslim community, and the world.

As to what should exactly be mentioned in that portion of the sermon, and what information is necessary to convey, it is best that we discuss this issue directly from the *aḥādīth*.

In the first volume of the book, *Wasāʾil al-Shīʿa*,[27] on page 357 under the section concerning the sermons of *Ṣalāt al-Jumuʿah*, there is a narration which is also mentioned in both

---

[27] The full name of this book is *Tafṣīl Wasāʾil al-Shīʿa ilā Taḥṣīl Masāʾil al-Sharīʿa*, and it was compiled by the late Shaykh Ḥurr al-ʿĀmilī (d.1104 AH/1693 AD). *Wasāʾil al-Shīʿa* is a twenty-volume extensive collection of narrations from the Prophet ﷺ and the Ahlul Bayt ؑ regarding Shīʿa jurisprudence and practical laws. The narrations are classified in fifty categories, and the final section presents various discussions about Ḥadīth Sources, the Chains of Narrators, and a study of the transmitters of the Ḥadīth. Shaykh Ḥurr al-ʿĀmilī compiled these narrations in twenty years, finishing them in 1082 AH/1671-2 AD. This great collection contains 36,000 narrations, dealing with practical laws, obligations, and rituals. The book is a scrutinized selection from authentic early Shīʿa Ḥadīth collections and primary manuscripts of early companions.

ʿIlal al-Sharāʾiʿ[28] and *ʿUyūn al-Akhbār al-Riḍā* 🕊.[29] This *ḥadīth* has been narrated from the known and trusted companion, Faḍl ibn al-Shādhān al-Nīshābūrī[30] – one of the greatest and most dependable narrators – in which he asked Imam ʿAlī ibn Mūsā al-Riḍā 🕊 a series of questions regarding aspects of Islamic Jurisprudence. In this *ḥadīth*, he quotes Imam al-Riḍā 🕊 as saying:[31]

---

[28] Written by the late Abū Jaʿfar Muḥammad ibn ʿAlī ibn Ḥusayn ibn Mūsā al-Qummī, better known as Shaykh Ṣadūq or Ibn Bābawayh (b. 917-8 AH – d. 991-992 AH). This book contains narrations from the Prophet 🕊 and immaculate Imams 🕊 regarding the reasons of religious obligations and theological beliefs. It also includes the reasons for naming some characters and events, and some information about creation of animals. Shaykh Ṣadūq mentioned some points on the behaviours and activities of the final Prophet 🕊 and the 12 Imams 🕊. This book can be read and downloaded in PDF from: www.ijtihadnet.com by searching for "Reasons of the Rulings."

[29] *ʿUyūn al-Akhbār al-Riḍā*, also known as *ʿUyūn al-Akhbār*, is a *Ḥadīth* reference compilation of the traditions from Imam ʿAlī ibn Mūsā al-Riḍā 🕊, compiled by Shaykh Ṣadūq. The *Ḥadīth* collected in this book are either the direct sayings of the 8th Imam, or those which he quoted from his forefathers 🕊. This book is among the most important Shīʿa references, covering topics such as History, Jurisprudence, Ethics, and Theology. This can be found online at:
www.al-islam.org/uyun-akhbar-ar-ridha-volume-1-shaykh-saduq
www.al-islam.org/uyun-akhbar-ar-ridha-volume-2-shaykh-saduq

[30] His full name was Abū Muḥammad Faḍl ibn al-Shādhān ibn Khalīl al-Azdī al-Nīshābūrī (d. 873-4 AH).

[31] *ʿUyūn al-Akhbār al-Riḍā*, Vol. 2.

فَإِنْ قَالَ فَلِمَ صَارَتْ صَلَاةُ الْجُمُعَةِ إِذَا كَانَتْ مَعَ الْإِمَامِ رَكْعَتَيْنِ وَإِذَا كَانَتْ بِغَيْرِ إِمَامٍ رَكْعَتَيْنِ وَرَكْعَتَيْنِ

If it is said: "Why is it that the Friday Prayer, when performed with the *imam* (prayer leader), is only two *rakaʿāt*, but when it is without the imam, it becomes two *rakaʿāt* and two *rakaʿāt* (i.e. four in total - meaning you are reciting *Ṣalāt al-Ẓuhr)*?'

قِيلَ لِعِلَلٍ شَتَّى مِنْهَا أَنَّ النَّاسَ يَتَخَطَّوْنَ إِلَى الْجُمُعَةِ مِنْ بُعْدٍ فَأَحَبَّ اللَّهُ عَزَّ وَجَلَّ أَنْ يُخَفِّفَ عَنْهُمْ لِمَوْضِعِ التَّعَبِ الَّذِي صَارُوا إِلَيْهِ.

The reply to this is: 'For various reasons, among them that people come to the Friday prayers from far distances, so Allah, the Mighty and Majestic, wished to make things easier for them because of the hardship they endured to get there.'

وَمِنْهَا أَنَّ الْإِمَامَ يَحْبِسُهُمْ لِلْخُطْبَةِ وَهُمْ مُنْتَظِرُونَ لِلصَّلَاةِ وَمَنِ انْتَظَرَ الصَّلَاةَ فَهُوَ فِي صَلَاةٍ فِي حُكْمِ التَّمَامِ.

'And among them (the reason for the shortened prayer for *Ṣalāt al-Jumuʿah*) is that the *imam* keeps them (the congregation) for the sermons and so they wait for the prayer [listening to the sermons], and whoever is waiting for the prayer [and is patiently listening to the sermons], is, in the ruling of the law [of Islam], considered as being in the state of prayer in its entirety [it is as if they have prayed their *ṣalāt* in full – in four *rakaʿāt*].'

وَمِنْهَا أَنَّ الصَّلَاةَ مَعَ الْإِمَامِ أَتَمُّ وَأَكْمَلُ لِعِلْمِهِ وَفِقْهِهِ وَعَدْلِهِ وَفَضْلِهِ.

'And among [the other reasons is that the performance of the] *ṣalāt* with the *imam* is more complete and more perfect due to his knowledge, understanding, justice, and virtue.'

وَمِنْهَا أَنَّ الْجُمُعَةَ عِيدٌ وَصَلَاةَ الْعِيدِ رَكْعَتَانِ وَلَمْ تُقْصَرْ لِمَكَانِ الْخُطْبَتَيْنِ.

'And among [the other reasons is that] Friday is a day of *ʿEid* (festivity), and the prayer on the day of *ʿEid* consists of two units *(rakaʿāt)*, and it was not shortened because of the two sermons.'

فَإِنْ قَالَ فَلِمَ جُعِلَتِ الْخُطْبَةُ

So then, if someone says: "Why has it been that (two) sermons [are to be delivered]?"

قِيلَ لِأَنَّ الْجُمُعَةَ مَشْهَدٌ عَامٌّ فَأَرَادَ أَنْ يَكُونَ الْإِمَامُ سَبَبًا لِمَوْعِظَتِهِمْ وَتَرْغِيبِهِمْ فِي الطَّاعَةِ وَتَرْهِيبِهِمْ مِنَ الْمَعْصِيَةِ وَتَوْفِيقِهِمْ عَلَى مَا أَرَادَ مِنْ مَصْلَحَةِ دِينِهِمْ وَدُنْيَاهُمْ وَيُخْبِرُهُمْ بِمَا وَرَدَ عَلَيْهِمْ مِنَ الْآفَاتِ وَمِنَ الْأَهْوَالِ الَّتِي لَهُمْ فِيهَا الْمَضَرَّةُ وَالْمَنْفَعَةُ.

It is said: 'Since Friday is a public gathering, and Allah wanted the *imam* to be a means for their admonition, for encouraging them towards obedience, for warning them against disobedience, for guiding them to what He desires of benefit for their religion and worldly life, and for informing them of what has befallen them [the Muslims] of tribulations and momentous events in which lie harm and benefit for them.'

فَإِنْ قَالَ فَلِمَ جُعِلَتْ خُطْبَتَيْنِ قِيلَ لِأَنْ يَكُونَ وَاحِدَةٌ لِلثَّنَاءِ وَالتَّمْجِيدِ وَالتَّقْدِيسِ لِلَّهِ عَزَّ وَجَلَّ وَالْأُخْرَى لِلْحَوَائِجِ وَالْإِعْذَارِ وَالْإِنْذَارِ وَالدُّعَاءِ وَمَا يُرِيدُ أَنْ يُعَلِّمَهُمْ مِنْ أَمْرِهِ وَنَهْيِهِ مَا فِيهِ الصَّلَاحُ وَالْفَسَادُ.

So then, if it is asked: 'Why were two sermons instituted?' It is said: 'So that one may be for praising, glorifying, and sanctifying Allah, the Mighty and Majestic; while the other one would be for addressing needs, offering excuses, warnings, for supplication, and for what he (the *imam*) wishes to each them of His commands and prohibitions – that which contains their welfare and what contains their corruption.'

فَإِنْ قَالَ فَلِمَ جُعِلَتِ الْخُطْبَةُ يَوْمَ الْجُمُعَةِ قَبْلَ الصَّلَاةِ وَجُعِلَتْ فِي الْعِيدَيْنِ بَعْدَ الصَّلَاةِ

So then, if it is asked: 'Why was the sermon on Friday placed before the prayer, while in the two *'Eid* Prayers it was placed after the prayer?'

قِيلَ لِأَنَّ الْجُمُعَةَ أَمْرٌ دَائِمٌ وَتَكُونُ فِي الشَّهْرِ مِرَارًا وَفِي السَّنَةِ كَثِيرًا فَإِذَا كَثُرَ ذٰلِكَ عَلَى النَّاسِ مَلُّوا وَتَرَكُوا وَلَمْ يُقِيمُوا عَلَيْهِ وَتَفَرَّقُوا عَنْهُ فَجُعِلَتْ قَبْلَ الصَّلَاةِ لِيُحْتَبَسُوا عَلَى الصَّلَاةِ وَلَا يَتَفَرَّقُوا وَلَا يَذْهَبُوا

It is said: 'Due to the fact that Friday is a regular, recurring matter and occurs repeatedly in a month and frequently in a year. If this became too much for the people, then they would grow weary, abandon it, not uphold it, and disperse from it. Thus, the sermons were placed before the prayer so that they, the people, remain waiting for the prayer and do not scatter or leave.'

وَأَمَّا الْعِيدَيْنِ فَإِنَّمَا هُوَ فِي السَّنَةِ مَرَّتَيْنِ وَهُوَ أَعْظَمُ مِنَ الْجُمُعَةِ وَالزِّحَامُ فِيهِ أَكْثَرُ وَالنَّاسُ فِيهِ أَرْغَبُ فَإِنْ تَفَرَّقَ بَعْضُ النَّاسِ بَقِيَ عَامَّتُهُمْ وَلَيْسَ هُوَ بِكَثِيرٍ فَيَمَلُّوا وَيَسْتَخِفُّوا بِهِ.

'As for the two *'Eids*, they are only twice a year, and they are greater than the Friday Prayer, with the crowd being larger and people more eager for them. So, even if some people disperse (after the prayer), most of them will remain (for the two sermons), and it does not happen often for them to become weary or to take it lightly.'"

قَالَ مُصَنِّفُ هٰذَا الْكِتَابِ رَحِمَهُ اللّٰهُ: جَاءَ هٰذَا الْخَبَرُ هٰكَذَا وَالْخُطْبَتَانِ فِي الْجُمُعَةِ وَالْعِيدَيْنِ بَعْدَ الصَّلَاةِ لِأَنَّهُمَا بِمَنْزِلَةِ الرَّكْعَتَيْنِ الْأُخْرَاوَيْنِ وَأَوَّلُ مَنْ قَدَّمَ الْخُطْبَتَيْنِ عُثْمَانُ بْنُ عَفَّانَ.

The author of this book (Shaykh Ṣadūq), may Allah have Mercy upon him, said: "This report has come in this manner – the two

إِنَّمَا جُعِلَتِ الْخُطْبَةُ يَوْمَ الْجُمْعَةِ لِأَنَّ الْجُمْعَةَ مَشْهَدٌ عَامٌ

"The sermon was instituted on Friday because Friday is a public gathering."

فَأَرَادَ أَنْ يَكُونَ لِلأَمِيرِ سَبَبٌ إِلَى مَوْعِظَتِهِمْ وَتَرْغِيبِهِمْ فِي الطَّاعَةِ وَتَرْهِيبِهِمْ مِنَ الْمَعْصِيَةِ

"So, it was desired (by Allah ﷻ) that the leader (of *Ṣalāt al-Jumuʿah*) would provide exhortation and encourage (the listeners) to get closer to the obedience (of Allah ﷻ) and admonish them concerning (the consequences of) going against (the laws of Allah ﷻ)."

وَتَوْقِيفِهِمْ عَلَى مَا أَرَادَ مِنْ مَصْلَحَةِ دِينِهِمْ وَدُنْيَاهُمْ

---

sermons on Friday and the two ʿĪd days were (originally) after the prayer, because they take the place of the last two *rakaʿāt* (of the *ṣalāt*). The first one who delivered the sermons before the prayer was ʿUthmān ibn ʿAffān (the third caliph).

Since the people detested him for his wrongdoings, after the *ṣalāt*, they would not listen to his sermons and thought to themselves that his sermons were of no use, since he did whatever he wanted to do [in corrupting the religion].

Therefore, [on *ʿEid* day] he delivered the two sermons before the prayers, so the people would have to wait for the *ṣalāt* and not disperse."

[It seems that the author (Shaykh Ṣadūq ؒ) has made a mistake here. ʿUthmān changed the order of delivery of the sermons for the *ʿEid* Prayer. The sermons for the Friday Prayer **are** to be delivered **before** the prayers, and the sermons for the *ʿEid* Prayer **are** to be delivered **after** the prayers.]

> "And so, the people would be made aware of what is good for them in relation to their religion and religious affairs, and the worldly events as well."

> وَيُخْبِرُهُمْ بِـمَا يَرِدُ عَلَيْهِمْ مِنَ الْآفَاقِ مِنَ الْأَحْوَالِ الَّتِي فِيهَا الْمُضَرَّةُ وَالْمَنْفَعَةُ

> "In addition, (the leader of *Ṣalāt al-Jumuʿah*) would also inform the people about what is happening far away – both the good and the bad – (to the Muslims of other lands and countries) and keep them informed about various occurrences (around the world)."

Events are always taking place in various regions of the world which other believers must know about – instances where advancements are made, which are a pride and upliftment for Islam and Muslims, so it is good that such things are conveyed to other believers. Certain times, damaging events afflict the world of Islam, and these too must be conveyed to people so that they are made aware about the plight of other individuals. For example, they should know what is happening to their brothers and sisters in various parts of the world in the past week.

Why then is it necessary that **two** sermons be given? Why not just suffice with one sermon? In addition, should there be a difference in the content of these two sermons?

In this same *ḥadīth* we previously mentioned, it is stated:

وَإِنَّمَا جُعِلَتْ خُطْبَتَيْنِ لِيَكُونَ وَاحِدَةٌ لِلثَّنَاءِ عَلَى اللهِ وَالتَحْمِيدِ وَالتَّقْدِيسِ لِلّهِ عَزَّ وَجَلَّ وَالأُخْرى لِلْحَوَائِجِ وَالْإِنْذَارِ وَالدُّعَاءِ لِمَا يُرِيدُ أَنْ يُعْلِمُهُمْ مِنْ أَمْرِهِ وَنَهْيِهِ وَمَا فِيهِ الصَّلَاحُ وَالْفَسَادُ.

> "And indeed, the two sermons were instituted so that one would be for praising Allah, glorifying, and sanctifying Allah, the Mighty and Majestic, while the other would be for presenting needs, giving warnings, supplications, and conveying to the people what he [the *imam*] wishes to inform them of His commands and prohibitions, and what contains their benefit and harm."

However, just as the late Shaykh Ḥurr al-Āmulī, the compiler of *Wasāʾil al-Shīʿa* stated, this does not need to take the entire time of the speech, so other content may also be discussed in these sermons.

This concludes the text of the late Āyatullāh Murtaḍā Muṭahharī regarding the philosophy of *Ṣalāt al-Jumuʿah.*

From here, we move into the second phase of this book, and we will review forty *ḥadīth* regarding *Ṣalāt al-Jumuʿah* and *Ṣalāt al-Jamāʿah.*

Forty Ḥadīth: Ṣalāt al-Jumuʿah and Ṣalāt al-Jamāʿah[32]

وَٱعْتَصِمُوا۟

بِحَبْلِ ٱللَّهِ جَمِيعًا وَلَا تَفَرَّقُوا۟ ۚ

وَٱذْكُرُوا۟ نِعْمَتَ ٱللَّهِ عَلَيْكُمْ إِذْ كُنتُمْ

أَعْدَآءً فَأَلَّفَ بَيْنَ قُلُوبِكُمْ فَأَصْبَحْتُم بِنِعْمَتِهِۦٓ إِخْوَٰنًا

وَكُنتُمْ عَلَىٰ شَفَا حُفْرَةٍ مِّنَ ٱلنَّارِ فَأَنقَذَكُم

مِّنْهَا ۗ كَذَٰلِكَ يُبَيِّنُ ٱللَّهُ لَكُمْ ءَايَٰتِهِۦ

لَعَلَّكُمْ تَهْتَدُونَ ١٠٣

---

[32] This section of forty *ḥadīth* regarding *Ṣalāt al-Jumuʿah* and *Ṣalāt al-Jamāʿah* was compiled by Maḥmūd Laṭīfī and is available at shorturl.at/AHLY3.

"And hold fast to the rope
of Allah all together and never be divided; and
remember the favour of Allah upon you – you were once
enemies, and He reconciled your hearts, so that through His
favour you became like brothers (and sisters). And you stood
on the brink of a pit of fire, and He delivered you from it.
Thus, Allah makes His signs of truth clear to you
that you may be guided."[33]

At one level, all Muslims are equal – just like the teeth of an even comb; or they are like the various organs of a living, well-balanced body, and any damage to one part of the body will cause disorder and upheaval within the entire body.

As such, what binds the global Muslim community together has its roots in the human institutions which are created for them – either by Allah ﷻ as in the case of *Ṣalāt al-Jumuʿah*, *Ṣalāt al-Jamāʿah*, the annual *Ḥajj* rites, and other such events; or those which people create to bind themselves together and arise from the necessity of continuity of societal life. Thus, Muslims must work together for their collective preservation, just as they work for their individual protection.

Allah ﷻ created the world and gave it a unique system such that its inhabitants do not end up in a vortex of confusion and mire like chaff, scattered on the water, wandering around aimlessly; or like a sheep cut off from its

[33] Quran, Sūrah Āle ʿImrān (3), Verse 103.

flock to be prey for the wolves lying in wait, falling into the eternal torment of division, hypocrisy, or even worse.

Thus, as the Quran confirms, the believers are brethren of one another, and they share one heart and one goal. They strike down on the belligerent disbelievers like an iron fist when under attack; they are like a strong wall built with solid foundations in the face of aggressions against their faith and the global community of believers. Above all, they avoid the evil whisperer – Satan – and strive together in their united ranks.

In this collection, we have selected and translated forty ḥadīth from the immaculate, chosen ones – Prophet Muḥammad ﷺ and the 12 Imams ﷺ. Our selection seeks to provide guidance and inspiration about the Friday Prayer, as well as the Congregational Prayers.

This selection is a gift to those who are seeking true Islam and want to keep alive the revolutionary spirit of the beautiful teachings of the faith. It is for those who are looking to enliven a greater level of commitment to faith in their lives. Lastly, this collection of *aḥādīth* is a beacon of inspiration for those prayer leaders who take on the mammoth task of leading either *Ṣalāt al-Jumuʿah* or *Ṣalāt al-Jamāʿah* – or both.

May the precious words of the immaculate personalities which Allah ﷻ sent for our guidance be our candle of inspiration and enlightenment in this world, and a means of salvation in the next.

... So be it, O the Lord of the Worlds!
Maḥmūd Laṭīfī

Ṣalāt al-Jumuʿah: In the Quran

قَالَ اللهُ تَبَارَكَ وَتَعَالَى: ﴿يَٰٓأَيُّهَا ٱلَّذِينَ ءَامَنُوٓاْ إِذَا نُودِىَ لِلصَّلَوٰةِ مِن يَوۡمِ ٱلۡجُمُعَةِ فَٱسۡعَوۡاْ إِلَىٰ ذِكۡرِ ٱللَّهِ وَذَرُواْ ٱلۡبَيۡعَۚ ذَٰلِكُمۡ خَيۡرٞ لَّكُمۡ إِن كُنتُمۡ تَعۡلَمُونَ ٩﴾

Allah, Blessed and All-High says (in the Quran): "O you who believe! When the call is made for the Prayer on Friday *(Ṣalāt al-Jumuʿah)*, then hasten to the remembrance of Allah, and leave aside business (and whatever else you may be preoccupied with). This is better for you if you only knew."[34]

1. Merits of Participating in Ṣalāt al-Jumuʿah

1. Ḥajj of the Deprived

عَنْ أَبِي عَبْدِ اللهِ عليه السلام: جَاءَ أَعْرَابِيٌّ إِلَى النَّبِيِّ صلى الله عليه وآله يُقَالُ لَهُ قُلَيْبٌ فَقَالَ لَهُ: يَا رَسُولَ اللهِ إِنِّي تَهَيَّأْتُ إِلَى الْحَجِ كَذَا وَكَذَا مَرَّةً فَمَا قُدِّرَ لِي. فَقَالَ لَهُ: يَا قُلَيْبُ عَلَيْكَ بِالْجُمُعَةِ فَإِنَّهَا حَجُّ الْمَسَاكِينِ.

It has been narrated from Abī ʿAbdillāh [Imam Jaʿfar al-Ṣādiq (a)] that: "One of the desert-dwelling [bedouin] Arabs, whom it is said was named Qulayb, once came to the Prophet (s) and said to him: 'O Messenger of Allah, I have done all of the preparations required for the *Ḥajj* many times, however, I

[34] Quran, Sūrah al-Jumuʿah (62), Verse 9.

have not been successful in performing it *[Ḥajj].*' The Prophet responded: 'O Qulayb! I advise you to attend *[Ṣalāt] al-Jumuʿah* as this is the *Ḥajj* of the deprived *(al-masākīn).*'"[35]

2. Performing Ḥajj and ʿUmrah Every Friday

قَالَ رَسُولُ اللّٰهِ ﷺ: إِنَّ لَكُمْ فِي كُلِّ جُمُعَةٍ حَجَّةً وَعُمْـرَةً فَالْحَجَّةُ الْهِجْـرَةُ إِلَى الْجُمُعَةِ وَالْعُمْـرَةُ انْتِظَارُ الْعَصْـرِ بَعْدَ الْجُمُعَةِ.

The Messenger of Allah ﷺ said: "Every Friday, you can have the reward of the performance of a *Ḥajj* and an *ʿUmrah*: as for the [reward of the] *Ḥajj*, it is to rush towards the (Friday) Prayers; and as for [the reward] of the *ʿUmrah*, it is your waiting for the establishment of the *ʿAṣr* prayers after *[Ṣalāt] al-Jumuʿah.*"[36]

3. Recommended Times for Hastening

قَالَ رَسُولُ اللّٰهِ ﷺ: ثَلَاثٌ لَوْ يَعْلَمُ النَّاسُ مَا فِيهِنَّ لَـرَكَضُوا الْإِبْلِ فِي طَلَبِهِنَّ: أَلْأَذَانُ وَالصَّفُّ الْأَوَّلُ وَالْغُدُوِّ إِلَى الْجُمُعَةِ.

The Messenger of Allah ﷺ said: "If people knew the importance which lies in three things, they would have raced on the backs of camels [or used whatever means is the fastest at the time] to reach them: The *adhān* (call to prayer); standing in the first line [of the Congregational Prayers]; and hastening towards *[Ṣalāt] al-Jumuʿah.*"[37]

---

[35] Shaykh Ṭūsī, *Tahdhīb al-Aḥkām*, Vol. 3, Pg. 237, Tradition 625.

[36] ʿAllāmah Majlisī, *Biḥār al-Anwār*, Vol. 86, Pg. 213.

[37] Ghazālī, *Iḥyāʾ ʿUlūm al-Dīn*, Vol. 1, Pg. 239.

4. Steps that Protect an Individual

قَالَ الْإِمَامُ جَعْفَر الصَّادِقُ عليه السلام: مَا مِنْ قَدَمٍ سَعَتْ إِلَى الْجُمُعَةِ إِلَّا حَرَّمَ اللهُ جَسَدَهُ عَلَى النَّارِ.

Imam Jaʿfar al-Ṣādiq said: "There is no step that is taken towards *[Ṣalāt] al-Jumuʿah* except that Allah makes it impermissible *(ḥarām)* for that person's body to enter the fire [of Hell]."[38]

5. Measure of One's Spiritual Proximity to Allah

قَالَ رَسُولُ اللّٰهِ صلى الله عليه وآله: يَجْلِسُ النَّاسُ مِنَ اللّٰهِ يَوْمَ الْقِيَامَةِ عَلَى قَدْرِ رَوَاحِهِمْ إِلَى الْجُمُعَاتِ الْأَوَّلُ وَالثَّانِي وَالثَّالِثِ.

The Messenger of Allah said: "The spiritual proximity of people to Allah on the Day of Resurrection will be in relation to their attendance of *[Ṣalāt] al-Jumuʿah* in order of the first, second, and third [of their reaching to the area where *Ṣalāt al-Jumuʿah* is taking place]."[39]

6. Insurance Policy to Enter Paradise

قَالَ الْإِمَامُ عَلِيٌّ عليه السلام: ضَمِنْتُ لِسِتَّةٍ عَلَى اللّٰهِ الْجَنَّةَ مِنْهُمْ رَجُلٌ خَرَجَ إِلَى الْجُمُعَةِ فَمَاتَ فَلَهُ الْجَنَّةُ.

Imam ʿAlī said: "I take an oath by Allah, I pledge that there are six groups [of people] who will enter Paradise, and

[38] Shaykh Ṣadūq, *Al-Amālī*, Pg. 366, Tradition 14.
[39] *Mustadrak al-Wasāʾil*, Vol. 6, Pg. 38, Tradition 6369.

amongst these groups is a person who leaves their home on the way to *[Ṣalāt] al-Jumuʿah* and passes away – Paradise will become incumbent for that person."[40]

7. The Traveller

قَالَ الْإِمَامُ جَعْفَرُ الصَّادِقُ عَلَيْهِ السَّلَامُ: أَيُّمَا مُسَافِرٍ صَلَّى الْجُمُعَةَ رَغْبَةً فِيهَا وَحُبًّا لَهَا أَعْطَاهُ اللَّهُ عَزَّ وَجَلَّ أَجْرَ مِائَةِ جُمُعَةٍ لِلْمُقِيمِ.

Imam Jaʿfar al-Ṣādiq (a) said: "Allah, the Noble and Grand, will grant a traveller who – due to their desire and love for *[Ṣalāt] al-Jumuʿah* – performs it, the reward of a non-traveller who has performed one hundred *[Ṣalāt] al-Jumuʿah.*"[41]

---

[40] Shaykh Ḥurr Āmulī, *Wasāʾil al-Shīʿa*, Vol. 7, Pg. 307, Tradition 9429.

[41] *Al-Amālī*, Pg. 11, Tradition 5. We will see in the section of Jurisprudence that there are certain individuals who are exempt from performing *Ṣalāt al-Jumuʿah*, and one of them is a traveller. Perhaps it is for this reason – since they are technically excused from attending it but still decide to perform it – that they will attain this great reward. (Tr.)

2. Necessity of Participation in Ṣalāt al-Jumuʿah

8. Minimal Amount of Participants

عَنْ زُرَارَةَ قَالَ: قُلْتُ لِأَبِي جَعْفَرٍ ﵇: عَلَى مَنْ تَجِبُ الْجُمُعَةُ؟ قَالَ ﵇: تَجِبُ عَلَى سَبْعَةِ نَفَرٍ مِنَ الْمُسْلِمِينَ وَلَا جُمُعَةَ لِأَقَلَّ مِنْ خَمْسَةٍ مِنَ الْمُسْلِمِينَ أَحَدُهُمُ الْإِمَامُ.

It has been narrated from Zurārah: "I said to Abī Jaʿfar ﵇ [Imam Muḥammad al-Bāqir ﵇]: 'Upon whom is [Ṣalāt] al-Jumuʿah an obligation [how many people must be present on a Friday for Ṣalāt al-Jumuʿah to be an obligation]?' To this, he ﵇ replied: 'It becomes obligatory when seven Muslims gather; and a person cannot perform [Ṣalāt] al-Jumuʿah if there are less than five Muslims [present] – one of them being the imam [of the congregation].'"[42]

---

[42] *Wasāʾil al-Shīʿa*, Vol. 7, Pg. 304, Tradition 9410. The ruling from the senior scholars is that there must be a minimum of five people for Ṣalāt al-Jumuʿah to be an obligation – as long as all other rules are also present. As we will see in the section on the Jurisprudential rulings, Ṣalāt al-Jumuʿah is not an obligation in our current era due to the lack of a directly appointed prayer leader from the immaculate Imam ﵇ who is in the occultation *(Ghaybah)*. Thus, in such times, even if a group of five people were to gather, they are not necessarily required to establish Ṣalāt al-Jumuʿah – especially if no one fits the criteria to deliver the sermons and lead the prayers. (Tr.)

9. Radius for Participation

قَالَ الْإِمَامُ جَعْفَرُ الصَّادِقُ عليه السلام: تَجِبُ الْجُمُعَةُ عَلَى كُلِّ مَنْ كَانَ مِنْها عَلَى فَرْسَخَيْنِ.

Imam Jaʿfar al-Ṣādiq said: *"[Ṣalāt] al-Jumuʿah* is obligatory upon all of those who live in the radius of two *farsakh*[43] [of where *Ṣalāt al-Jumuʿah* is taking place]."[44]

10. Who is Excused from Attending?

عَنْ حَفْصِ بْنِ غِيَاثٍ: إِنَّ اللّهَ عَزَّ وَجَلَّ فَرَضَ الْجُمُعَةَ عَلَى جَمِيعِ الْمُؤْمِنِينَ وَالْمُؤْمِنَاتِ وَرَخَّصَ لِلْمَرْئَةِ وَالْعَبْدِ وَالْمُسَافِرِ أَنْ لَا يَأْتُوهَا فَلَمَّا حَضَرُوا سَقَطَتِ الرُّخْصَةُ وَلَزِمَهُمُ الْفَرْضُ الْأَوَّلُ فَمِنْ أَجْلِ ذٰلِكَ أَجْزَءَ عَنْهُمْ. فَقُلْتُ: عَمَّنْ هٰذَا؟ قَالَ: عَنْ مَوْلَانَا أَبِي عَبْدِ اللّهِ عليه السلام.

It has been narrated from Ḥafṣ ibn Ghiyāth: "Indeed, Allah, the Noble and Grand, has obligated [the performance of *Ṣalāt*] *al-Jumuʿah* upon all believing men and believing women; and He has granted a concession to a woman, a slave, and a traveller that they do not have to attend. However, if they are present (in the gathering where *Ṣalāt al-Jumuʿah* is about to take place), then it is an obligation upon them to perform it *[Ṣalāt al-Jumuʿah]*, and they cannot abstain from

---

[43] A *farsakh* is a measure of distance equaling about 5.76 km or 3.42 miles, thus, two farsakh is approximately 11.52 km or 6.84 miles.

[44] *Al-Kāfī*, Vol. 2, Pg. 419, Tradition 2. Refer to the section on Islamic Jurisprudence in this book or the *Marjaʿ Taqlīd* you follow for further details. (Tr.)

its performance. In this case, *Ṣalāt al-Jumuʿah* will suffice for them in place [of the performance of] *Ṣalāt al-Ẓuhr.*" The companion who narrated this *ḥadīth* then asked: "Who is this [ruling] from?" To this, Ḥafṣ replied: "It is from our master *(Maulānā)* Abī ʿAbdillāh ﷺ [Imam Jaʿfar al-Ṣādiq ﷺ]."[45]

11. Consequences for Intentionally Abandoning

قَالَ رَسُولُ اللهِ ﷺ فِي خُطْبَةٍ طَوِيلَةٍ نَقَلَهَا الْمُخَالِفُ وَالْمُؤَالِفُ: إِنَّ اللهَ تَبَارَكَ وَتَعَالَى فَرَضَ عَلَيْكُمُ الْجُمُعَةَ فَمَنْ تَرَكَهَا فِي حَيَاتِي أَوْ بَعْدَ مَوْتِي اسْتِخْفَافًا بِهَا أَوْ جُحُودًا لَهَا فَلَا جَمَعَ اللهُ شَمْلَهُ وَلَا بَارَكَ لَهُ فِي أَمْرِهِ أَلَا وَلَا صَلَاةَ لَهُ أَلَا وَلَا زَكَاةَ لَهُ أَلَا وَلَا حَجَّ لَهُ أَلَا وَلَا صَوْمَ لَهُ أَلَا وَلَا بِرَّ لَهُ حَتَّى يَتُوبَ.

During a lengthy sermon which both the Sunnī *(al-Mukhālif)* and the Shīʿa *(al-Muʾālif)* narrate, Prophet Muḥammad ﷺ said: "Indeed Allah, Blessed and All-Exalted, placed an obligation upon all of you with respect to *[Ṣalāt] al-Jumuʿah.* So, then the person who forsakes it during my lifetime or after my death – due to considering it trivial or denying it [its importance] – Allah will not organize that person's affairs, nor will they have any blessings in their actions. Realize that a person's *ṣalāt, zakāt, Ḥajj, ṣawm,* and goodness to their parents will not be accepted until they repent (to Allah ﷻ and make amends) [and give importance to *Ṣalāt al-Jumuʿah*]."[46]

[45] *Wasāʾil al-Shīʿa*, Vol. 7, Pg. 337, Tradition 9518.

[46] Ibid., Pg. 302, Tradition 9,409.

12. Outcome of Spiritual Negligence (Ghaflah)

قَالَ رَسُولُ اللّٰهِ ﷺ: لَيَنْتَهِيَنَّ أَقْوَامٌ عَنْ وَدْعِهِمُ الْجُمُعَاتِ أَوْ لَيُخْتَمَنَّ عَلَى قُلُوبِهِمْ ثُمَّ لَيَكُونُنَّ مِنَ الْغَافِلِينَ.

The Messenger of Allah ﷺ said: "Certainly people [will come in the future, who] will persist in abandoning the Friday Prayers and through this, their hearts will become sealed, and they will definitely be (regarded as being) among the heedless ones *(al-ghāfilīn).*"[47]

13. Demolition of a Community

قَالَ عَلِيٌّ ؑ: ثَلَاثَةٌ إِنْ أَنْتُمْ خَالَفْتُمْ فِيهِنَّ أَئِمَّتَكُمْ هَلَكْتُمْ جُمُعَتُكُمْ وَجِهَادُ عَدُوِّكُمْ وَمَنَاسِكُكُمْ.

Imam ʿAlī ؑ said: "There are three things that if you disobey your leaders in these, you will be destroyed: your *[Ṣalāt] al-Jumuʿah*; your standing in the sacred defense *(jihād)* against your enemies; and your rites (and duties in regard to) the *Ḥajj* pilgrimage."[48]

14. A Way to Identify a Hypocrite

قَالَ رَسُولُ اللّٰهِ ﷺ: مَنْ تَرَكَ ثَلَاثَ جُمُعَاتٍ مِنْ غَيْرِ عُذْرٍ كُتِبَ مِنَ الْمُنَافِقِينَ.

---

[47] *Wasāʾil al-Shīʿa,* Vol. 7, Pg. 337, Tradition 9,407.

[48] *Mustadrak Wasāʾil al-Shīʿa,* Vol. 5, Pg. 7, Tradition 6,286.

The Messenger of Allah ﷺ said: "A person who does not attend *[Ṣalāt] al-Jumuʿah* for three consecutive Fridays without a valid reason will be regarded as being among the hypocrites *(al-munāfiqīn)*."[49]

15. Working During Prayer Time

قَالَ رَسُولُ اللهِ ﷺ: مَنِ اسْتَأْجَرَ أَجِيراً فَلَا يَحْبِسْهُ عَنِ الْجُمُعَةِ فَيَأْثَمَ وَإِنْ لَمْ يَحْبِسْهُ عَنِ الْجُمُعَةِ اشْتَرَكَا فِي الْأَجْرِ.

The Messenger of Allah ﷺ said: "A person who hires a worker to do some work but does not permit them to take time off for *[Ṣalāt] al-Jumuʿah* has committed a sin; and if they do not prevent them from performing *[Ṣalāt] al-Jumuʿah,* then they will share in the rewards [of that person performing *Ṣalāt al-Jumuʿah*]."[50]

16. Incarcerated Muslims

عَنْ أَبِي عَبْدِ اللهِ عليه السلام قَالَ: إِنَّ عَلَى الْإِمَامِ أَنْ يُخْرِجَ الْمُحْبَسِينَ فِي الدَّيْنِ يَوْمَ الْجُمُعَةِ إِلَى الْجُمُعَةِ وَيَوْمَ الْعِيدِ إِلَى الْعِيدِ وَيُرْسِلَ مَعَهُمْ فَإِذَا قَضَوُا الصَّلَاةَ وَالْعِيدَ رَدَّهُمْ إِلَى السِّجْنِ.

Abū ʿAbdillāh [Imam Jaʿfar al-Ṣādiq عليه السلام] said: "The leader *(imam)* must ensure that the incarcerated Muslims who have been put into prison due to their debts (that they could not pay) are taken out of prison on Friday to perform *[Ṣalāt] al-Jumuʿah,* and also on the Day of *ʿEid* to perform *[Ṣalāt] al-*

[49] *Man lā Yaḥḍhuruhu al-Faqīh,* Vol. 1, Pg. 375, Tradition 1,090.
[50] *Mustadrak Wasāʾil al-Shīʿa,* Vol. 6, Pg. 7, Tradition 6,285.

Eid, then sent back to prison once the prayers and/or the *Eid* [celebrations] are completed."[51]

17. How to Prepare

قَالَ أَبُو جَعْفَرٍ ؏: وَاللهِ لَقَدْ بَلَغَنِي أَنَّ أَصْحَابَ النَّبِيِّ ﷺ كَانُوا يَتَجَهَّزُونَ لِلْجُمُعَةِ يَوْمَ الْخَمِيسِ لِأَنَّهُ يَوْمٌ مُضَيَّقٌ عَلَى الْمُسْلِمِينَ.

Abū Ja'far ؏ [Imam Muḥammad al-Bāqir ؏] said: "I take an oath by Allah that news has reached me that the companions of the Prophet ﷺ would prepare themselves for *[Ṣalāt] al-Jumu'ah* on Thursday because they recognized it [Friday] as being a very pressing day for the Muslims [as there was so much work to do they felt that they did not have enough time to get everything done to prepare for Friday]."[52]

3. Etiquettes to Observe

18. Manners to Observe

قَالَ أَبُو عَبْدِ اللهِ ؏ لِيَتَزَيَّنْ أَحَدُكُمْ يَوْمَ الْجُمُعَةِ يَغْتَسِلُ وَيَتَطَيَّبُ وَيُسَرِّحُ لِحْيَتَهُ وَيَلْبَسُ أَنْظَفَ ثِيَابِهِ وَلْيَتَهَيَّأْ لِلْجُمُعَةِ وَلْيَكُنْ عَلَيْهِ فِي ذٰلِكَ الْيَوْمِ السَّكِينَةُ وَالْوَقَارُ وَلْيُحْسِنْ عِبَادَةَ رَبِّهِ وَلْيَفْعَلِ الْخَيْرَ مَا اسْتَطَاعَ فَإِنَّ اللهَ يَطَّلِعُ عَلَى أَهْلِ الْأَرْضِ لِيُضَاعِفَ الْحَسَنَاتِ.

---

[51] Shaykh Ṭūsī, *Tahdhīb al-Aḥkām*, Vol. 3, Pg. 285, Tradition 852.
[52] *Al-Kāfī*, Vol. 3, Pg. 415, Tradition 10.

Abū ʿAbdillāh ⁕ [Imam Jaʿfar al-Ṣādiq ⁕] said: "Each one of you should beautify yourselves on Friday: you should take a bath *(ghusl)*, apply perfume, comb your beard (hair), wear the cleanest of clothing, and prepare yourself for *[Ṣalāt] al-Jumuʿah* – of course, you should act with tranquillity and dignity [in getting ready and carrying out the activities of the day]; and (more so) need to beautify your worship to your Lord and perform acts of goodness as much as you are able to, for indeed, Allah has informed the people of the Earth that good deeds will receive an increased reward [on Friday]."[53]

19. Recompense for Sins of the Previous Week

قَالَ رَسُولُ اللهِ ﷺ: مَنِ اغْتَسَلَ يَوْمَ الْجُمُعَةِ وَمَسَّ مِنْ طِيبِ امْرَأَتِهِ إِنْ كَانَ لَهَا وَلَبِسَ مِنْ صَالِحِ ثِيَابِهِ ثُمَّ لَمْ يَتَخَطَّ رِقَابَ النَّاسِ وَلَمْ يَلْغُ عِنْدَ الْمَوْعِظَةِ كَانَ كَفَّارَةً لِمَا بَيْنَهُمَا وَمَنْ لَغَا وَتَخَطَّى رِقَابَ النَّاسِ كَانَتْ لَهُ ظُهْرًا.

The Messenger of Allah ⁕ said: "A person who performs a *ghusl* on Friday, then uses his wife's perfume [if he does not have any of his own to use], then puts on his best clothing; and when he walks through the rows of the people attending *[Ṣalāt] al-Jumuʿah,* he does so ensuring that he does not step on the clothing of the people, and does not utter any words while the two sermons are being delivered will find that [his *Ṣalāt al-Jumuʿah*] will be a recompense *(kaffārah)* for the sins performed between two *[Ṣalāt al-Jumuʿah]* sessions. However, if a person speaks during the two sermons, then *Ṣalāt al-Jumuʿah* will only be regarded as *Ṣalāt al-Ẓuhr*

---

[53] *Al-Kāfī*, Vol. 3, Pg. 418, Tradition 1.

(meaning that the aspect of attending *Ṣalāt al-Jumuʿah* as being an atonement *(kaffārah)* of their sins will be removed from them)."[54]

20. The Angels are Obligated to Record

قَالَ النَّبِيُّ ﷺ: إِذَا كَانَ يَوْمُ الْجُمُعَةِ كَانَ عَلَى كُلِّ بَابٍ مِنْ أَبْوَابِ الْمَسْجِدِ مَلَائِكَةٌ يَكْتُبُونَ الْأَوَّلَ فَالْأَوَّلَ فَإِذَا جَلَسَ الْإِمَامُ طَوَوُا الصُّحُفَ وجَاءُوا يَسْتَمِعُونَ الذِّكْرَ.

The Prophet ﷺ said: "When Friday comes along [and the people gather to take part in *Ṣalāt al-Jumuʿah*], angels are stationed at every door of the *masjid,* and they record the names of the people in the order in which they enter. When the *imam* [of *Ṣalāt al-Jumuʿah*] sits in his spot [awaiting the time to start the sermons], the angels close the book of records [in which they were recording the names of the people as they entered], and they take their own places [in the *masjid*] to listen to the reminder [the sermons]."[55]

21. Greeting the Individuals Attending

قَالَ الْإِمَامُ عَلِيٌّ عليه السلام: مِنَ السُّنَّةِ إِذَا صَعِدَ الْإِمَامُ الْمِنْبَرَ أَنْ يُسَلِّمَ إِذَا اسْتَقْبَلَ النَّاسَ.

Imam ʿAlī عليه السلام said: "From the *Sunnah* [of Prophet Muḥammad ﷺ] is that when the *imam* ascends the *mimbar* [to begin to

---

[54] *Biḥār al-Anwār,* Vol. 86, Pg. 212, Tradition 57.
[55] *Mustadrak al-Wasāʾil,* Vol. 6, Pg. 38, Tradition 6,368.

deliver the sermons for *Ṣalāt al-Jumuʿah*], he starts by greeting (saying *Salāmun ʿAlaykum* to) the people."[56]

22. The Political and Ethical Program for a Believer

عَنِ الْإِمَامُ عَلِيُّ ابْنِ مُوسَى الرِّضَا عليه السلام قَالَ: إِنَّـمَا جُعِلَتِ الْخُطْبَةُ يَوْمَ الْجُمُعَةِ لِأَنَّ الْجُمُعَةَ مَشْهَدٌ عَامٌّ فَأَرَادَ أَنْ يَكُونَ لِلْأَمِيرِ سَبَبٌ إِلَى مَوْعِظَتِهِمْ وَتَرْغِيبِهِمْ فِي الطَّاعَةِ وَتَرْهِيبِهِمْ مِنَ الْمَعْصِيَةِ وَتَوْقِيفِهِمْ عَلَى مَا أَرَادَ مِنْ مَصْلَحَةِ دِينِهِمْ وَدُنْيَاهُمْ وَيُخْبِرُهُمْ بِـمَا وَرَدَ عَلَيْهِمْ مِنَ (الْآفَاقِ مِنَ) الْأَهْوَالِ الَّتِي لَهُمْ فِيهَا الْمَضَرَّةُ وَالْمَنْفَعَةُ وَلَا يَكُونُ الصَّابِرُ فِي الصَّلَاةِ مُنْفَصِلًا وَلَيْسَ بِفَاعِلٍ غَيْرُهُ مِمَّنْ يَؤُمُّ النَّاسَ فِي غَيْرِ يَوْمِ الْجُمُعَةِ وَإِنَّـمَا جُعِلَتْ خُطْبَتَيْنِ لِيَكُونَ وَاحِدَةٌ لِلثَّنَاءِ عَلَى اللهِ وَالتَّمْجِيدِ وَالتَّقْدِيسِ لِلَّهِ عَزَّ وَجَلَّ وَالْأُخْرَى لِلْحَوَائِجِ وَالْإِعْذَارِ وَالْإِنْذَارِ وَالدُّعَاءِ وَلِمَا يُرِيدُ أَنْ يُعَلِّمَهُمْ مِنْ أَمْرِهِ وَنَهْيِهِ مَا فِيهِ الصَّلَاحُ وَالْفَسَادُ.

It has been narrated that Imam ʿAlī ibn Mūsā al-Riḍā عليه السلام said: "The sermons were designated [specifically] for the day of Friday because the Friday Prayer is a public gathering, so He (Allah عزّ وجلّ) wanted to provide a way for the leader *(imam)* to admonish and encourage them [the people] towards obedience, warn them against disobedience, and remind them about what He intends in regards of reforming their religious issues and worldly affairs, and to inform them about the calamities that could bring them harm or benefit. The one who is patient for the sake of the prayer (i.e., patiently

[56] *Tahdhīb al-Aḥkām*, Vol. 3, Pg. 244, Tradition 662.

waiting for the prayer) is not distanced from it [from receiving the rewards]; nor shall another person who normally leads in other than the Friday prayer do [the above – the individual that is regarded as the regular, appointed *imam* of the centre should always be leading *Ṣalāt al-Jumuʿah*]. The sermons were made (to be) two so that one is dedicated to praising, glorifying, and sanctifying Allah Almighty; while the other one is for [discussing] the affairs, discharging the duty of warning, making supplications, and for what he (the *imam*) intends of teaching them from His commands and prohibitions what brings benefit and detriment [to the people]."[57]

23. Remaining Silent During Time of Sermons

عَنْ أَبِي عَبْدِ اللّهِ عليه السلام قَالَ: إِذَا خَطَبَ الْإِمَامُ يَوْمَ الْجُمُعَةِ فَلَا يَنْبَغِي لِأَحَدٍ أَنْ يَتَكَلَّمَ حَتَّى يَفْرُغَ الْإِمَامُ مِنْ خُطْبَتِهِ وَإِذَا فَرَغَ الْإِمَامُ مِنَ الْخُطْبَتَيْنِ تَكَلَّمَ مَا بَيْنَهُ وَبَيْنَ أَنْ تُقَامَ الصَّلَاةُ فَإِنْ سَمِعَ الْقِرَاءَةَ أَوْ لَمْ يَسْمَعْ أَجْزَأَهُ.

It is narrated from Abī ʿAbdillāh [Imam Jaʿfar al-Ṣādiq (a)] that he said: "When the *imam* is delivering the Friday sermons (for *Ṣalāt al-Jumuʿah*), it is not appropriate for anyone to speak until the *imam* completes his sermons. Thus, when the *imam* completes the two sermons, then a person is permitted to speak from that time until the time when the prayer (*Ṣalāt al-Jumuʿah*) is established. Whether a person hears the recitation [of the *imam*] or does not hear it, one is discharged of this duty (to remain silent and does not recite

---

[57] *Wasāʾil al-Shīʿa*, Vol. 7, Pg. 333, Tradition 9,510.

the two chapters of the Quran – Sūrah al-Fātiḥa and the second chapter in both *rakaʿāt*)."[58]

24. The Sermon is Equivalent to Two-Rakaʿāt of Ṣalāt

عَنْ أَبِي عَبْدِ اللّٰهِ عليه السلام قَالَ: إِنَّمَا جُعِلَتِ الْجُمُعَةُ رَكْعَتَيْنِ مِنْ أَجْلِ الْخُطْبَتَيْنِ فَهِيَ صَلَاةٌ حَتَّى يَنْزِلَ الْإِمَامُ.

It is narrated from Abī ʿAbdillāh [Imam Jaʿfar al-Ṣādiq ﷺ] that he said: "[The reason] *[Ṣalāt] al-Jumuʿah* is two *rakaʿāt* is due to the two sermons. Thus, those two sermons are 'equivalent' to two *rakaʿāt* of *ṣalāt* [and while the people (who are participating in *Ṣalāt al-Jumuʿah*) are listening to the two sermons, they are regarded as being in a state of *ṣalāt*] until the *imam* completes them [the two sermons]."[59]

25. Acceptance of One's Supplications

قَالَ الْإِمَامُ الصَّادِقُ عليه السلام: أَلسَّاعَةُ الَّتِي تُسْتَجَابُ فِيهَا الدُّعَاءُ يَوْمَ الْجُمُعَةِ مَا بَيْنَ فَرَاغِ الْإِمَامِ مِنَ الْخُطْبَةِ إِلَى أَنْ يَسْتَوِيَ النَّاسُ فِي الصُّفُوفِ، وَسَاعَةٌ أُخْرَى مِنْ آخِرِ النَّهَارِ وَإِلَى غُرُوبِ الشَّمْسِ.

It is narrated from [Imam Jaʿfar] al-Ṣādiq ﷺ that he said: "There is a time on Friday in which supplications are answered [by Allah ﷻ]. [One of them is] between the time when the *imam* finishes the [second] sermon, and people are

[58] *Al-Kāfī*, Vol. 3, Pg. 421, Tradition 2.

[59] *Wasāʾil al-Shīʿa*, Vol. 7, Pg. 313, Tradition 9,441.

moving into place in the rows [to offer *Ṣalāt al-Jumuʿah*]; and [the second time] is at the end of Friday in its final hours just before the setting of the sun."[60]

Since *Ṣalāt al-Jumuʿah* can only be performed in congregation *(jamāʿah)*, we also need to better understand the traditions which speak about the Congregational Prayers *(Ṣalāt al-Jamāʿah)* – a selection of which we present below.

4. Merits of Participation in Ṣalāt al-Jamāʿah

26. The Greatness of Congregational Prayers

إِنَّ رَسُولَ اللّٰهِ ﷺ قَالَ: صَلَاةُ الْجَمَاعَةِ أَفْضَلُ مِنْ صَلَاةِ الْفَرْدِ بِخَمْسٍ وَعِشْرِينَ دَرَجَةً.

Indeed, the Messenger of Allah ﷺ said: "The Congregational Prayers *(Ṣalāt al-Jamāʿah)* are twenty-five levels [times] better than a prayer performed individually *(furāda)*."[61]

---

[60] Shaykh Ḥurr al-ʿĀmilī, *Hidāyatul Ummah ilā Aḥkām al-Aʾimmah* ﷺ, Vol. 3, Pg. 251, Tradition 111.

[61] Shaykh Ṣadūq, *Al-Khiṣāl,* Vol. 2, Pg. 521, Tradition 10.

27. Wisdom behind Congregational Prayers

عَنِ الرِّضَا عليه السلام قَالَ: إِنَّمَا جُعِلَتِ الْجَمَاعَةُ لِئَلَّا يَكُونَ الْإِخْلَاصُ وَالتَّوْحِيدُ وَالْإِسْلَامُ وَالْعِبَادَةُ لِلّٰهِ إِلَّا ظَاهِرًا مَكْشُوفًا مَشْهُورًا لِأَنَّ فِي إِظْهَارِهِ حُجَّةً عَلَى أَهْلِ الشَّرْقِ وَالْغَرْبِ لِلّٰهِ وَحْدَهُ وَلِيَكُونَ الْمُنَافِقُ وَالْمُسْتَخِفُّ مُؤَدِّيًا لِمَا أَقَرَّ بِهِ يُظْهِرُ الْإِسْلَامَ وَالْمُرَاقَبَةَ وَلِيَكُونَ شَهَادَاتُ النَّاسِ بِالْإِسْلَامِ بَعْضِهِمْ لِبَعْضٍ جَائِزَةً مُمْكِنَةً مَعَ مَا فِيهِ مِنَ الْمُسَاعَدَةِ عَلَى الْبِرِّ وَالتَّقْوَى وَالزَّجْرِ عَنْ كَثِيرٍ مِنْ مَعَاصِي اللّٰهِ عَزَّ وَجَلَّ.

[Imam ʿAlī ibn Mūsā] al-Riḍā said: "The Congregational Prayers *(Ṣalāt al-Jamāʿah)* have been instituted in Islam so that sincerity *(ikhlāṣ)*, the belief in the Oneness of Allah *(Tawḥīd)*, Islam, and the worshipping *(ʿibādah)* of Allah are publicly seen and known – since this will serve as a proof *(ḥujjah)* upon the people of the East and the West, about Allah, the One. It also serves as a means by which the hypocrites, and those who underestimate the prayer would at least have to publicly perform what they claim to adhere to. Further, it serves as a means for Muslims to testify to the adherence of their fellow Muslim brethren to Islam. There are certain other benefits for Congregational Prayers as well, such as encouragement to do good deeds, advising (oneself and others) to God-consciousness *(taqwā)*, and admonishing against doing many of the acts of disobedience to Allah, the Noble and Grand.'"[62]

[62] *Wasāʾil al-Shīʿa*, Vol. 8, Pg. 287, Tradition 10,683.

28. Two Pages of Liberation

عَنِ النَّبِيِّ ﷺ: مَنْ صَلَّى أَرْبَعِينَ يَوْمًا فِي جَمَاعَةٍ يُدْرِكُ التَّكْبِيرَةَ الْأُولَى كُتِبَ لَهُ بَرَاءَتَانِ بَرَاءَةٌ مِنَ النَّارِ وَبَرَاءَةٌ مِنَ النِّفَاقِ.

The Prophet [Muḥammad] ﷺ said: "A person who partakes in Congregational Prayers for forty days such that they witness the *Takbīratul Iḥrām* [in congregation – meaning they join in the prayers right from when they start] should know that two forms of liberation will be written for them: One is the liberation from the fire of Hell, and (the other is the) liberation from hypocrisy *(nifāq)*."[63]

29. Lines of Those in Jihād (Sacred Struggle)

قَالَ الْإِمَامُ مُوسَى بْنُ جَعْفَرٍ عليه السلام: إِنَّ الصَّلَاةَ فِي الصَّفِ الْأَوَّلِ كَالْجِهَادِ فِي سَبِيلِ اللّٰهِ عَزَّ وَجَلَّ.

Imam Mūsā ibn Jaʿfar عليه السلام said: "Indeed, the performance of *Ṣalāt [al-Jamāʿah]* in [which the person is standing in] the first row is like being engaged in the sacred struggle *(jihād)* in the Way of Allah, the Noble and Grand."[64]

---

[63] *Mustadrak al-Wasāʾil*, Vol. 6, Pg. 447, Tradition 7,192.

[64] *Man lā Yaḥḍhuruhu al-Faqih*, Vol. 1, Pg. 385, Tradition 1,140.

30. The First Rows of the Prayers

قَالَ الْإِمَامُ عَلِيٌّ عليه السلام: سُدُّوا فُرَجَ الصُّفُوفِ مَنِ اسْتَطَاعَ أَنْ يُتِمَّ الصَّفَّ الْأَوَّلَ وَالَّذِي يَلِيهِ فَلْيَفْعَلْ فَإِنَّ ذٰلِكُمْ أَحَبُّ إِلَى نَبِيِّكُمْ وَأَتِمُّوا الصُّفُوفَ فَإِنَّ اللّٰهَ وَمَلَائِكَتَهُ يُصَلُّونَ عَلَى الَّذِينَ يُتِمُّونَ الصُّفُوفَ.

Imam ʿAlī ﷺ said: "Fill up the gaps in the rows. Those who can complete the first row and the next one should do so, for that is more beloved to your Prophet; and complete the rows, for Allah and His Angels send blessings upon those who complete the rows [before starting the next rows for *Ṣalāt al-Jamāʿah*]."[65]

5. The Necessity of Ṣalāt al-Jamāʿah

31. Being Present in the Community

قَالَ رَسُولُ اللّٰهِ ﷺ: إِنَّ الشَّيْطَانَ ذِئْبُ الْإِنْسَانِ كَذِئْبِ الْغَنَمِ يَأْخُذُ الشَّاةَ الْقَاصِيَةَ وَالنَّاحِيَةَ فَإِيَّاكُمْ وَالشِّعَابَ وَعَلَيْكُم بِالْجَمَاعَةِ وَالعَامَّةِ وَالْمَسْجِدِ.

The Messenger of Allah ﷺ said: "Indeed, *Shayṭān* (Satan) is (like) a wolf towards people [seeking to attack them] just like a wolf is a beast towards the sheep [seeking to attack and kill them] and always tries to take those sheep who are the farthest away [from the flock and the shepherd]. Thus, avoid classifications [groupism and separation]; and I advise you to

[65] *Mustadrak al-Wasāʾil*, Vol. 6, Pg. 505, Tradition 7,373.

be present in the congregations *[Ṣalāt al-Jamāʿah]*, in general gatherings (which are righteous ones), and in the *masjid*."[66]

32. Severing Relations with Some People

قَالَ رَسُولُ اللّٰهِ ﷺ: لَا صَلَاةَ لِمَنْ لَا يُصَلِّي فِي الْمَسْجِدِ مَعَ الْمُسْلِمِينَ إِلَّا مِنْ عِلَّةٍ.

The Messenger of Allah ﷺ said: "The *ṣalāt* of a person who does not pray *(Ṣalāt al-Jamāʿah)* with the other Muslims in a *masjid* without a valid reason is not counted."[67 and 68]

قَالَ رَسُولُ اللّٰهِ ﷺ: لَا غِيبَةَ إِلَّا لِمَنْ صَلَّى فِي بَيْتِهِ وَرَغِبَ عَنْ جَمَاعَتِنَا وَمَنْ رَغِبَ عَنْ جَمَاعَةِ الْمُسْلِمِينَ وَجَبَ عَلَى الْمُسْلِمِينَ غِيبَتُهُ وَسَقَطَتْ بَيْنَهُمْ عَدَالَتُهُ وَوَجَبَ هِجْرَانُهُ وَإِذَا رُفِعَ إِلَى إِمَامِ الْمُسْلِمِينَ أَنْذَرَهُ وَحَذَّرَهُ فَإِنْ حَضَرَ جَمَاعَةَ الْمُسْلِمِينَ وَإِلَّا أَحْرَقَ عَلَيْهِ بَيْتَهُ وَمَنْ لَزِمَ جَمَاعَتَهُمْ حَرُمَتْ عَلَيْهِمْ غِيبَتُهُ وَثَبَتَتْ عَدَالَتُهُ بَيْنَهُمْ.

The Messenger of Allah ﷺ said: "A person cannot backbite (a believer) except [meaning there are certain instances when one is permitted to backbite]: a person who prays in one's own house [and intentionally does not perform the Congregational Prayers] with others in a gathering. Thus, one who dislikes being amongst the community of Muslims,

---

[66] *Al-Muʿjizāt al-Nabawīyyah*, Pg. 405.

[67] *Man lā Yaḥḍhuruhu al-Faqīh*, Vol. 3, Pg. 39, Tradition 3,280.

[68] Such a *ṣalāt* **may** be 'accepted' by Allah ﷻ as in the person has fulfilled one's obligation of the prayers, however, they will not receive the rewards promised. (Tr.)

it becomes permissible upon other Muslims to engage in backbiting (about) that person, and such a person (who does not perform the prayers in congregation), their state of being morally-just and upright *(ʿadālah)* is dropped, and it is obligatory to desert this individual. When the situation of this individual is raised to the *imam* of the Muslim community, they must be admonished and warned; then if they attend the gatherings of the Muslims *(Ṣalāt al-Jamāʿah)* [then all is well and good]; however, if they still desist and do not [attend *Ṣalāt al-Jamāʿah*], then their house should be burned down.[69] Whoever adheres to the community (and attends *Ṣalāt al-Jamāʿah*), it is forbidden to backbite that individual, and their being just *(ʿādil)* is confirmed."[70]

33. Not Giving Importance

قَالَ الْإِمَامُ عَلِيٌّ عليه السلام: مَنْ سَمِعَ النِّدَاءَ فَلَمْ يُجِبْهُ مِنْ غَيْرِ عِلَّةٍ فَلَا صَلَاةَ لَهُ.

[Imam] ʿAlī (a) said: "A person who hears the call [for the establishment of *Ṣalāt al-Jamāʿah*] and does not answer it without a valid reason [and therefore, performs their *ṣalāt*

---

[69] Phrases like **"their house should be burned down,"** in *Ḥadīth* literature are "stern warnings" meant to strongly discourage abandoning religious duties, not actual commands to carry out such an action. They highlight how serious it is to neglect significant religious obligations; and in this instance, the *ḥadīth* draw the attention of the Muslims to the great value of communal worship in Islam. (Tr.)

[70] *Tahdhīb al-Aḥkām*, Vol. 7, Pg. 241. Tradition 1.

individually, rather than in congregation], they have no *ṣalāt* [meaning that their *ṣalāt* will not be accepted by Allah ﷻ]."[71]

34. Penalty for Intentionally being Absent

قَالَ رَسُولُ اللّٰهِ ﷺ: لَيَنْتَهِيَنَّ أَقْوَامٌ لَا يَشْهَدُونَ الصَّلَاةَ أَوْ لَآمُرَنَّ مُؤَذِّنًا يُؤَذِّنُ ثُمَّ يُقِيمُ ثُمَّ لَآمُرَنَّ رَجُلًا مِنْ أَهْلِ بَيْتِي وَهُوَ عَلِيُّ بْنُ أَبِي طَالِبٍ فَلَيُحْرِقَنَّ عَلَى أَقْوَامٍ بُيُوتَهُمْ بِحُزَمِ الْحَطَبِ لِأَنَّهُمْ لَا يَأْتُونَ الصَّلَاةَ.

The Messenger of Allah ﷺ said: "Those who do not attend the Congregational Prayers need to stop doing this, otherwise I will order the *muadhdhin* to call the *adhān* and *iqāmah*. Then (once the people gather), I will order a man from my family, and he is ʿAlī ibn Abī Ṭālib, to take bundles of firewood and set fire to the[ir] houses because they do not attend the (Congregational) Prayers."[72]

35. The Scale of Recognition

قَالَ رَسُولُ اللّٰهِ ﷺ: إِذَا سُئِلْتَ عَمَّنْ لَا يَشْهَدُ الْجَمَاعَةَ فَقُلْ لَا أَعْرِفُهُ.

The Messenger of Allah ﷺ said: "If you are asked about someone [to testify in their respect for something that requires this – such as a marriage proposal, or business transactions] who does not attend the congregation [of *Ṣalāt*

---

[71] *Al-Kāfī*, Vol. 3, Pg. 382, Tradition 5.

[72] *Wasāʾil al-Shīʿa*, Vol. 5, Pg. 195, Tradition 6,310. Refer to footnote 69 for an interpretation of what such a phrase can mean.

al-Jamāʿah], then respond to that individual by saying: 'I do not know that person.'"[73]

6. Manners of Ṣalāt al-Jamāʿah

36. Rushing to be Present

قَالَ رَسُولُ اللّهِ ﷺ: إِذَا سَمِعْتَ الْأَذَانَ فَأْتِ وَلَوْ حَبْوًا.

The Messenger of Allah ﷺ said: "When you hear the *adhān* (for the Congregational Prayers), then come [to the *masjid* as fast as possible] even with your chest raised [meaning even if you have to run to get there]."[74]

37. The Prayer Leader

قَالَ رَسُولُ اللّهِ ﷺ: إِمَامُ الْقَوْمِ وَافِدُهُمْ فَقَدِّمُوا أَفْضَلَكُمْ.

The Messenger of Allah ﷺ said: "The leader *(imam)* of the Congregational Prayers is the representative [of the followers – in the presence of Allah ﷻ] thus, choose the worthiest person [to be the prayer leader]."[75]

38. Unification of the Hearts

قَالَ رَسُولُ اللّهِ ﷺ: إِسْتَووا تَسْتَوِ قُلُوبُكُمْ وَتَمَاسُوا تَرَاحَمُوا.

Prophet Muḥammad ﷺ said: "Arrange the lines [of the Congregational Prayers] so that your hearts are also

---

[73] *Biḥār al-Anwār*, Vol. 85, Pg. 5, Tradition 6.

[74] Muttaqī al-Hindī, *Kanz al-ʿUmmāl*, Vol. 7, Pg. 548.

[75] *Wasāʾil al-Shīʿa*, Vol. 8, Pg. 348, Tradition 10,867.

organized and ensure that your shoulders are touching [in the rows] so that your mercy for one another increases."[76]

39. The Prayer Leader is Not Accountable

عَنْ أَبِي عَبْدِ اللّٰهِ عليه السلام أَنَّهُ سَأَلَهُ رَجُلٌ عَنِ الْقِرَاءَةِ خَلْفَ الْإِمَامِ فَقَالَ: لَا إِنَّ الْإِمَامَ ضَامِنٌ لِلْقِرَاءَةِ وَلَيْسَ يَضْمَنُ الْإِمَامُ صَلَاةَ الَّذِينَ هُمْ مِنْ خَلْفِهِ إِنَّمَا يَضْمَنُ الْقِرَاءَةَ.

A man once asked Abī ʿAbdillāh [Imam al-Ṣādiq] ﷺ regarding the recitation [of the two *sūrahs* in the *ṣalāt* – meaning, Sūrah al-Fātiḥa and another chapter of the Quran] in the Congregational Prayers. To this question, the Imam ﷺ replied: "No, they (meaning the followers) must not recite [either *sūrah*] as the *imam* [of the Congregational Prayers] is responsible for the recitation [of these two chapters], but he is not responsible for the [rest] of the recitations of the followers – indeed, he is only responsible for the recitation [of the two chapters – meaning that the people praying behind the *imam* need to recite everything else on their own]."[77]

40. Being Swift in Completing the Prayers

عَنْ أَبِي عَبْدِ اللّٰهِ عليه السلام قَالَ: صَلَّى رَسُولُ اللّٰهِ صلى الله عليه وآله الظُّهْرَ وَالْعَصْرَ فَخَفَّفَ الصَّلَاةَ فِي الرَّكْعَتَيْنِ فَلَمَّا انْصَرَفَ قَالَ لَهُ النَّاسُ: يَا رَسُولَ اللّٰهِ أَ حَدَثَ فِي الصَّلَاةِ شَيْءٌ؟

[76] *Nahj al-Faṣāḥa*, Pg. 210, Tradition 289.

[77] *Man lā Yaḥḍhuruhu Faqīh*, Vol. 1, Pg. 378, Tradition 1,103.

قَالَ: وَمَا ذَاكَ؟ قَالُوا: خَفَّفْتَ فِي الرَّكْعَتَيْنِ الْأَخِيرَتَيْنِ. فَقَالَ لَهُمْ: أَ مَا سَمِعْتُمْ صُرَاخَ الصَّبِيِّ؟

Abī ʿAbdillāh ﵇ said: "The Messenger of Allah ﷺ performed *(Ṣalāt) al-Ẓuhr* and *al-ʿAṣr,* and he performed the last two *rakaʿāt* slightly faster [than the first two *rakaʿāt*]. When he finished [the *ṣalāt*], one of the people present said: 'O Messenger of Allah, did some new rulings come [from Allah ﷻ] during the *ṣalāt*?' He (the Prophet ﷺ) replied: 'Why would you ask this?' The people responded: 'You prayed the last two *rakaʿāt* faster [than the first two *rakaʿāt*].' Then he (the Prophet ﷺ) replied to them (the people): 'Did you not hear the young child crying!?'"[78]

This concludes the section on forty *ḥadīth* regarding both *Ṣalāt al-Jumuʿah* and *Ṣalāt al-Jamāʿah* as compiled by Maḥmūd Laṭīfī.

[78] *Tahdhīb al-Aḥkām*, Vol. 3, Pg. 284. Tradition 116.

Practical Rulings of Ṣalāt al-Jumuʿah[79]

1.1 Introduction

Ṣalāt al-Jumuʿah is an act of worship and a prayer which is considered as being within the scope of the daily prayers; however, it is unique in that it can only be performed on Friday at midday (the time of *ẓuhr*) if all its specific conditions are fulfilled.

Regarding its merits, it suffices to note that an entire chapter of the Quran has been named after it [Sūrah al-Jumuʿah (62)]; and in this chapter, the believers have been invited to take part in the Friday Prayers, as Allah ﷻ says:

﴿يَا أَيُّهَا الَّذِينَ آمَنُوا إِذَا نُودِيَ لِلصَّلَاةِ مِن يَوْمِ الْجُمُعَةِ فَاسْعَوْا إِلَىٰ
ذِكْرِ اللَّهِ وَذَرُوا الْبَيْعَ ۚ ذَٰلِكُمْ خَيْرٌ لَّكُمْ إِن كُنتُمْ تَعْلَمُونَ﴾

---

[79] These rulings of His Eminence, Āyatullāh Sayyid ʿAlī al-Ḥusaynī al-Sīstānī, have been extracted and translated from his four-volume *Comprehensive Islamic Laws* manual published by the office of His Eminence, in Mashad, Iran.

> O you who have faith! When the call is proclaimed to prayer on the Day of *Jumuʿah* (Friday – the day of assembly) then hasten to the remembrance of Allah and leave aside all business. That is best for you if you only knew![80]

In addition, it has been mentioned in the *aḥādīth* that:

1. The performance of *Ṣalāt al-Jumuʿah* is one of the factors which can prevent an individual from entering the fire of Hell.
2. Performing *Ṣalāt al-Jumuʿah* can grant an individual a reduction in the pains and sufferings on the [Day of] Judgement.
3. The performance of *Ṣalāt al-Jumuʿah* could allow for the [metaphorical] pen of forgiveness to be employed in pardoning one's previous acts of transgression against the laws of Allah ﷻ.
4. Finally, we are also told in the *aḥādīth* that the reward for taking part in *Ṣalāt al-Jumuʿah* is equivalent to the performance of *Ḥajj* for those who are not obligated to perform *Ḥajj* [as they do not meet the criteria for those who must perform this act of worship].

Let us now review the Jurisprudential Rulings *(Aḥkām)* of this important act of worship.

---

[80] Quran, Sūrah al-Jumuʿah (62), Verse 9.

1.2 Jurisprudential Rulings

Ruling 1: *Ṣalāt al-Jumuʿah* is what is referred to as an optional obligation[81] *(Wājib al-Taʾkhīrī)* which means that on Friday, an individual who is obligated to perform their religious duties – known as a *mukallaf* – has the option to either perform *Ṣalāt al-Jumuʿah* (if all of its conditions are met), or perform *Ṣalāt al-Ẓuhr* – however, the performance of *Ṣalāt al-Jumuʿah* is better. In addition, if an individual performs *Ṣalāt al-Jumuʿah* while maintaining all its conditions, then this will suffice in place of *Ṣalāt al-Ẓuhr* [and therefore, one does not have to perform *Ṣalāt al-Ẓuhr*].[82]

---

[81] *Wājib al-Taʾkhīrī* is a concept in Islamic Jurisprudence referring to an optional obligation. It denotes a situation where a person is given a choice among different actions, and any one of them will fulfill the requirement of the obligation. This contrasts with *Wājib al-Taʿyīnī,* where a specific act is mandated without any alternatives.

[82] Please note that scholars have varying opinions regarding the performance of *Ṣalāt al-Ẓuhr* on Friday after having performed *Ṣalāt al-Jumuʿah,* and they include the following – from among the living scholars [in alphabetical order of their last name]:

1. **Āyatullāh Shaykh Jawādī Āmulī** – No need.
2. **Āyatullāh Shaykh Isḥāq al-Fayyāḍ** – No need.
3. **Āyatullāh Shaykh Nūrī Hamadānī** – Yes, according to recommended precaution *(iḥtiyāṭ mustaḥabb).*
4. **Āyatullāh Sayyid ʿAlī Ḥusaynī Khāmeneʾī**– Yes, according to recommended precaution *(iḥtiyāṭ mustaḥabb).*
5. **Āyatullāh Shaykh Waḥīd Khurāsānī** – Yes, according to obligatory precaution *(iḥtiyāṭ wājib).*
6. **Āyatullāh Shaykh Ḥusayn Maẓāherī** – No need.

---

7. **Āyatullāh Shaykh Bashīr al-Najafī** – Yes, according to obligatory precaution *(iḥtiyāṭ wājib).*
8. **Āyatullāh Sayyid ʿAlī al-Ḥusaynī al-Sīstānī** – No need.
9. **Āyatullāh Shaykh Nāṣir Makārim Shīrāzī** – No need.
10. **Āyatullāh Shaykh Jaʿfar Subḥānī** – Yes, according to recommended precaution *(iḥtiyāṭ mustaḥabb).*
11. **Āyatullāh Sayyid Shubayrī Zanjānī** – Yes, according to obligatory precaution *(iḥtiyāṭ wājib).*

As for the scholars who have passed away, their opinions are as follows [in alphabetical order of their last name]:

1. **Āyatullāh Shaykh Muḥammad ʿAlī Arākī** – No need.
2. **Āyatullāh Shaykh Muḥammad Taqī Behjat** – No need.
3. **Āyatullāh Sayyid Muḥammad Ḥusayn Faḍlullāh** – No need.
4. **Āyatullāh Shaykh Luṭfullāh Ṣāfī Gulpāygānī** – Yes, according to obligatory precaution *(iḥtiyāṭ wājib).*
5. **Āyatullāh Sayyid Muḥammad Riḍā Gulpāygānī** – Yes, according to obligatory precaution *(iḥtiyāṭ wājib).*
6. **Āyatullāh Sayyid Saʿīd Ṭabāʾṭabāʾī al-Ḥakīm** – Yes, according to obligatory precaution *(iḥtiyāṭ wājib).*
7. **Āyatullāh Sayyid Abul Qāsim al-Khūʾī** – No need.
8. **Āyatullāh Sayyid Rūḥollāh Khumaynī** – Yes, according to obligatory precaution *(iḥtiyāṭ wājib).*
9. **Āyatullāh Shaykh Fāḍil Lankarānī** – No need.
10. **Āyatullāh Shaykh Jawād Tabrīzī** – No need.
11. **Āyatullāh Sayyid Ṣādiq Rūḥānī** – Yes, according to obligatory precaution *(iḥtiyāṭ wājib).*
12. **Āyatullāh Sayyid Muḥammad Shīrāzī** – No need.

1.2.1 Method of Performing Ṣalāt al-Jumuʿah

Ruling 2: *Ṣalāt al-Jumuʿah* is a two *rakaʿāt* prayer, and the method of performing it is like *Ṣalāt al-Ṣubḥ (al-Fajr)* with the difference that in *Ṣalāt al-Jumuʿah*, it is a requirement that two sermons must be delivered **before** the performance of the prayers.

Ruling 3: *Ṣalāt al-Jumuʿah* has two *qunūt* which are recommended *(mustaḥabb)* to perform – the initial *qunūt* is **before** the *rukūʿ* in the first *rakʿah*, while the next *qunūt* is **after** the *rukūʿ* in the second *rakʿah.*

Ruling 4: In the first *rakʿah* of the *ṣalāt*, it is recommended that the prayer leader *(imam)* of *Ṣalāt al-Jumuʿah* recites *Sūrah al-Jumuʿah* [Chapter 62] after reciting *Sūrah al-Ḥamd*; and in the second *rakʿah*, he recites *Sūrah al-Munāfiqūn* [Chapter 63] after *Sūrah al-Ḥamd.*

Ruling 5: According to obligatory precaution *(iḥtiyāṭ wājib)*, it is necessary that the recitation of *Sūrah al-Ḥamd* and the second *sūrah* in both the first and second *rakʿah* of the *ṣalāt* be done in an **audible voice** [as opposed to the "audible whisper" which is employed for *Ṣalāt al-Ẓuhr* and *Ṣalāt al-ʿAṣr*].

Ruling 6: *Ṣalāt al-Jumuʿah* contains two sermons, and just like the actual *ṣalāt* itself, they are obligatory *(wājib)* and must be delivered by the prayer leader *(imam)* of the Friday Prayers [the same one who is leading the *ṣalāt*]. Without the delivery of these two sermons, *Ṣalāt al-Jumuʿah* is not actualized.

Ruling 7: It is obligatory that the two sermons are delivered **before** performing *Ṣalāt al-Jumuʿah*, and if a person performs *Ṣalāt al-Jumuʿah* first, then delivers the sermons - that *Ṣalāt al-Jumuʿah* will be considered invalid. If someone performed the *ṣalāt* first, then offered the two sermons, and time is remaining, one must deliver the sermons again and then perform *Ṣalāt al-Jumuʿah;* however, if the time of *Ṣalāt al-Jumuʿah* has passed, then one must perform *Ṣalāt al-Ẓuhr*.

1.2.2 Conditions for its Obligation

Ruling 8: *Ṣalāt al-Jumuʿah* becomes obligatory when certain conditions are fulfilled, and these are the following:

1. The time of *ṣalāt* must have started [meaning the time of *ẓuhr* or midday].
2. The number of participants [who are physically present] much have reached at least five [including the prayer leader *(imam)* of *Jumuʿah*].
3. The prayer leader of *Jumuʿah* must fulfill all the requisites for leading the prayers – whose conditions will be mentioned shortly in another ruling.

1.2.3 Condition One: Time

Ruling 9: The time for *Ṣalāt al-Jumuʿah* is from the beginning of the time just after midday when the sun begins its decline *(zawāl)*, or in other words, the time when *Ṣalāt al-Ẓuhr* begins. Its instance is that initial time which is regarded by the common people *(ʿurf)* to be the beginning of the decline [of the sun]. Therefore, if the actual starting of the *Ṣalāt al-Jumuʿah* (meaning the beginning of the delivery of the two sermons) is delayed beyond this time, then its period is deemed to be over, which then means that *Ṣalāt al-Ẓuhr* **must** also be performed.[83]

Ruling 10: It is not permissible for the prayer leader of *Jumuʿah* to prolong the two sermons to such an extent that the time of *Ṣalāt al-Jumuʿah* passes, and if he does so, then everyone **must** also perform *Ṣalāt al-Ẓuhr*, as *Ṣalāt al-Jumuʿah* which is performed out of its time does not have a *qaḍā* associated with it.[84]

---

[83] According to Āyatullāh al-Sīstānī, this is a period of 10 minutes. Thus, for example, if the time of *ẓuhr* – which is also the time of the beginning of the decline of the sun – is 12:30 PM, then the *adhān* and the sermon need to start by 12:40 PM. If they are delayed past the 10-minute mark after the time of the beginning of the decline of the sun for any reason (such as the prayer leader arriving late, not having the required quorum of five people, or any other reason), then *Ṣalāt al-Ẓuhr* **must** be performed as well. In such a scenario, the sermons can still be delivered, and the participants can technically still perform *Ṣalāt al-Jumuʿah*, however, it will not suffice, and all present must still perform *Ṣalāt al-Ẓuhr*. (Tr.)

[84] According to Āyatullāh al-Sīstānī, in his updated Arabic manual, *Minhāj al-Ṣālīḥīn*, if the two sermons take up to 40 minutes to deliver, and immediately thereafter, *Ṣalāt al-Jumuʿah* starts, then this is valid; however, if the two sermons take 40 to 75 minutes to deliver, then according to obligatory precaution *(iḥtiyāṭ wājib)*, it is also necessary to perform *Ṣalāt al-Ẓuhr*; and if the two sermons go on for more than 75 minutes, then one must, as an obligation *(wājib)*, also perform *Ṣalāt al-Ẓuhr*. (Tr.)

Ruling 11: It is problematic to start to deliver the two sermons **before** the time of *adhān* of *ẓuhr* sets in, even if the ending of the two sermons was timed such that it would fall within the time of the *ẓuhr* period. Therefore, according to obligatory precaution *(iḥtiyāṭ wājib)*, one cannot suffice with a *Ṣalāt al-Jumuʿah* in which its sermons were started before the time of the *adhān* of *ẓuhr*, even if it was only the first sermon which was delivered before the start of the *adhān* of *ẓuhr*.

1.2.4 Condition Two: Participants

Ruling 12: The minimum number of people who must be present for *Ṣalāt al-Jumuʿah*, including the prayer leader of *Jumuʿah* is five; and anytime the minimum number of five Muslims do not gather [at the time of the Friday Prayer], one of them being the prayer leader, *Ṣalāt al-Jumuʿah* will not be an obligation.

1.2.5 Condition Three: Prayer Leader (Imam)

Ruling 13: It is obligatory that the prayer leader of the *Jumuʿah* service fulfills certain conditions for the task of leading the prayers. These conditions are the following:

1. He must be *ʿāqil* – of sound mind and not mentally unstable.
2. He must be *ʿādil* – of good moral probity and just.
3. He must be a *Shīʿa Ithnā-ʿAsherī* – a follower of the 12 Divinely-appointed leaders after Prophet Muḥammad ﷺ – starting with Imam ʿAlī ibn Abī Ṭālib ؑ; followed by Imam Ḥasan ibn ʿAlī ؑ; then Imam Ḥusayn ibn ʿAlī ؑ; then Imam ʿAlī ibn Ḥusayn al-Sajjād ؑ; then

Imam Muḥammad ibn ʿAlī al-Bāqir (عليه السلام); then Imam Jaʿfar ibn Muḥammad al-Ṣādiq (عليه السلام); then Imam Mūsā ibn Jaʿfar al-Kāẓim (عليه السلام); then Imam ʿAlī ibn Mūsā al-Riḍā (عليه السلام); then Imam Muḥammad ibn ʿAlī al-Jawād (عليه السلام); then Imam ʿAlī ibn Muḥammad al-Hādī (عليه السلام); then Imam Ḥasan ibn ʿAlī al-ʿAskarī (عليه السلام); then the 12th and final leader, Imam Muḥammad ibn Ḥasan al-Mahdī (عجّل الله تعالى فرجه الشريف).

4. His recitation *(qirāʾat)* of the Arabic portions of the prayers, such as the two chapters of the Quran and other recitations in the prayers, must be correct.
5. In addition, all the other conditions which are applicable for the prayer leader of the congregational prayers *(imam* of *Ṣalāt al-Jamāʿah)* are also necessary for the prayer leader of *Ṣalāt al-Jumuʿah.* If any of these conditions are not met, then *Ṣalāt al-Jumuʿah* is not obligatory. One must note that children and women acting as the prayer leader in *Ṣalāt al-Jumuʿah* is not permissible.

1.2.5.1 Conditions of the Prayer Leader (Imam)[85]

Ruling 14: The prayer leader *(imam)* of the Congregational Prayers *(Ṣalāt al-Jamāʿah/Ṣalāt al-Jumuʿah)* must fulfill the criteria below, so that praying behind him is deemed correct and valid:

1. The individual must be of maturity age *(bāligh).*
2. The individual must be sane *(ʿāqil).*

---

[85] We include further clarifications and specifics with regards to the criteria of the prayer leader *(imam)* of Congregational Prayers as mentioned in the Islamic Laws manual. (Tr.)

3. The individual must be born legitimately (his parents must have been married when he was conceived).
4. The individual must be a *Shīʿa Ithnā-ʿAsherī.*[86]
5. The individual must be just *(ʿādil).*
6. The recitation *(qirāʾat)* of the Arabic portions of the prayers must be correct.
7. If the participants include any men, then the prayer leader of the congregational prayers must be a man.
8. According to obligatory precaution *(iḥtiyāṭ wājib),* any Islamic legal-code punishment must never have been meted out against the prayer leader.
9. If the followers are performing their prayers standing [as opposed to sitting or lying down due to medical or health reasons], then the prayer leader must also be performing his prayers standing.
10. The direction of the *qiblah* [direction of Mecca] of the prayer leader and the followers must be the same.
11. From the point of view of the followers, the *ṣalāt* of the prayer leader must be correct.

A further explanation behind each of these criteria will be offered next.

---

[86] Performing *Ṣalāt al-Jumuʿah* (as well as Ṣalāt *al-Jamāʿah)* behind a Sunnī prayer leader is not sufficient, and in such instances, the believer must also perform *Ṣalāt al-Ẓuhr.* A Shīʿa can still listen to the sermons and perform *Ṣalāt al-Jumuʿah,* however, it will not be counted as being valid. (Tr.)

1.2.5.2 One: Age of Maturity (Bāligh[87])

Ruling 15: The prayer leader of the Congregational Prayers must be *bāligh* as it is not correct to perform *ṣalāt* behind a prayer leader who is a non-*bāligh* child even though there is a [legal] possibility that it may be permissible to offer the prayers behind a child who has fully completed ten years of age; however, according to obligatory precaution *(iḥtiyāṭ wājib)*, one should refrain from this. In addition, the leading of the Congregational Prayers by a child who is not *bāligh* for children who are also not *bāligh* is an area of doubt.

1.2.5.3 Two and Three: Sane (ʿĀqil) and Legitimate Birth

Ruling 16: The prayer leader of the Congregational Prayers must not be one who is mentally unstable, so he must be sane. As well, he must not be of illegitimate birth – meaning that he must not have been born out of wedlock [or conceived out of wedlock].

---

[87] The age of maturity is that point in time when, for the male, it becomes an obligation to perform their acts of worship to Allah ﷻ. In the Shīʿa Jurisprudence, boys enter this stage at a minimum of 12 lunar years. If the signs of maturity are not seen in a boy, then by default they enter the stage of being *bāligh* at age 15 based on the lunar calendar. (Tr.)

1.2.5.4 Four: Shīʿa Ithnā-ʿAsherī

Ruling 17: The prayer leader of the Congregational Prayers must be a follower of the Shīʿa Ithnā-ʿAsherī Imamī tradition. Therefore, it is incumbent upon those who are performing their prayers in congregation behind a prayer leader from the Ahlul Sunnah to recite *Sūrah al-Ḥamd* and the second *sūrah* on their own – even in as much as reciting them in a quiet whisper [as opposed to reciting the two chapters out loud as is normally done for the *Fajr*, *Maghrib*, and *ʿIshā* prayers]. If a Shīʿa is performing *Ṣalāt al-Jumuʿah* within an Ahlul Sunnah congregation, then they must also perform *Ṣalāt al-Ẓuhr* (after *Ṣalāt al-Jumuʿah* is finished). In the event that the prayers of the Ahlul Sunnah begin before the legal Islamic time [of the prayer] – either due to a legal ruling *(fatwa)*, or because of precaution [which they are following] – then such a prayer will not be sufficient to be considered valid as an obligatory prayer (for a Shīʿa Ithnā-ʿAsherī), according to a legal ruling, or due to precaution.[88] For example, if their (Ahlul Sunnah) call to prayer for *Maghrib* is given before the actual time – during the period between the beginning of the setting of the sun and the actual *Maghrib* time (the disappearance of the redness in the eastern sky), and the person performing the prayer performs *Maghrib* with them (the Ahlul Sunnah) right when the time in which they pray

---

[88] Therefore, this prayer must be repeated, either based on a legal ruling, or because of precaution. For example, if a person prays with the Sunnīs right at sunset (before the time of *Maghrib*), then one must repeat that prayer – as an obligatory precaution *(iḥtiyāṭ wājib)* – after the time of *Maghrib* sets in. (Tr.)

sets in, then according to obligatory precaution *(iḥtiyāṭ wājib)*, that person must make up that prayer by performing it again in its religiously prescribed time.

1.2.5.5 Five: Just (ʿĀdil)

Ruling 18: The prayer leader *(imam)* of the congregational prayers must be just, and as such, performing the *ṣalāt* behind a prayer leader of the congregation who is unknown [as to their status of whether they are just or not], or are an open sinner *(fāsiq)* is not correct. The meaning of justice *(ʿadālah)* in this discussion is that the individual (the prayer leader) performs all of their obligations *(wājibāt)*, and keeps away from all of the prohibitions *(mūḥarramāt)*; and a sign of this is their well-mannered apparent nature in how they speak, act, and carry themselves; with the condition that an individual has no other knowledge of the prayer leader acting contrary to these indicators in any other way. A detailed and complete discussion of the meaning of *ʿadālah* – justice, and the ways to determine this trait has been discussed in the section on *Taqlīd* in ruling 5.[89]

---

[89] For the benefit of the readers of this book, we provide the translation of this ruling:

1. A just *(ʿādil)* person is an individual who carries out all the responsibilities which are obligatory upon them, and refrains from all actions which are impermissible upon them. An individual who, without a valid Islamic reason does not perform the obligatory actions, or performs the impermissible actions, is **not just**, and in this issue, there is no difference between the major or minor sins. The justice of an individual can be proven through the following ways:

Ruling 19: If a person has a doubt regarding the prayer leader of the congregation who was known to be just in the past, as to whether they are still just or not, then an individual can perform one's *ṣalāt* behind such an individual.

1.2.5.6 Six: Quality of Recitation (Qirāʾat)

Ruling 20: The recitation *(qirāʾat)* of the prayer leader of the Congregational Prayers must be correct [according to the rules of Arabic recitation], and the recitation of *Sūrah al-Ḥamd* and the second *sūrah* of the *ṣalāt* must be recited following the correct Arabic pronunciation. Therefore, it is not right for an individual whose recitation is correct to

---

a. Personal knowledge or certainty through a medium which would be recognized as valid by a lay person.
b. Two other just individuals bear witness to that person's justice.
c. The individual has a good outward manifestation and conduct – meaning that from the apparent point of view, they are a good person, and in their speaking, actions, and way they carry themself, there is nothing seen which goes against the Islamic legal code. For example, if one was to ask the people of the region in which they live, or ask their neighbours, or those people who have close ties and connection to them about that individual, they would confirm their goodness and would easily tell you that: 'We have no knowledge of them doing anything against the Islamic legal code.' It is important to mention that the definition of justice and the ways of proving this for an individual are the same in the various sections of Islamic Jurisprudence.

perform the *ṣalāt* behind a prayer leader of the congregation whose recitation is not correct, even if the prayer leader has a legal religious justification for their method of recitation.

In addition, if the quality of recitation of both the prayer leader and the followers is not correct, and if their mistakes in the pronunciation of the words are different between one another [but both are still making errors], then it is still not permissible to perform the *ṣalāt* behind such a person. Rather, if in the pronunciation of the words, there are mistakes which they [the prayer leader and the followers] make which are like one another [in those words being recited], then even in this scenario, according to obligatory precaution *(iḥtiyāṭ wājib)*, it is not valid to perform the *ṣalāt* behind such a person.

It is important to mention that it is not a problem to pray behind a prayer leader in other than those areas in which the prayer leader is tasked with reciting on behalf of those praying behind them – meaning in the recitation of *Sūrah al-Ḥamd* and the second *sūrah*, and whose pronunciation of *Sūrah al-Ḥamd* and the second *sūrah* is not correct; however, they have a valid legal reason for not correcting their recitation. For example, if the followers of the prayers arrive [late] and join in the Congregational Prayers at the time of the *rukūʿ* of the second, third, or fourth *rakaʿāt* in which case they would have already passed the stage of performing the recitation [of the two chapters of the Quran in congregation] – then one can join in and pray in congregation behind that prayer leader for that prayer.

In addition, it is not a problem to follow behind a prayer leader who, in the recitation of the remembrances *(adhkār)* in the *rukūʿ*, *sajdah*, *tashahhud*, or the *tasbiḥāt al-arbaʿah* and all other such areas, is not reciting them correctly, and has a valid legal reason for not being able to correct them [their recitation].

Ruling 21: If an individual has a doubt as to whether the recitation of a prayer leader of the congregation is correct for *Sūrah al-Ḥamd* and the other *sūrah*, then according to obligatory precaution *(iḥtiyāṭ wājib)*, an individual cannot perform one's *ṣalāt* behind that individual in those instances in which the prayer leader is reciting *Sūrah al-Ḥamd* and the second *sūrah* on behalf of the followers. So, for example, in the first or second *rakʿah* of the *ṣalāt*, one cannot join in the congregation before the state of *rukūʿ*. However, if an individual knows that the prayer leader of the congregation has correct recitation, there is a possibility that due to forgetfulness or a mistake, they may recite something incorrectly, then the individual should not pay attention to such a possibility [of an error] and should presume the recitation of the prayer leader to be correct and therefore pray behind them in the Congregational Prayers.

Ruling 22: If during the recitation of *Sūrah al-Ḥamd* and the second *sūrah*, the prayer leader of the Congregational Prayers, mistakenly and unintentionally misses a verse (of the *sūrah*), or recites it incorrectly and does not notice their own mistake, then in the event that the followers notice the mistake of the prayer leader and they change [the intention of their prayers] to be an individual *(furāda)* prayer and continue in that fashion, their *ṣalāt* will be correct. According to obligatory precaution *(iḥtiyāṭ wājib)*, the followers need to recite *Sūrah al-Ḥamd* and the second *sūrah* right from the beginning and must not suffice with merely reciting that portion which the prayer leader recited incorrectly.

However, if the followers did not notice the mistake of the prayer leader and the period of the recitation passes by – for example, they go into the position of *rukūʿ*, or they realize after the *ṣalāt* finishes that there was a mistake, then their *ṣalāt* and the Congregational Prayers which were performed are deemed as correct, and the *ṣalāt* of the prayer leader who did not notice the mistake which they made at that period of time, will also be considered as correct.

Ruling 23: It is not a problem for an individual whose recitation is eloquent *(faṣīḥ)* and beautiful and maintains all the rules of Quranic recitation *(tajwīd)* to pray behind a prayer leader who is not eloquent and may only be able to correctly pronounce and recite the minimal obligatory portions of the *ṣalāt*; or if they do not observe all of the rules of beautification of the Quranic recitation.

1.2.5.7 Seven: Gender

Ruling 24: If the followers in the Congregational Prayer are all men (or there is a mix of men and women praying in congregation), then the prayer leader **must** be a man; and it is not a problem for women who are praying [if there are **only** women and no men are present in the Congregational Prayer, and no men can hear the voices of the women] to follow a woman who is leading the *ṣalāt*. It is **not** permissible for a woman to lead a congregation [neither any of the congregational five daily prayers, nor the Friday Prayers] in which men are also participating in the *ṣalāt* – even if those men are her blood or marriage-related individuals *(maḥārim)*.

1.2.5.8 Eight: Never Been a Recipient of the Islamic Penal Code

Ruling 25: According to obligatory precaution *(iḥtiyāṭ wājib)*, an individual who has had a legal Islamic penalty meted out upon them cannot ever be the prayer leader of the Congregational Prayers – even if they have asked for forgiveness and repented (done *tawbah*).

1.2.5.9 Nine: Method of Performing the Prayers

Ruling 26: An individual who is performing the *ṣalāt* standing up (in the usual manner) is not permitted to follow a prayer leader who is performing the daily obligatory *ṣalāt* sitting or lying down.

Ruling 27: An individual who is sitting and performing the *ṣalāt* is not permitted to follow a prayer leader who is performing the *ṣalāt* lying down; however, if a follower's responsibility is to perform the *ṣalāt* sitting down, and the prayer leader of the Congregational Prayer is performing the *ṣalāt* standing up, then this is not a problem.

Ruling 28: An individual who is sitting down to perform the *ṣalāt* is permitted to follow a prayer leader who is also performing their *ṣalāt* sitting down; however, it is an area of doubt for a person who is performing one's *ṣalāt* lying down to follow anyone in prayer [even those praying who are also lying down] – whether the prayer leader is standing, sitting, or lying down.

1.2.5.10 Ten: Direction of Prayers (Qiblah)

Ruling 29: It is not permissible for an individual who truly believes that the *qiblah* is in a certain direction to follow the prayer leader of the congregation who believes that the *qiblah* is in another direction; except if the difference between the two directions is so small which would commonly be acknowledged by others that they are all praying in congregation in a similar direction; so in this case, there is no problem following behind such a prayer leader.

1.2.5.11 Eleven: Prayers Must be Correct

Ruling 30: If between the followers and the prayer leader of the Congregational Prayers, there are some differences in the workings of the *ṣalāt*, and its conditions from the point of view of their [the prayer leader's own] *ijtihād* or *taqlīd*[90] (and as such, the rulings which both follow may differ), then in the event that the followers, based on the rationale of their own *ijtihād* or *taqlīd*, believe that the *ṣalāt* of the prayer leader is invalid, then they are **not** permitted to perform their prayers behind such an individual; and indeed this is the ruling in the event that there is a difference in the subjects and the external manifestations of the portions of *ṣalāt* – and in the case of the followers of that Congregational Prayer being

[90] The expression used here: "...the point of view of [one's own] *ijtihād* or *taqlīd*..." refers to a person praying behind the prayer leader – and either because he/she is a *mujtahid*, or one is a *muqallid* and the *Marjaʿ* whom one follows has a particular ruling in such an instance. (Tr.)

unaware of these rulings, this will invalidate their *ṣalāt.* We present the following examples to clarify this ruling:

1. If the palm of the prayer leader's hand has some impediment on it [such as a cast] which cannot be removed at all, and the prayer leader, based on their own reasoning *(ijtihād)* or emulation of a scholar *(taqlīd)*, strongly believes that their responsibility in such a circumstance is to perform *wuḍūʾ* for the one who has a bandage on that part of the body *(jabīrah),* or to perform the *ghusl* of one who has a bandage/cast on, however, the followers – either based on their own reasoning or emulation of another scholar believe that the responsibility of the prayer leader is to perform *tayammum* [based on one's own unique circumstances], then in such a scenario, the followers are not permitted to perform their prayers behind this prayer leader who has performed the *wuḍūʾ* or *ghusl* of one who has a bandage/cast.
2. If the followers in the Congregational Prayer, either based on their own reasoning *(ijtihād)* or emulation of a scholar *(taqlīd)*, believe it to be obligatory to recite one complete *sūrah* after the recitation of *Sūrah al-Ḥamd,* however, the prayer leader of the congregation believes, based on their own reasoning *(ijtihād)* or emulation of a scholar *(taqlīd)*, that it is **not** obligatory to recite one complete *sūrah* after *Sūrah al-Ḥamd,* and in their Congregational Prayer, they merely suffice with the full recitation of *Sūrah al-Ḥamd,* then in this event, the followers are **not** permitted to join in such a Congregational Prayer in the position of *qiyām* or any time before going into

rukūʿ [of the second *rakʿah*]. As for following this prayer leader by joining the congregation while they are in the state of *rukūʿ* of the second *rakʿah,* or in the third or fourth *rakʿah,* is not a problem.

3. If the followers in a Congregational Prayer **know for certain** that the water which the prayer leader used to perform their *wuḍūʾ* was impure *(najis),* however, the prayer leader themself believed the water to be pure, then in this scenario, it will **not** be permissible for the people to perform their *ṣalāt* behind that person, because performing *wuḍūʾ* with water which is impure – even if one is unaware of it as being such – would render the *wuḍūʾ* invalid and subsequently, also render the *ṣalāt* invalid.
4. If the prayer leader of a Congregational Prayer forgets one of the *rukn* from the *arkān* in the *ṣalāt* – for example, they forget to perform *takbīratul iḥrām,* or a *rukūʿ*, or the two *sajdah* in one *rakʿah,* then it is not permissible to offer one's *ṣalāt* behind this individual [in that particular instance], even if the prayer leader themself did not realize that they missed these things.
5. However, if in the view of the followers, the *ṣalāt* of the prayer leader of the Congregational Prayers is correct according to what they are to follow, then they are permitted to follow behind that person. For example, in those instances in which a prayer leader was an inculpably ignorant person *(jāhil al-qāṣir)*[91] –

[91] *Jāhil al-qāṣir* is a term in Islamic Jurisprudence and Theology referring to a person who is ignorant but is excused due to their circumstances. The term distinguishes between types of ignorance,

then in such a case, if the individual is also an inculpably ignorant individual, then one's *ṣalāt* will be valid.

Further to the above examples, if a prayer leader, based on their own reasoning *(ijtihād)* or emulation of a scholar *(taqlīd)*, truly believes that in the third and fourth *rakʿah* of the *ṣalāt*, it is permissible for an individual to recite the *tasbiḥāt al-arbaʿah* only one time, however, those following the *imam* believe that it is an obligation *(wājib)* to recite the *tasbiḥāt al-arbaʿah* three times, then in this case, it is permissible for the followers to pray behind the prayer leader who is reciting the *tasbiḥāt al-arbaʿah* only once (and in such a case, the follower should recite it three times and join the *imam* in the state of *rukūʿ*).

In addition, if the lack of knowledge on the difference in the subject and its outward manifestation is such that it does not cause any harm to the validity of the *ṣalāt* [for example, if the followers of a Congregational Prayer notice that the clothing of the prayer leader is impure, however, the prayer leader oneself does not know that their clothing is impure], then in this case, there is no problem praying behind such an individual, and it is not necessary for the followers to inform the prayer leader about the issue.

---

and the accountability of individuals based on their levels of access to knowledge and capacity to understand it.

1.3 Conditions for a Correct Ṣalāt al-Jumuʿah

Ruling 31: For *Ṣalāt al-Jumuʿah* to be correct, the following conditions must be fulfilled:

1. It must be performed in congregation *(jamāʿah).*
2. The prayer leader of *Ṣalāt al-Jumuʿah* must deliver two sermons **before** the performance of *Ṣalāt al-Jumuʿah.*
3. The distance between two different occurrences of *Ṣalāt al-Jumuʿah* **must not** be less than one *farsakh* (5.76 km or 3.52 miles).
4. The conditions which are related to the *Ṣalāt al-Jamāʿah* for its validity must also be present for *Ṣalāt al-Jumuʿah.*

The explanation of each of the above conditions will be explained in detail below.

1.3.1 Condition One: Congregation

Ruling 32: *Ṣalāt al-Jumuʿah* must be performed in congregation, and it is not sufficient to perform it as an individual prayer. However, if some followers reach *Ṣalāt al-Jumuʿah* **before** the prayer leader goes into *rukūʿ* of the second *rakʿah,* then they are permitted to join in and follow in that prayer. In such a case, they will have to perform one more *rakʿah* (on their own), and in doing so, their *Ṣalāt al-Jumuʿah* will be valid. However, if a person makes it to *Ṣalāt al-Jumuʿah* while the prayer leader is in the state of *rukūʿ* of the second *rakʿah*, then according to obligatory precaution *(iḥtiyāṭ wājib)* one cannot suffice with Ṣalāt al-Jumuʿah, and according to obligatory precaution, one must perform Ṣalāt al-Ẓuhr as well.

1.3.2 Condition Two: Two Sermons

Ruling 33: The prayer leader *(imam)* of Ṣalāt al-Jumuʿah must deliver two sermons **before** the performance of the *ṣalāt*. The first sermon must *(wājib)* contain the praise *(ḥamd)* and glorification *(thanāʾ)* of Allah ﷻ, and he must advise the believers to observe piety *(taqwā)*, and he needs to recite a short chapter of the Quran.

In the second sermon, it is also obligatory *(wājib)* that the prayer leader engage in the praise and glorification of Allah ﷻ, and that prayers are sent upon Prophet Muḥammad ﷺ and the immaculate Imams ؑ; and according to recommended precaution *(iḥtiyāṭ mustaḥabb)* he should also ask for forgiveness for the believing men and the believing women.

Ruling 34: The praise of Allah ﷻ and the evoking of prayers upon the Noble Prophet ﷺ and the immaculate Imams ؑ, according to obligatory precaution *(iḥtiyāṭ wājib)*, must be done in Arabic, however, for the rest of the sermon, such as the glorification of Allah ﷻ and the advising to observe piety, it is not necessary to recite these in ʿArabic. In fact, if most of the people present do not understand ʿArabic, then according to obligatory precaution *(iḥtiyāṭ wājib)*, the advising to observe piety must be done in the language of the majority of the people present.

Ruling 35: It is obligatory that the prayer leader of *Ṣalāt al-Jumuʿah* delivers the two sermons **while standing**. Therefore, if the sermons are delivered sitting down, then this will not be correct. In addition, it is also obligatory that between the two sermons, the prayer leader of *Ṣalāt al-Jumuʿah* sits down for a brief period – and this sitting down should be very brief. It is also necessary that the prayer leader of *Ṣalāt al-Jumuʿah* himself delivers the two sermons; therefore, if the prayer leader of *Ṣalāt al-Jumuʿah* is not able to deliver the two sermons, or he is not able to deliver the two sermons standing up, then someone else must be directed to deliver the two sermons and that person [who delivered the sermons] must also take on the responsibility of leading *Ṣalāt al-Jumuʿah* as well.

1.3.3 Condition Three: Physical Distance

Ruling 36: The distance between two occurrences of *Ṣalāt al-Jumuʿah* cannot be less than one *farsakh* (approximately 5.76 km or 3.42 miles). Therefore, if another instance of *Ṣalāt al-Jumuʿah* is taking place at a different location which is less than one *farsakh* from the other *Ṣalāt al-Jumuʿah*, then if both have started at the exact same time [on that day], then both will be invalid.

However, if one of them began slightly before the other one, even if it be the pronouncement of the *takbīratul iḥrām*, then that *Ṣalāt al-Jumuʿah* will be valid, and the second one [which started slightly later] will be invalid.

However, if after the establishment of the *Ṣalāt al-Jumuʿah* [for that day], one becomes aware that another *Ṣalāt al-Jumuʿah* had been initiated at either the same time or just before that one (which the person took part in), and it was within the range of one *farsakh*, then it will not be obligatory to perform *Ṣalāt al-Ẓuhr.*

Furthermore, the establishment of one *Ṣalāt al-Jumuʿah* can only have a prohibitive effect on another one taking place within the stipulated distance of one *farsakh* if it is a valid prayer and if it fulfills all the required conditions – otherwise it does not have any prohibitive effect.[92]

---

[92] This ruling means that if: Centre "A" establishes *Ṣalāt al-Jumuʿah* at a particular point in time, and later on, another community, centre "B"– a new centre is established – and they also decide to have their own *Ṣalāt al-Jumuʿah,* and if they are less than one *farsakh* range from one another, then: If centre "A" and their *Ṣalāt al-Jumuʿah* fulfill all of the required criteria for *Ṣalāt al-Jumuʿah* to be valid, and if the prayer leader has all of the credentials to lead the *Ṣalāt al-Jumuʿah* (such as being of age, being a *Shīʿa Ithnā-ʿAsherī,* etc.), then and only then will the *Ṣalāt al-Jumuʿah* of centre "B" be problematic if they also fulfill all of the criteria for *Ṣalāt al-Jumuʿah* to be valid, and if their prayer leader *(imam)* has all of the credentials to lead the *Ṣalāt al-Jumuʿah* (such as being of age, being a *Shīʿa Ithnā-ʿAsherī,* etc.), and they both started at the exact same time.

1. However, if centre "A" does not fulfill all the criteria (for example, not enough people attending, or the prayer leader is a non-*Shīʿa*), then there is no problem whatsoever in centre "B" establishing *Ṣalāt al-Jumuʿah* – although they may be within the one *farsakh* range of the other centre. (Tr.)

1.3.4 Condition Four: General Conditions

Ruling 37: All of the conditions which are required in *Ṣalāt al-Jamāʿah* to be valid are also required for a valid *Ṣalāt al-Jumuʿah* – such as there being no barrier between the participants [other than the physical barrier between men and women]; the prayer leader not standing at a place which is noticeably higher than the followers; maintaining the distances between the lines of believers praying, and the other conditions [mentioned in the detailed books of Islamic Jurisprudence].

1.4 Participation in Ṣalāt al-Jumuʿah

Ruling 38: Any time *Ṣalāt al-Jumuʿah*, with all of its necessary prerequisites takes place, and the one who establishes it is the immaculate Imam ﷺ himself, or one of his specific [directly appointed] representatives,[93] it becomes an obligation to attend that *Ṣalāt al-Jumuʿah* – except in cases which will be mentioned in the next ruling. In other than this scenario, meaning in the time of the occultation of Imam al-ʿAṣr ﷺ, taking part in *Ṣalāt al-Jumuʿah* is **not** an obligation *(wājib)*.

Ruling 39: Anytime *Ṣalāt al-Jumuʿah* is established with the mentioned conditions, and the one who is establishing it is the [immaculate] Imam ﷺ himself, or his specific [directly

[93] Which is not the fact currently in 2025 – however, we constantly pray for the advent of the Imam of our Time, may Allah ﷻ hasten his return. (Tr.)

appointed] representative, there are certain groups who are (still) not obligated to attend, and they include:

1. Women.
2. Slaves.
3. Travellers – even if their responsibility while on the journey is to perform their prayers in full – such as a traveller who has made the intention to remain at a destination for ten days [or more – and thus, would be offering their prayers in full].
4. Those who are sick, the blind, and the elderly.
5. Individuals whose residence is more than two *farsakh* [11 km or 6.84 miles] away from the place where *Ṣalāt al-Jumuʿah* is taking place.
6. Individuals for whom attending *Ṣalāt al-Jumuʿah* will be difficult due to rain, cold, or other such conditions.

Ruling 40: For those people upon whom attending and taking part in *Ṣalāt al-Jumuʿah* is a fixed obligation *(Wājib al-Taʿyīnī)*, if they perform *Ṣalāt al-Ẓuhr* in place of *Ṣalāt al-Jumuʿah*, then their prayers are correct, despite the fact of having committed a sin [due to not attending and performing *Ṣalāt al-Jumuʿah*].[94]

---

[94] This is a reference to the time when the advent of the 12th Imam عجل الله تعالى فرجه الشريف takes place, and either he or his directly appointed deputies, will take the lead in establishing *Ṣalāt al-Jumuʿah* around the globe. In that era, as it will be a fixed obligation for certain groups of believers to attend, if they refuse to do so and perform *Ṣalāt al-Ẓuhr*, even though they have fulfilled their prayers for that day, however, as they were obligated to perform *Ṣalāt al-Jumuʿah*, they have committed a sin. (Tr.)

1.4.1 Women and Ṣalāt al-Jumuʿah

Ruling 41: Women are permitted to take part in *Ṣalāt al-Jumuʿah* and their prayers are valid, and it is sufficient for them to not have to perform *Ṣalāt al-Ẓuhr* [afterwards]; however, if there are only women attending *Ṣalāt al-Jumuʿah* (with no men in attendance), then they do not form the 'completion' of the participants required for *Ṣalāt al-Jumuʿah* as the necessary prerequisite for having a minimum of five people present for *Ṣalāt al-Jumuʿah* to be established (and sufficient over *Ṣalāt al-Ẓuhr*) is that it is a minimum of five **men** present to establish *Ṣalāt al-Jumuʿah* for it to be sufficient to take the place of *Ṣalāt al-Ẓuhr* [for the men and women present].

1.4.2 Travellers Taking Part

Ruling 42: Travellers are permitted to take part in and perform *Ṣalāt al-Jumuʿah* – whether that person is the prayer leader of the congregation, or a follower in the prayer – and if *Ṣalāt al-Jumuʿah* is one in which all of the conditions [which were previously mentioned] are fulfilled, then *Ṣalāt al-Ẓuhr* will be dropped from them [and they only need to perform *Ṣalāt al-Jumuʿah*].

1.4.3 Ṣalāt al-Jumuʿah of Travellers

Ruling 43: Those travellers whose [religious] responsibility is to perform their prayers in the shortened form *(qaṣr)* are not allowed to, on their own and without the participation of local people being present (who are locals to that city or region), form the minimum requirements for the number of people required to establish *Ṣalāt al-Jumuʿah.* In such a situation [if their presence is to complete the number of people required for *Ṣalāt al-Jumuʿah*], then *Ṣalāt al-Ẓuhr* will become obligatory upon them to perform. In addition, that traveller whose prayers are done in a shortened form **cannot** be one of those who makes up the minimum requirements for *Ṣalāt al-Jumuʿah* (meaning the five people minimum needed).[95]

Question: Is a traveller who has the intention of staying ten days in one location, or for another reason has the responsibility of performing their *ṣalāt* in full, permitted to be counted as one of those individuals who could make up the minimum number of people required to establish a *Ṣalāt al-Jumuʿah*?

Answer: This is a matter of doubt; thus, one should observe precautions on such an issue.

1.4.4 Speaking During the Sermons

Ruling 44: When the prayer leader is delivering the sermons for *Ṣalāt al-Jumuʿah*, it is reprehensible *(makrūh)* to talk; however, if talking will prevent others from listening to the sermons, then in this case, according to obligatory precaution *(iḥtiyāṭ wājib)*, it is not permissible to talk.

---

[95] This means that if there are five people present, including the prayer leader of *Ṣalāt al-Jumuʿah,* and of the five people, one is a traveller who will be performing the prayers in the shortened form, then they **do not count** in making the minimum of five people for *Ṣalāt al-Jumuʿah* to be an obligation.

1.4.5 Listening to the Sermons

Ruling 45: According to obligatory precaution *(iḥtiyāṭ wājib)*, those who can understand the [language of the] sermons, must listen to both, however, it is not obligatory upon those who do not understand the [language of the] sermons to listen to them.

1.4.6 Missing the Two Sermons

Ruling 46: It is not obligatory to be present while the prayer leader of *Ṣalāt al-Jumuʿah* is delivering the sermons, and if a person who wants to join the prayers did not take part in the two sermons, however, reaches during the actual performance of the *ṣalāt*, then their *Ṣalāt al-Jumuʿah* will be valid and will still suffice for *Ṣalāt al-Ẓuhr* (meaning that they do not have to recite *Ṣalāt al-Ẓuhr*).

1.5 Those Who Do Not Attend Ṣalāt al-Jumuʿah

Ruling 47: It has been stated that during the period of the occultation of Imam al-ʿAṣr عجل الله تعالى فرجه الشريف [Imam al-Mahdī عجل الله تعالى فرجه الشريف] *Ṣalāt al-Jumuʿah* is **not** a fixed obligation; therefore, an individual is permitted to perform *Ṣalāt al-Ẓuhr* right at the first instance when the time of *ẓuhr* begins [rather than waiting for *Ṣalāt al-Jumuʿah* to finish and then recite *Ṣalāt al-Ẓuhr*].

1.6 Business Dealings During the Time of Adhān

Ruling 48: During the Period of the Occultation of [Imam] Walī al-ʿAṣr ﷻ in which it is not an obligation to take part in *Ṣalāt al-Jumuʿah*, engaging in business dealings and all other such transactions, after the time of the *adhān* of *Ẓuhr* is not forbidden.

However, when the immaculate 12th Imam ﷻ establishes the prayers, and it becomes obligatory upon individuals to take part in *Ṣalāt al-Jumuʿah*, then to engage in business transactions and all forms of commerce, after the *adhān* of *Ẓuhr* has been pronounced, if this detracts people from taking part in *Ṣalāt al-Jumuʿah*, will be impermissible.

In such a scenario, even though they will be counted as sinners, their business dealings will still be valid from a religious perspective.

1.7 Step by Step Method of the Performance of the Actual Ṣalāt

After ensuring that a person has completed the necessary mode of purification *(wuḍūʾ, ghusl, tayammum)*, and the intention *(niyyah)* has been made, and the Friday Prayers have been initiated, one should follow the below steps.

As *Ṣalāt al-Jumuʿah* is performed in congregation *(jamāʿah)*, it is only a requirement for the *imam* to recite the two *sūrahs* of the Quran [on behalf of the people in attendance performing the *ṣalāt*] – thus, the participants must remain silent and simply listen to the recitation. However, the followers **must recite everything else** in the *ṣalāt* on their own – meaning, the *dhikr* in *rukūʿ*, *sujūd*, *qunūt*, *tashahhud*, and *salām*. All of these **must** be recited in what scholars refer to as an 'audible whisper' – such that the person beside them can hear what is being said, however, it should be done in such a way that the *imam* of the congregation does not hear the individual recitations.

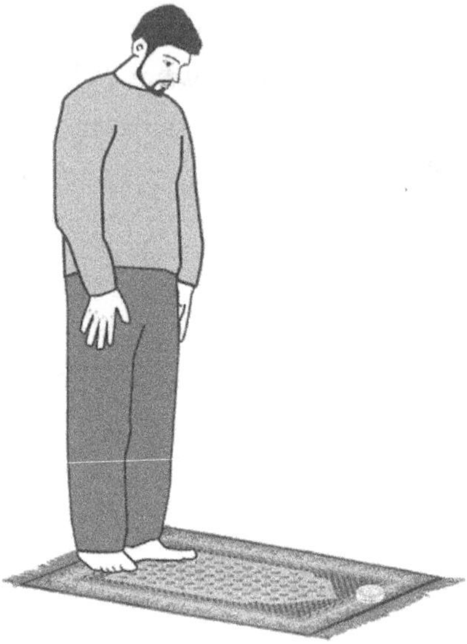

Intention for Ṣalāt al-Jumuʿah

The intention *(niyyah)* for our acts of worship does not have to be 'verbal' – meaning, it is not necessary to say/verbalize what we are about to do. Therefore, for *Ṣalāt al-Jumuʿah*, it is sufficient that a person is at the religious centre and knows why they are there – to perform a two *rakaʿāt* prayer on Friday in congregation to attain spiritual proximity to Allah ﷻ.

Takbīratul Iḥrām

It is recommended to raise the hands such that they are parallel to the ears, and for men and women to look at the place of prostration when pronouncing *takbīratul iḥrām* and all subsequent *takbīrāt* in the *ṣalāt.* One would then say:

أَللّٰهُ أَكْبَرُ

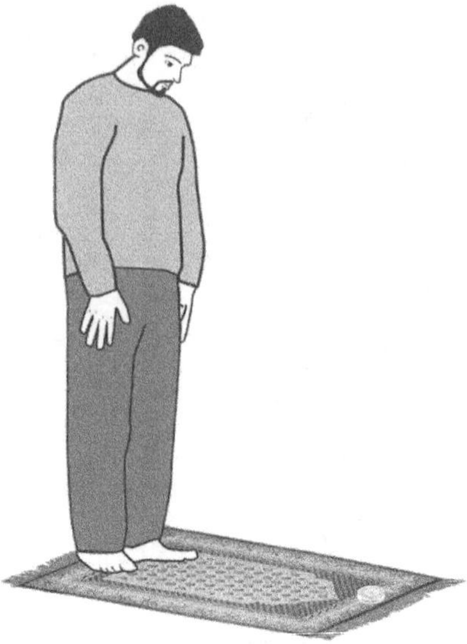

Sūrah al-Fātiḥa

بِسۡمِ ٱللَّهِ ٱلرَّحۡمَٰنِ ٱلرَّحِيمِ ١ ٱلۡحَمۡدُ لِلَّهِ رَبِّ
ٱلۡعَٰلَمِينَ ٢ ٱلرَّحۡمَٰنِ ٱلرَّحِيمِ ٣ مَٰلِكِ يَوۡمِ ٱلدِّينِ ٤
إِيَّاكَ نَعۡبُدُ وَإِيَّاكَ نَسۡتَعِينُ ٥ ٱهۡدِنَا ٱلصِّرَٰطَ
ٱلۡمُسۡتَقِيمَ ٦ صِرَٰطَ ٱلَّذِينَ أَنۡعَمۡتَ عَلَيۡهِمۡ غَيۡرِ
ٱلۡمَغۡضُوبِ عَلَيۡهِمۡ وَلَا ٱلضَّآلِّينَ ٧

Sūrah al-Jumuʿah

It is recommended to recite Sūrah al-Jumuʿah (Chapter 62) in the first *rakʿah* (after Sūrah al-Fātiḥa) of the Friday Prayers, however, it is **NOT** an obligation.

بِسۡمِ ٱللَّهِ ٱلرَّحۡمَٰنِ ٱلرَّحِيمِ

يُسَبِّحُ لِلَّهِ مَا فِى ٱلسَّمَاوَاتِ وَمَا فِى ٱلۡأَرۡضِ ٱلۡمَلِكِ
ٱلۡقُدُّوسِ ٱلۡعَزِيزِ ٱلۡحَكِيمِ ١ هُوَ ٱلَّذِى بَعَثَ فِى ٱلۡأُمِّيِّـۧنَ
رَسُولٗا مِّنۡهُمۡ يَتۡلُواْ عَلَيۡهِمۡ ءَايَٰتِهِۦ وَيُزَكِّيهِمۡ وَيُعَلِّمُهُمُ
ٱلۡكِتَٰبَ وَٱلۡحِكۡمَةَ وَإِن كَانُواْ مِن قَبۡلُ لَفِى ضَلَٰلٖ مُّبِينٖ
٢ وَءَاخَرِينَ مِنۡهُمۡ لَمَّا يَلۡحَقُواْ بِهِمۡۚ وَهُوَ
ٱلۡعَزِيزُ ٱلۡحَكِيمُ ٣ ذَٰلِكَ فَضۡلُ ٱللَّهِ
يُؤۡتِيهِ مَن يَشَآءُۚ وَٱللَّهُ ذُو ٱلۡفَضۡلِ
ٱلۡعَظِيمِ ٤ مَثَلُ ٱلَّذِينَ حُمِّلُواْ ٱلتَّوۡرَىٰةَ ثُمَّ
لَمۡ يَحۡمِلُوهَا كَمَثَلِ ٱلۡحِمَارِ يَحۡمِلُ أَسۡفَارَۢاۚ
بِئۡسَ مَثَلُ ٱلۡقَوۡمِ ٱلَّذِينَ

كَذَّبُوا۟ بِـَٔايَٰتِ ٱللَّهِ ۚ وَٱللَّهُ لَا يَهْدِى ٱلْقَوْمَ ٱلظَّٰلِمِينَ ﴿٥﴾
قُلْ يَا أَيُّهَا ٱلَّذِينَ هَادُوٓا۟ إِن زَعَمْتُمْ أَنَّكُمْ أَوْلِيَآءُ لِلَّهِ مِن
دُونِ ٱلنَّاسِ فَتَمَنَّوُا۟ ٱلْمَوْتَ إِن كُنتُمْ صَادِقِينَ ﴿٦﴾ وَلَا
يَتَمَنَّوْنَهُۥٓ أَبَدًۢا بِمَا قَدَّمَتْ أَيْدِيهِمْ ۚ وَٱللَّهُ عَلِيمٌۢ بِٱلظَّالِمِينَ
﴿٧﴾ قُلْ إِنَّ ٱلْمَوْتَ ٱلَّذِى تَفِرُّونَ مِنْهُ فَإِنَّهُۥ مُلَاقِيكُمْ ۖ ثُمَّ
تُرَدُّونَ إِلَىٰ عَالِمِ ٱلْغَيْبِ وَٱلشَّهَادَةِ فَيُنَبِّئُكُم بِمَا كُنتُمْ
تَعْمَلُونَ ﴿٨﴾ يَا أَيُّهَا ٱلَّذِينَ ءَامَنُوٓا۟ إِذَا نُودِىَ لِلصَّلَاةِ مِن
يَوْمِ ٱلْجُمُعَةِ فَٱسْعَوْا۟ إِلَىٰ ذِكْرِ ٱللَّهِ وَذَرُوا۟ ٱلْبَيْعَ ۚ ذَالِكُمْ
خَيْرٌ لَّكُمْ إِن كُنتُمْ تَعْلَمُونَ ﴿٩﴾ فَإِذَا قُضِيَتِ ٱلصَّلَاةُ
فَٱنتَشِرُوا۟ فِى ٱلْأَرْضِ وَٱبْتَغُوا۟ مِن فَضْلِ ٱللَّهِ وَٱذْكُرُوا۟ ٱللَّهَ
كَثِيرًا لَّعَلَّكُمْ تُفْلِحُونَ ﴿١٠﴾ وَإِذَا رَأَوْا۟ تِجَارَةً أَوْ لَهْوًا
ٱنفَضُّوٓا۟ إِلَيْهَا وَتَرَكُوكَ قَآئِمًا ۚ قُلْ مَا عِندَ ٱللَّهِ خَيْرٌ مِّنَ
ٱللَّهْوِ وَمِنَ ٱلتِّجَارَةِ ۚ وَٱللَّهُ خَيْرُ ٱلرَّازِقِينَ ﴿١١﴾

Takbīr

أَللّٰهُ أَكْبَرُ

Qunūt in the First Rakʿah

NOTE: This *qunūt* is **before** *rukūʿ* in the first *rakʿah,* and ANY supplication can be recited – however, the following recitation is recommended.

لَا إِلٰهَ إِلَّا اللّٰهُ الْحَلِيمُ الْكَرِيمُ، لَا إِلٰهَ إِلَّا اللّٰهُ الْعَلِيُّ الْعَظِيمُ. سُبْحَانَ اَللّٰهِ رَبِّ السَّمَوَاتِ السَّبْعِ، وَرَبِّ الأَرْضِينَ السَّبْعِ، وَمَا فِيهِنَّ وَمَا بَيْنَهُنَّ وَرَبِّ الْعَرْشِ الْعَظِيمِ، وَالْحَمْدُ لِلّٰهِ رَبِّ الْعَالَمِينَ.

Takbīr

أَللهُ أَكْبَرُ

Rukūʿ

سُبْحَانَ اللهِ، سُبْحَانَ اللهِ، سُبْحَانَ اللهِ.

or

سُبْحَانَ رَبِّيَ الْعَظِيمِ وَبِحَمْدِهِ.

Standing Before Sajdah

It is recommended that the following phrase is recited (while standing) before a person goes down to *sajdah.*

سَمِعَ اللّٰهُ لِـمَنْ حَمِدَهُ.

Takbīr

أَللّٰهُ أَكْبَرُ

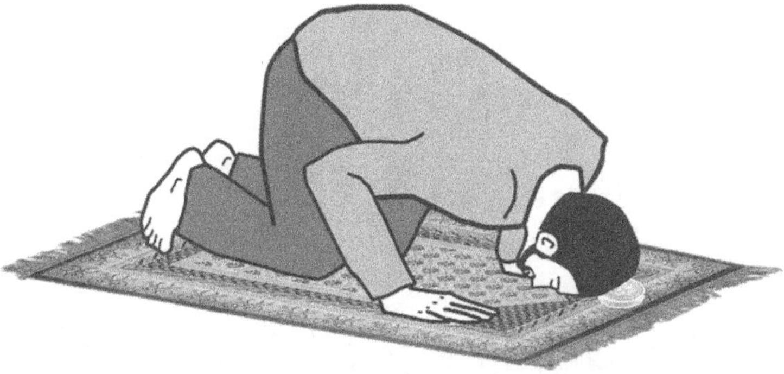

First Sajdah

سُبْحَانَ اللّٰهِ، سُبْحَانَ اللّٰهِ، سُبْحَانَ اللّٰهِ.

or

سُبْحَانَ رَبِّيَ الأَعْلٰى وَ بِحَمْدِهِ.

Takbīr

أَللّٰهُ أَكْبَرُ

Sitting in between Sajdah

It is recommended that the following phrase is recited (while sitting) before a person goes back into *sajdah.*

أَسْتَغْفِرُ اللّٰهَ رَبِّي وَ أَتُوبُ إِلَيْهِ.

Takbīr

أَللهُ أَكْبَرُ

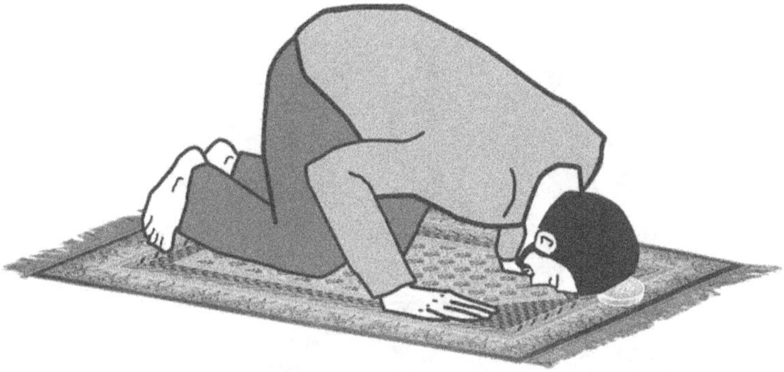

First Sajdah

سُبْحَانَ اللّٰهِ، سُبْحَانَ اللّٰهِ، سُبْحَانَ اللّٰهِ.

or

سُبْحَانَ رَبِّيَ الأَعْلٰى وَ بِحَمْدِهِ.

Takbīr

أَللّٰهُ أَكْبَرُ

End of First Rakʿah

It is recommended that the following phrase is recited while one is standing up for the next *rakʿah.*

بِـحَوْلِ اللهِ وَقُوَّتِهِ أَقُومُ وَأَقْعُدُ.

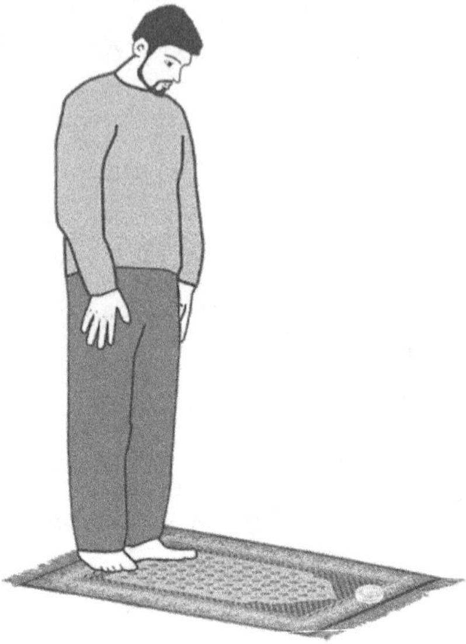

Sūrah al-Fātiḥa

بِسْمِ ٱللَّهِ ٱلرَّحْمَٰنِ ٱلرَّحِيمِ ﴿١﴾ أَلْحَمْدُ لِلَّهِ رَبِّ
ٱلْعَالَمِينَ ﴿٢﴾ أَلرَّحْمَٰنِ ٱلرَّحِيمِ ﴿٣﴾ مالِكِ يَوْمِ ٱلدِّينِ ﴿٤﴾
إِيَّاكَ نَعْبُدُ وَإِيَّاكَ نَسْتَعِينُ ﴿٥﴾ ٱهْدِنَا ٱلصِّرَاطَ
ٱلْمُسْتَقِيمَ ﴿٦﴾ صِرَاطَ ٱلَّذِينَ أَنْعَمْتَ عَلَيْهِمْ غَيْرِ
ٱلْمَغْضُوبِ عَلَيْهِمْ وَلَا ٱلضَّآلِّينَ ﴿٧﴾

Sūrah al-Munāfiqūn

It is highly recommended to recite Sūrah al-Munāfiqūn (Chapter 63) in the second *rakʿah* of the Friday Prayer, however, it is **NOT** an obligation.

بِسْمِ ٱللَّهِ ٱلرَّحْمَٰنِ ٱلرَّحِيمِ

إِذَا جَآءَكَ ٱلْمُنَٰفِقُونَ قَالُوا۟ نَشْهَدُ إِنَّكَ لَرَسُولُ ٱللَّهِ ۗ وَٱللَّهُ
يَعْلَمُ إِنَّكَ لَرَسُولُهُۥ وَٱللَّهُ يَشْهَدُ إِنَّ ٱلْمُنَٰفِقِينَ لَكَٰذِبُونَ ١
ٱتَّخَذُوٓا۟ أَيْمَٰنَهُمْ جُنَّةً فَصَدُّوا۟ عَن سَبِيلِ ٱللَّهِ ۚ إِنَّهُمْ سَآءَ مَا
كَانُوا۟ يَعْمَلُونَ ٢ ذَٰلِكَ بِأَنَّهُمْ ءَامَنُوا۟ ثُمَّ كَفَرُوا۟ فَطُبِعَ عَلَىٰ
قُلُوبِهِمْ فَهُمْ لَا يَفْقَهُونَ ٣ وَإِذَا رَأَيْتَهُمْ تُعْجِبُكَ أَجْسَامُهُمْ ۖ
وَإِن يَقُولُوا۟ تَسْمَعْ لِقَوْلِهِمْ ۖ كَأَنَّهُمْ خُشُبٌ
مُّسَنَّدَةٌ ۖ يَحْسَبُونَ كُلَّ صَيْحَةٍ عَلَيْهِمْ ۚ هُمُ
ٱلْعَدُوُّ فَٱحْذَرْهُمْ ۚ قَٰتَلَهُمُ ٱللَّهُ ۖ أَنَّىٰ يُؤْفَكُونَ
٤ وَإِذَا قِيلَ لَهُمْ تَعَالَوْا۟ يَسْتَغْفِرْ لَكُمْ
رَسُولُ ٱللَّهِ لَوَّوْا۟ رُءُوسَهُمْ وَرَأَيْتَهُمْ يَصُدُّونَ
وَهُم مُّسْتَكْبِرُونَ ٥

سَوَآءٌ عَلَيۡهِمۡ أَسۡتَغۡفَرۡتَ لَهُمۡ أَمۡ لَمۡ تَسۡتَغۡفِرۡ لَهُمۡ لَن يَغۡفِرَ
ٱللَّهُ لَهُمۡۚ إِنَّ ٱللَّهَ لَا يَهۡدِي ٱلۡقَوۡمَ ٱلۡفَٰسِقِينَ ٦ هُمُ ٱلَّذِينَ
يَقُولُونَ لَا تُنفِقُواْ عَلَىٰ مَنۡ عِندَ رَسُولِ ٱللَّهِ حَتَّىٰ يَنفَضُّواْۗ
وَلِلَّهِ خَزَآئِنُ ٱلسَّمَٰوَٰتِ وَٱلۡأَرۡضِ وَلَٰكِنَّ ٱلۡمُنَٰفِقِينَ لَا
يَفۡقَهُونَ ٧ يَقُولُونَ لَئِن رَّجَعۡنَآ إِلَى ٱلۡمَدِينَةِ لَيُخۡرِجَنَّ
ٱلۡأَعَزُّ مِنۡهَا ٱلۡأَذَلَّۚ وَلِلَّهِ ٱلۡعِزَّةُ وَلِرَسُولِهِۦ وَلِلۡمُؤۡمِنِينَ وَلَٰكِنَّ
ٱلۡمُنَٰفِقِينَ لَا يَعۡلَمُونَ ٨ يَٰٓأَيُّهَا ٱلَّذِينَ ءَامَنُواْ لَا تُلۡهِكُمۡ
أَمۡوَٰلُكُمۡ وَلَآ أَوۡلَٰدُكُمۡ عَن ذِكۡرِ ٱللَّهِۚ وَمَن يَفۡعَلۡ ذَٰلِكَ
فَأُوْلَٰٓئِكَ هُمُ ٱلۡخَٰسِرُونَ ٩ وَأَنفِقُواْ مِن مَّا رَزَقۡنَٰكُم مِّن
قَبۡلِ أَن يَأۡتِيَ أَحَدَكُمُ ٱلۡمَوۡتُ فَيَقُولَ رَبِّ لَوۡلَآ أَخَّرۡتَنِيٓ إِلَىٰٓ
أَجَلٖ قَرِيبٖ فَأَصَّدَّقَ وَأَكُن مِّنَ ٱلصَّٰلِحِينَ ١٠ وَلَن يُؤَخِّرَ
ٱللَّهُ نَفۡسًا إِذَا جَآءَ أَجَلُهَاۚ وَٱللَّهُ خَبِيرُۢ بِمَا تَعۡمَلُونَ ١١

Takbīr

أَللّٰهُ أَكْبَرُ

Rukūʿ

سُبْحَانَ اللهِ، سُبْحَانَ اللهِ، سُبْحَانَ اللهِ.

or

سُبْحَانَ رَبِّيَ الْعَظِيمِ وَبِحَمْدِهِ.

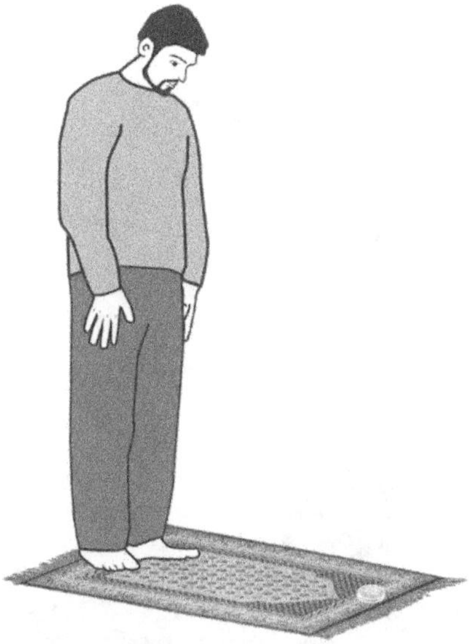

Standing After Rukūʿ

It is recommended that the following phrase is recited (while standing) before a person recites the *qunūt.*

سَمِعَ اللّٰهُ لِـمَنْ حَمِدَهُ.

Takbīr

أَللّٰهُ أَكْبَرُ

Qunūt in the Second Rakʿah

NOTE: This *qunūt* is **after** *rukūʿ* in the second *rakʿah,* and ANY supplication can be recited – however, the following recitation is recommended.

لَا إِلٰهَ إِلَّا اللّٰهُ الْحَلِيمُ الْكَرِيمُ، لَا إِلٰهَ إِلَّا اللّٰهُ الْعَلِيُّ الْعَظِيمُ. سُبْحَانَ اَللّٰهِ رَبِّ السَّمَوَاتِ السَّبْعِ، وَرَبِّ الأَرْضِينَ السَّبْعِ، وَمَا فِيهِنَّ وَمَا بَيْنَهُنَّ وَرَبِّ الْعَرْشِ الْعَظِيمِ، وَالْحَمْدُ لِلّٰهِ رَبِّ الْعَالَمِينَ.

Takbīr

أَللّٰهُ أَكْبَرُ

First Sajdah of Second Rakʿah

سُبْحَانَ اللّٰهِ، سُبْحَانَ اللّٰهِ، سُبْحَانَ اللّٰهِ.

or

سُبْحَانَ رَبِّيَ الأَعْلٰى وَ بِحَمْدِهِ.

Sitting in between Sajdah

It is recommended that the following phrase is recited (while sitting) before a person goes back into *sajdah.*

أَسْتَغْفِرُ اللّٰهَ رَبِّي وَ أَتُوبُ إِلَيْهِ.

Takbīr

أَللهُ أَكْبَرُ

Second Sajdah

سُبْحَانَ اللّٰهِ، سُبْحَانَ اللّٰهِ، سُبْحَانَ اللّٰهِ.

or

سُبْحَانَ رَبِّيَ الأَعْلٰى وَ بِحَمْدِهِ.

Takbīr

أَللّٰهُ أَكْبَرُ

Sitting After the Second Sajdah and Reciting Tashahhud

أَشْهَدُ أَنْ لَا إِلٰهَ إِلَّا اللّٰهُ وَحْدَهُ لَا شَرِيكَ لَهُ
وَأَشْهَدُ أَنَّ مُحَمَّدًا عَبْدُهُ وَرَسُولُهُ. أَللّٰهُمَّ صَلِّ
عَلٰى مُحَمَّدٍ وَّآلِ مُحَمَّدٍ.

Salām

أَلسَّلَامُ عَلَيْكَ أَيُّهَا النَّبِيُّ وَرَحْمَةُ اللّٰهِ وَبرَكَاتُهُ.

أَلسَّلَامُ عَلَيْنَا وَعَلىٰ عِبَادِ اللّٰهِ الصَّالِحِينَ.

أَلسَّلَامُ عَلَيْكُمْ وَ رَحْمَةُ اللّٰهِ وَ برَكَاتُهُ.

Three Takbīr

This is the first part of the *taʿqibāt* after the completion of *ṣalāt*.

أَللّٰهُ أَكْبَرُ. أَللّٰهُ أَكْبَرُ. أَللّٰهُ أَكْبَرُ.

1.8 Conclusion

Believers who follow a *Marjaʿ Taqlīd* who deem that *Ṣalāt al-Jumuʿah* is sufficient will be able to conclude their afternoon prayers by performing *Ṣalāt al-ʿAṣr*; others will need to perform *Ṣalāt al-Ẓuhr,* and then *Ṣalāt al-ʿAṣr.* Details for this were discussed in Footnote 82.

Ṣalāt al-Jumuʿah During the Occultation (Ghaybah)

Abstract[96]

The primary discussion regarding *Ṣalāt al-Jumuʿah* concerns the legitimacy of holding this act of worship during the Era of Occultation *(ʿAṣr al-Ghaybah)* of the 12th Imam, al-Ḥujjah ibn Ḥasan عجل الله تعالى فرجه الشريف. During the time of the presence of the immaculate Imam عجل الله تعالى فرجه الشريف, it will be an Individual Obligation *(Wājib al-ʿAynī)*;[97] and this is unanimously agreed upon by

---

[96] This research article was written by Sayyid Shāhid Ḥusayn Naqavī and was extracted from: www.hawzah.net/fa/Magazine/View/2691/6563/76322/مذاهب-اسلامی (Last accessed on July 14, 2025 – This was translated into English by Saleem Bhimji.)

[97] There are several legal terms used in this article that the reader needs to be aware of their precise legal definitions before moving forward:

1. *Wājib al-ʿAynī*: Means "Individual Obligation" and is a type of religious obligation in which each person is accountable for one's own deeds in the presence of Allah ﷻ *(mukallaf)*, thus everyone needs to perform them individually. These

Obligations are opposite to Collective Obligations. Some examples of Individual Obligations include the five daily prayers *(ṣalāt);* fasting *(ṣawm);* pilgrimage *(Ḥajj);* obligatory charity *(zakāt)*; doing good to one's parents; and strengthening ties with blood relatives.

2. *Wājib al-Kifā'ī*: Means "Collective Obligation;" and this is a type of religious obligation that falls upon the shoulders of every person accountable in the presence of Allah ﷻ *(mukallaf);* however, if enough Muslims perform that act, then all others are discharged of the responsibility. Some examples of Collective Obligations include: Burial rites of a Muslim for all of those who are informed about a death (thus, if a group of people step forward to fulfill this responsibility, then other Muslims who were informed about the death are absolved of that responsibility); and replying to the greeting of *salām* for all of those who hear it.
3. *Wājib al-Ta'khyīrī*: Means "Optional Obligation;" and this is a type of obligation in which a person who is accountable in the presence of Allah ﷻ *(mukallaf)* can choose one from among certain actions which one they want to do. Some examples of Optional Obligation include: Expiation for fasting: A person who intentionally missed a fast during the month of Ramaḍān has the choice to either emancipate a slave, fast for two months, or feed 60 needy people – they are required to carry out one of these three actions; another example is whether one wants to recite *Ṣalāt al-Ẓuhr,* or *Ṣalāt al-Jumuʿah* on the Day of Friday, if all of the conditions are met.
4. *Wājib al-Taʿyīnī*: Means "Fixed Obligation;" and this is a type of obligation in which a person is required to perform a specific action oneself, and there is no alternative for it. For example: The obligations of prayers and fasting are

all Muslims; however, during the current period of the occultation, [amongst the Muslims] the Ahlul Sunnah consider *Ṣalāt al-Jumuʿah* obligatory; whereas among the *Imāmīyyah (Shīʿa Ithnā-ʿAsherī),* this issue is disputed [keep in mind that the non-Shīʿa do not acknowledge an immaculate Imam directly appointed by Prophet Muḥammad ﷺ to be on Earth at all times].

In brief [we can state that], some Shīʿa scholars consider *Ṣalāt al-Jumuʿah* a Definite Obligation *(Wājib al-Taʿyīnī)*; while others consider it a choice that a believer has on Friday *(Wājib al-Taʾkhyīrī)* – [such that if all conditions are met, then a believer has the choice of either performing *Ṣalāt al-Jumuʿah* or performing *Ṣalāt al-Ẓuhr*]; while yet another group of Shīʿa Jurists consider it forbidden *(ḥarām)* to establish and perform *Ṣalāt al-Jumuʿah* during the Era of Occultation of the 12th Imam عجل الله تعالى فرجه الشريف [as there is no official or direct appointment of the Friday Prayer leader].

The root of the disagreement lies in whether the presence of an immaculate Imam or his direct, explicit permission is required for holding *Ṣalāt al-Jumuʿah.*

This article reviews this topic and provides an analysis on the various opinions of the Ahlul Sunnah scholars, and more importantly, a detailed review of the Shīʿa *Imāmīyyah [Ithnā-ʿAsherī]* opinion.

---

such that every able-bodied Muslim is obligated to perform their five daily prayers during their prescribed times, and these set of prayers cannot be replaced with any other form of worship, nor can anyone else perform the prayers on their behalf. (Tr.)

The Primary Discussion

The first issue regarding the Friday Prayer is whether holding *Ṣalāt al-Jumuʿah* during the Era of Occultation of the immaculate Imam of the Age عجل الله تعالى فرجه الشريف is legitimate or not. While during the presence of an Imam, the Individual Obligation *(Wājib al-ʿAynī)* of *Ṣalāt al-Jumuʿah* is unanimously agreed upon by all Muslims, the issue this research focuses on is during the time in which the 12th Imam عجل الله تعالى فرجه الشريف is not accessible and is in occultation.

The difference between the *Imāmīyyah* and the Ahlul Sunnah concerns the performance of *Ṣalāt al-Jumuʿah* during the Era of the Occultation of the immaculate Imam عجل الله تعالى فرجه الشريف [or for the Sunnī community, a caliph who acts as the head of the Muslim *ummah*].

The Ahlul Sunnah scholars consider *Ṣalāt al-Jumuʿah* obligatory during this period [our current era], because most of the Sunnī Schools of Jurisprudence do not recognize the condition of the presence of an immaculate Imam, or the permission of the [just] appointed ruler [caliph] for *Ṣalāt al-Jumuʿah* to be established, and for people to be permitted to take part in it [meaning that they do not require a caliph of the Muslim community to establish and appoint the prayer leaders for *Ṣalāt al-Jumuʿah* around the world].

However, among the *Imāmīyyah* scholars, this issue is disputed as follows:

1. Some scholars consider it a Definite Obligation *(Wājib al-Taʿyīnī)* [and that it **must** be performed regardless of the presence of an immaculate Imam or his appointment of a prayer leader].

2. Other scholars consider it an Optional Obligation *(Wājib al-Taʾkhyīrī)* [such that on Friday, a believer can either perform *Ṣalāt al-Jumuʿah* or *Ṣalāt al-Ẓuhr* and if they perform the former, then there is no need to perform the latter].
3. The last group considered holding *Ṣalāt al-Jumuʿah* as being forbidden *(ḥarām).*

The core of the disagreement is the necessity of the presence of an immaculate Imam, or his explicit permission for establishing *Ṣalāt al-Jumuʿah.* This divergence, which ranges from *Ṣalāt al-Jumuʿah* being an obligation to its being prohibited, has various reasons – the most important of which is ambiguity [in the *aḥādīth*] regarding the essential role of *wilāyah* (guardianship/authority over the Muslim community) as it relates to *Ṣalāt al-Jumuʿah.*

From this perspective, as noted, there are three Jurisprudential bases:

1. Some scholars do not consider *Ṣalāt al-Jumuʿah,* whether during the presence of the immaculate Imam or his occultation, as among the functions of *wilāyah* [Divinely-appointed authority on Earth] to establish and believe that holding *Ṣalāt al-Jumuʿah* (like the establishment of the other daily prayers) does not require his [the immaculate Imam's] permission. Therefore, some senior scholars, like the late Shahīd al-Thānī ﵀, considered *Ṣalāt al-Jumuʿah* a Definite Obligation *(Wājib al-Taʿyīnī)* during both the presence and occultation of a Divinely-appointed Imam ﵇.[98]

---

[98] Shahīd al-Thānī, Zayn al-Dīn ibn ʿAlī, *Risālah fī Ṣalāt al-Jumuʿah,* Jāmiʿa al-Mudarrisīn, Qum, 1410 AH, Pg. 46.

2. Other scholars consider it among the functions of *wilāyah* during the presence of an immaculate Imam, but do not believe in this relationship during the Period of Occultation of the Imam.

Supporters of this second basis have adopted different opinions: after forming a consensus in their opinion of the establishment of *Ṣalāt al-Jumuʿah* during the time of the presence of an immaculate Imam, when it comes to the Era of Occultation, due to the lack of access to an immaculate Imam, the condition of the presence of a [fair and just] Muslim ruler is dropped, and thus, they have considered *Ṣalāt al-Jumuʿah* as being an Optional Obligation *(Wājib al-Taʾkhyīrī).*

Some great scholars, like the late Grand Āyatullāh al-Khoei have noted that even though holding *Ṣalāt al-Jumuʿah* is an Optional Obligation *(Wājib al-Taʾkhyīrī)*, they consider attendance at *Ṣalāt al-Jumuʿah* as being a Fixed Obligation.[99]

3. The last group of Shīʿa Jurists consider the establishment of *Ṣalāt al-Jumuʿah* entirely among the

---

[99] Khoei, Abūl Qāsim al-, *Al-Mustanad fī Sharḥ al-ʿUrwatul Wuthqā*, Muʾassasa lī-Iḥyāʾ Āthār al-Imam al-Khoei, Qum, 2nd Edition, 1421 AH, Vol. 11, Pg. 31.

In short, what the late Āyatullāh al-Khoei is saying is that he accepted that praying itself on Friday is *Wājib al-Taʾkhyīrī* – you must pray either *Ṣalāt al-Jumuʿah* or *Ṣalāt al-Ẓuhr*. However, he considered that if *Ṣalāt al-Jumuʿah* is being properly held in your city/area, then attending it becomes a Fixed Obligation *(Wājib al-Taʿyīnī)*: thus, a believer must not skip *Ṣalāt al-Jumuʿah* and perform *Ṣalāt al-Ẓuhr* at home. (Tr.)

functions of *wilāyah,* and do not distinguish between the time of the presence of an immaculate Imam or his occultation in this regard. Therefore, according to this belief, during the occultation of the 12th Imam عجل الله تعالى فرجه الشريف, holding *Ṣalāt al-Jumuʿah* is forbidden and an impermissible religious innovation *(bidʿah).* Some scholars have noted that in the presence of a just *[ʿādil]* jurist, believers have the option to attend *Ṣalāt al-Jumuʿah* or not attend it; and if there is permission from a just jurist, they have considered holding *Ṣalāt al-Jumuʿah* as being a Definite Obligation *(Wājib al-Taʿyīnī),* and in other than such a circumstance, have issued a *fatwa* that establishing *Ṣalāt al-Jumuʿah* is an Optional Obligation *(Wājib al-Taʾkhyīrī).*

In summary, one of the important factors of disagreement among the Shīʿa Jurists is the role and scope of *wilāyah* in the establishment and attendance of *Ṣalāt al-Jumuʿah.*

Therefore, this article is an attempt to discuss and investigate why some scholars of the Ahlul Sunnah do not consider the Islamic ruler (caliph) or his permission necessary [to establish *Ṣalāt al-Jumuʿah*]; and on what basis do people like Abū Ḥanīfah and his followers consider the Muslim ruler's permission obligatory [in order to establish a valid *Ṣalāt al-Jumuʿah*]; and [more importantly] why the *Imāmīyyah* Jurists have various opinions, and what arguments they present for their stances.

Due to the brevity of the discussion of the Jurists of the Ahlul Sunnah, first the views of the Four Schools *(Madhāhib Arbaʿa)* will be presented, and then the detailed view of the *Imāmīyyah* Jurists will be discussed.

Mālikī School of Jurisprudence

The Mālikī School of Jurisprudence in Sunnī Islam consider holding *Ṣalāt al-Jumuʿah* without a religiously appointed *imam* [appointed by a caliph of the Prophet ﷺ], or by a ruler as being valid, and they do not consider the [legitimate] ruler a condition for the validity or obligation of *Ṣalāt al-Jumuʿah.*

According to the narration of Saḥfūn ibn Saʿīd from Mālik ibn Anas, in response to the people of the Maghrib (Morocco) who asked: "We do not have a governor [to preside] over *Ṣalāt al-Jumuʿah,*" he replied: "They should [still] hold *Ṣalāt al-Jumuʿah* even if there is no governor."[100]

That is, if there is no [Muslim] governor [over the land – or no caliph to appoint one], *Ṣalāt al-Jumuʿah* should be held by the people, because according to him, *Ṣalāt al-Jumuʿah* is among the obligations that nothing can inhibit.

In addition, he is quoted as saying: "Allah has obligations on His Earth that nothing can diminish, whether a [Muslim] governor is in charge or not;"[101] meaning that on Earth, there are obligations towards Allah ﷻ that nothing can overlook

---

[100] Aṣbaḥī, Mālik ibn Anas al-, *Al-Mudawwana al-Kubrā,* Dār al-Kutub al-ʿIlmīyyah, Beirut, 1st Edition, 1994; see also: Marwārīd, ʿAlī Aṣghar, *Al-Maṣādir al-Fiqhiyyah,* Dār al-Turāth, Beirut, 1st Edition, 1419 AH, Vol. 4, Pg. 730. The Arabic text of this is as follows:

يَجْمَعُونَ الْجُمُعَةَ إِنْ لَمْ يَكُنْ وَالٍ.

[101] *Al-Mudawwana al-Kubrā,* Vol. 1, Pg. 233. The Arabic text of this is as follows:

إِنَّ لِلّٰهِ فَرَائِضَ فِي أَرْضِهِ لَا يَنْقُصُهَا شَيْءٌ إِنْ وَلِيَهَا وَالٍ أَوْ لَمْ يَلِهَا.

their desertion, even if a [Muslim] governor does not strive to implement them [such as *Ṣalāt al-Jumuʿah*].

Therefore, followers of the Mālikī School of Jurisprudence have explicitly ruled that although *Ṣalāt al-Jumuʿah* without a sermon, and not being performed in congregation is not valid, it is valid to be established without a [Muslim] governor or ruler. As they state: "As for *Ṣalāt al-Jumuʿah,* there are conditions which are not fulfilled except by them [meaning these conditions must be met], and they are: the city... the *imam*, the sermon, the congregation, the standing, and the day... and *Ṣalāt al-Jumuʿah* is valid without a [Muslim] ruler [establishing *Ṣalāt al-Jumuʿah*], but not valid without a sermon, nor without a congregation [that it is performed in], nor without an *imam* [to deliver the sermons and lead *Ṣalāt al-Jumuʿah*]."[102]

Therefore, in the view of Mālikī jurists, *Ṣalāt al-Jumuʿah* requires an *imam* [to lead the sermons and the *ṣalāt*] because the essence of *Ṣalāt al-Jumuʿah* is [that it is performed in] congregation; but *Ṣalāt al-Jumuʿah* is not a governmental position, so it does not require a [Muslim] ruler's permission [to be established].

Muḥammad ibn Aḥmad ibn ʿAbdullāh al-Jazmī in *Al-Qawānīn al-Fiqhiyyah* has also ruled that the *imam* of *Ṣalāt*

---

[102] *Al-Kāfī fī Fiqh al-Madīna*; Badāʾiʿ al-Ṣanāʾiʿ al-Kāshānī, *Al-Maṣādir al-Fiqhiyyah*, Vol. 4, Pg. 920. The Arabic text of this is as follows:

وَلِلْجُمُعَةِ شُرُوطٌ وَهِيَ لاَ تَتِمُّ إِلَّا بِهَا وَهِيَ الْمِصْرُ... وَالْإِمَامُ وَالْخُطْبَةُ وَالْجَمَاعَةُ وَالْوَقْفُ وَالْيَوْمُ... وَتَصِحُّ الْجُمُعَةُ بِغَيْرِ سُلْطَانٍ، وَلَا تَصِحُّ بِغَيْرِ خُطْبَةٍ وَلَا بِغَيْرِ جَمَاعَةٍ وَلَا بِغَيْرِ إِمَامٍ.

al-Jumuʿah does not have to be a governor [of the Muslim state].[103]

Thus, according to the Mālikī school, *Ṣalāt al-Jumuʿah* is not (like) an official position that one must be appointed to lead [by the caliph of the Prophet ﷺ], because *Ṣalāt al-Jumuʿah* is an obligation like other religious obligations, and there is no evidence to prove the condition of the ruler's permission [to be required to establish *Ṣalāt al-Jumuʿah* in any given locality].

Shāfiʿī School of Jurisprudence

In the book *Al-Umm*, Imam al-Shāfiʿī states: "As for the *Ṣalāt al-Jumuʿah* behind any *imam* who leads it, whether he is the *amīr* [leader of the Muslim state], a subordinate, someone who has taken control of a town, or not an *amīr*, [such a *Ṣalāt al-Jumuʿah*] is sufficient."[104]

Ibrāhīm ibn Muḥammad al-Shīrāzī, a jurist of the Shāfiʿī school, says: "*Ṣalāt al-Jumuʿah* is a Divinely ordained obligation like other acts of worship, so it is not conditional on the ruler's permission [to establish and lead it]."

He then states his reason: "It is narrated that ʿAlī [ibn Abī Ṭālib] led the *ʿEid* Prayer while ʿUthmān [ibn ʿAffān] was besieged."[105]

---

[103] *Al-Maṣādir al-Fiqhiyyah*, Vol. 4, Pg. 1036.

[104] Shāfiʿī, Muhammad ibn Idrīs, *Al-Umm*, Dār al-Kutub al-ʿIlmīyyah, Dār al-Fikr, Beirut, 1st Edition, 1419 AH, Vol. 1, Pg. 331. The Arabic text of this is as follows:

وَالْجُمُعَةُ خَلْفَ كُلِّ إِمَامٍ صَلَّاهَا مِنْ أَمِيرٍ وَمَأْمُورٍ وَمُتَغَلِّبٍ عَلَى بَلْدَةٍ وَغَيْرِ أَمِيرٍ، مُجْزِئَةٌ.

[105] The Arabic text of this is as follows:

Therefore, according to the Shāfiʿī jurists, the leadership of *Ṣalāt al-Jumuʿah* is not an office [that one must be appointed to fulfill by the Prophet ﷺ, the caliph of the Prophet ﷺ or one that the Prophet ﷺ or the caliph designates] because:

1. *Ṣalāt al-Jumuʿah* is an obligation like other Divinely designated obligations, and there is no evidence that it [the establishment of it] is conditional on the ruler's permission [for it to be established and attended].
2. The action of the Commander of the Faithful, Imam ʿAlī ibn Abī Ṭālib ؑ, during the siege of the third caliph [ʿUthmān ibn ʿAffān] is cited [as proof that the permission of the caliph is not required], even though according to the Ahlul Sunnah, Imam ʿAlī ؑ was not yet the ruler [as his official caliphate had not begun at that time].

Ḥanbalī School of Jurisprudence

The Ḥanbalīs, like the Shāfiʿīs and Mālikīs, have explicitly rejected the need for a [Muslim] ruler's permission to establish and attend *Ṣalāt al-Jumuʿah,* and have said: "And the [appointment of an] *imam* is not a condition."[106]

They say: "Time [for *Ṣalāt al-Jumuʿah* must have set in], congregation [meaning it must be performed in congregation and not individually], the sermons [two sermons must be

---

لَمَّا رُوِيَ أَنَّ عَلِيًّا صَلَّى الْعِيدَ وَعُثْمَانُ مَحْصُورٌ.

[106] Ibn Qudāma, ʿAbdullāh ibn Aḥmad, *Al-Muqniʿ*; *Al-Maṣādir al-Fiqhiyyah*, Vol. 6, Pg. 1839. The Arabic text of this is as follows:

وَلَا يُشْتَرَطُ الْإِمَامُ.

delivered], and the like, are among the conditions for the validity of *Ṣalāt al-Jumuʿah,* but a [Muslim] ruler's permission is not among the conditions for its validity."

The evidence of the Ḥanbalī jurists for rejecting the condition of the [Muslim] ruler's permission is the same as that of the Shāfiʿīs, i.e., the action of the Commander of the Faithful, Imam ʿAlī ؑ, and the lack of evidence for the ruler's permission [as he did not have the explicit permission of ʿUthmān ibn ʿAffān to lead *Ṣalāt al-Jumuʿah,* but did so anyway].

They also have a third basis upon which they pass a verdict, and that is they refer to the practice of the people of Syria (Shām) during the period of chaos and sedition, when *Ṣalāt al-Jumuʿah* was held without the [Muslim] ruler's permission.

In addition, during the governorship of Walīd ibn ʿUqba, a companion named ʿAbdullāh ibn Masʿūd, took the lead and held *Ṣalāt al-Jumuʿah* with the people in Kūfa.

Similarly, during the governorship of Saʿīd ibn ʿĀṣ in Madina, Abū Mūsā al-Ashʿarī also held *Ṣalāt al-Jumuʿah*.[107]

Ḥanafī School of Jurisprudence

Among the four famous Schools of Jurisprudence of the Ahlul Sunnah, only the Ḥanafīs unequivocally state the condition of the requirement of a [Muslim] ruler [to explicitly sanction] the holding of *Ṣalāt al-Jumuʿah*.

Abūl Ḥasan Aḥmad ibn Muḥammad al-Qarawī (362–428 AH), head of the Ḥanafīs in Iraq, says the following in his

---

[107] Ḥāwardī, ʿAlī ibn Muḥammad ibn Ḥabīb al-, *Al-Ḥāwī al-Kabīr*, Dār al-Kutub al-ʿIlmīyyah, Beirut, 1414 AH, Vol. 2, Pg. 46.

famous book: "*Ṣalāt al-Jumuʿah* is not valid except in a city, or in a city's prayer place [which has been established for *Ṣalāt al-Jumuʿah*]; and it is not allowed [to be performed] in villages; nor is it allowed to hold it except with a [Muslim] ruler or someone appointed by the ruler [leading the sermons and the *ṣalāt*]."[108]

ʿAlāʾ al-Dīn al-Kāshānī in *Badāʾiʿ al-Ṣanāʾiʿ fī Tartīb al-Sharāʾiʿ*, lists five main conditions for *Ṣalāt al-Jumuʿah*, one of which is the [permission of a Muslim] ruler: "The gathering city, the ruler, the sermon, the congregation, and the time [are all conditions which must be in place before *Ṣalāt al-Jumuʿah* can be established]."[109]

In explaining the second condition, he says: "For us, the [Muslim] ruler is a condition for performing *Ṣalāt al-Jumuʿah*, and without the presence of a [Muslim] ruler, holding *Ṣalāt al-Jumuʿah* is not allowed."[110]

The Ḥanafī jurists have based their view that *Ṣalāt al-Jumuʿah* is an official position *(manṣab)* on two types of evidence: transmitted *(naqlī)* and rational *(ʿaqlī)*. These two

---

108 ʿUmar, ʿAbdullāh ibn, *Mawsūʿah Fiqhiyyah*, Pg. 521, Dār al-Nafās, Beirut, 1416 AH; *Al-Maṣādir al-Fiqhiyyah*, Vol. 3, Pg. 12. The Arabic text of this is as follows:

لَا تَصِحُّ الْجُمُعَةُ إِلَّا بِمِصْرٍ أَوْ فِي مُصَلَّى وَلَا تَجُوزُ فِي الْقُرَى وَلَا تَجُوزُ إِقَامَتُهَا إِلَّا بِالسُّلْطَانِ أَوْ مَنْ أَمَرَهُ السُّلْطَانُ.

109 *Al-Maṣādir al-Fiqhiyyah*, Vol. 3, Pg. 374. The Arabic text of this is as follows:

أَلْمِصْرُ الْجَامِعُ وَالسُّلْطَانُ وَالْخُطْبَةُ وَالْجَمَاعَةُ وَالْوَقْتُ.

110 Ibid., Pg. 378.

reasons serve as specific qualifiers or limiters of the general rules and supplementary laws regarding *Ṣalāt al-Jumuʿah.*

1. Transmitted *(Naqlī)* Evidence: There is a well-known *ḥadīth* cited by both Shīʿa and Ahlul Sunnah [scholars], in which the Prophet ﷺ said: "Allah Almighty made *Ṣalāt al-Jumuʿah* obligatory upon you in this place of mine, on this day of mine, in this month of mine, and in this year of mine. Whoever abandons it during my life and after my death, out of contempt, denial, or negligence of its right, and has a just or unjust *imam* [who presides over them], Allah will not unite them and will not bless their affairs."[111]

According to this *ḥadīth*, although the Messenger of Allah ﷺ warns and threatens those who abandon *Ṣalāt al-Jumuʿah* with Divine punishment, he conditions *ʿEid* (i.e., *Ṣalāt al-Jumuʿah*) on the presence of a just or [even an] unjust *imam* [delivering the sermons and leading the *ṣalāt*].

In another narration, the Prophet ﷺ assigned four important offices to the [Muslim] rulers: "Four things belong to the rulers [to implement in the society]: *Ṣalāt al-Jumuʿah*, the legal punishments, [the collection and distribution of the] war spoils, and alms *[ṣadaqāt].*"[112]

That is, just as the implementation of legal punishments, distribution of war spoils, and collection of *zakāt* and *ṣadaqāt*

---

[111] The Arabic text of this is as follows:

إِنَّ اللّٰهَ تَعَالَى فَرَضَ عَلَيْكُمُ الْجُمُعَةَ فِي مَقَامِي هٰذَا، فِي يَوْمِي هٰذَا، فِي شَهْرِي هٰذَا، وَفِي سَنَتِي هٰذِهِ. فَمَنْ تَرَكَهَا فِي حَيَاتِي وَبَعْدَ مَمَاتِي إِسْتِخْفَافًا بِهَا وَجُحُودًا عَلَيْهَا وَتَهَاوُنًا بِحَقِّهَا وَلَهُ إِمَامٌ عَادِلٌ أَوْ جَائِرٌ فَلَا جَمَعَ اللّٰهُ شَمْلَهُ وَلَا بَارَکَ لَهُ فِي أَمْرِهِ.

[112] The Arabic text of this is as follows:

أَرْبَعَةٌ إِلٰى الْوُلَاةِ، أَلْجُمُعَةُ وَالْحُدُودُ، وَالْفَيْءُ وَالصَّدَقَاتُ.

are among the responsibilities of the Islamic government [led by the Muslim head of state to implement], so is the establishment of *Ṣalāt al-Jumuʿah.*

Of course, to what extent these *aḥādīth* can prove the official nature of *Ṣalāt al-Jumuʿah* requires further investigation [which we will not delve into here].

2. Rational *(ʿAqlī)* Evidence: ʿAlāʾ al-Dīn ibn Masʿūd al-Kāshānī says: "If the [establishment of *Ṣalāt al-Jumuʿah* under a Muslim] ruler is not a condition, then holding the prayer will lead to chaos and sedition [in society], and preventing chaos is a necessity, and as such, preventing disorder [in the Muslim society] can only be achieved through a ruler, because the ruler has power [over the masses]."

In other words, he says: In *Ṣalāt al-Jumuʿah,* a large group of believers gather, and the leadership of *Ṣalāt al-Jumuʿah* [that is, the person that delivers the sermons and leads the prayers] has precedence over all the people of the city and as such, this brings about honour, high status, and increased social standing [for that prayer leader]. Therefore, those who are naturally overly ambitious and engrossed [in assuming societal] leadership [but do not have the requisite credentials] will naturally compete and dispute over this [position], which could ultimately lead to bloodshed [within the Muslim society].[113]

That is to say, the main nature of *Ṣalāt al-Jumuʿah* is political, and the leader of *Ṣalāt al-Jumuʿah* has significant social power, being the foremost of all the people of that city. Thus, those who aggressively seek leadership and power will

---

[113] *Al-Maṣādir al-Fiqhiyyah,* Vol. 39, Pg. 387.

fight one another to seize this power and [will do whatever they can to] take charge of the sacred pulpit *(mimbar)*, and this will ignite a fire of sedition and bloodshed. However, if the authority of this office is given to the legitimate leader (the caliph or *imam*) of the Muslims, all these seditions will be extinguished. Therefore, one of the duties of the Muslim government is to establish security in society. Thus, *Ṣalāt al-Jumuʿah* should be considered an official office [of the Muslim state], and a part of the governmental authorities [to appoint a prayer leader].

Therefore, the Mālikī, Shāfiʿī, and Ḥanbalī schools [of Jurisprudence of the Ahlul Sunnah] do not consider the ruler or his permission necessary for the establishment of *Ṣalāt al-Jumuʿah*, and their main reason is that there is no evidence [in the Quran or *aḥādīth*] for its being a condition. Moreover, the practice of some companions also shows that the ruler's permission is not a condition, as Imam ʿAlī ﷺ led prayers for the community during the siege of ʿUthmān ibn ʿAffān. However, the Ḥanafī jurists are among those who consider the [Muslim] ruler and his [explicit] permission a condition for *Ṣalāt al-Jumuʿah*, and rely on the following points:

- The practice of the Prophet ﷺ and the caliphs after him.
- A narration in the Prophet's ﷺ famous sermon on the Plains of ʿArafāt.
- A narration indicating that *Ṣalāt al-Jumuʿah*, like war spoils and alms, is a governmental matter [to oversee].

Shīʿa Imāmīyyah Jurisprudence

The study of *Ṣalāt al-Jumuʿah* from the perspective of governmental requirements [for its establishment] suggests a sort of negative reaction among Shīʿa Jurists, and this reaction overshadows the various opinions about the ruling of the permissibility of establishing *Ṣalāt al-Jumuʿah* in the absence of an immaculate Imam عليه السلام.

Some Shīʿa Jurists have ruled for the suspension of *Ṣalāt al-Jumuʿah* – meaning that they have considered it forbidden *(ḥarām)* to establish it during the Era of the Occultation (of the 12th Imam عجل الله تعالى فرجه الشريف); others have considered the [temporary] suspension of *Ṣalāt al-Jumuʿah* as being permissible [during the Era of the Occultation] and have ruled that the believers have a choice *(taʾkhīr)* in establishing *Ṣalāt al-Jumuʿah* (or reciting *Ṣalāt al-Ẓuhr);* and lastly, some scholars, regardless of the governmental situation, and irrespective of the era of the immaculate Imam's presence or absence, have considered *Ṣalāt al-Jumuʿah* to be obligatory to establish and attend in all situations.

Perhaps the reason for such a wide variety of opinions is that due to centuries of facing restrictions and challenges with illegitimate governments, Shīʿa Jurists could not reach a clear viewpoint in terms of how the rulings of Islamic Jurisprudence were impacted by various types of governments, such as those related to *Ṣalāt al-Jumuʿah* and the like. In addition, the limitations during the periods of restrictions prevented them from planning for the periods of expansion [and being free from unjust, tyrannical "Muslim" led governments].

Therefore, the most important factor causing the disagreement among the Shīʿa Jurists is the ambiguity regarding the essential role of the authority *(wilāyah)* as it relates to the ruling of *Ṣalāt al-Jumuʿah* [during the Era of Occultation of the 12th Imam ﷻ], even though the definite obligation of *Ṣalāt al-Jumuʿah* existed during the presence of the immaculate Imams ﷺ.

Thus, there are multiple opinions about [the permissibility of establishing and attending] *Ṣalāt al-Jumuʿah* that the Shīʿa Jurists hold, however, the main opinions which ultimately return to the three opinions noted previously, are the following:

1. *Ṣalāt al-Jumuʿah* is a Definite Obligation *(Wājib al-Taʿyīnī)*, conditional on the permission of an immaculate Imam, and this permission is available [for us in our current era].
2. *Ṣalāt al-Jumuʿah* is a Definite Obligation *(Wājib al-Taʿyīnī)*, and the immaculate Imam's permission is not a condition for the obligation to establish *Ṣalāt al-Jumuʿah*.
3. It is a Definite Obligation *(Wājib al-Taʿyīnī)*, however it is conditional on the presence of a fully qualified jurist *(faqīh jāmiʿ al-sharāʾiʿ)* to establish it.
4. It is an Optional Obligation *(Wājib al-Taʾkhyīrī)* – meaning that on Friday, a believer has the option of either performing the Noon Prayer *(Ṣalāt al-Ẓuhr)* or *Ṣalāt al-Jumuʿah.*
5. It is forbidden *(ḥarām)*, because *Ṣalāt al-Jumuʿah* is the function of the immaculate Imam [to establish, and to appoint its leader] and without his [explicit] permission, holding or initiating *Ṣalāt al-Jumuʿah* is

regarded as the usurpation of an immaculate Imam's authority, and obtaining the permission of the 12th Imam ﷺ in the Era of his Occultation is not possible.

Non-Legitimacy of Ṣalāt al-Jumuʿah in the Era of Occultation

Those Shīʿa scholars who believe in the non-legitimacy of establishing *Ṣalāt al-Jumuʿah* in the Era of Occultation of the 12th Imam ﷺ have provided several arguments:

First Argument: Consensus (Ijmāʿ)

The existence of an immaculate Imam [and his silent, tacit approval], or his [explicit] permission is a condition for convening *Ṣalāt al-Jumuʿah*. This condition is based on consensus of Shīʿa scholarship, and during the Era of Occultation of Imam al-Mahdī ﷺ, this condition is absent. Therefore, the conditioned matter, that is, holding *Ṣalāt al-Jumuʿah*, is also absent [so it cannot be held].[114]

The Status of Consensus

When we study the history of *Ṣalāt al-Jumuʿah* [and its Jurisprudential rulings within Shīʿa Islam], we find that until the time of Sayyid Murtaḍā, ʿAlam al-Hudā ﷺ (d. 1044 AD), no jurists addressed the requirement of an immaculate Imam's presence or his permission [to be required for *Ṣalāt al-Jumuʿah* to be held]. Therefore, when personalities like

---

[114] Shahīd al-Thānī, Zayn al-Dīn ibn ʿAlī, *Risālah fī Ṣalāt al-Jumuʿah*, Muʾassasa al-Nashr al-Islāmī, Jāmiʿa Mudarrisīn Qum, 1st Edition, 1410 AH, Pg. 45.

Shaykh Ṣadūq and Shaykh Mufīd are not part of the consensus, this consensus has no value.[115]

Shahīd Thānī says: "The opinion of the non-legitimacy [of holding *Ṣalāt al-Jumuʿah* during the Era of Occultation of the 12th Imam] is limited to [scholars] such as the late Sallār and Ibn Idrīs al-Ḥillī, but others [other scholars] in one place [in their writings] also leaned towards this opinion, however, in their other books, they opposed it - like Shaykh Ṭūsī."

Shahīd Thānī also said: "Even if we accept this consensus, still the absolute prohibition of holding *Ṣalāt al-Jumuʿah* will not necessarily follow, because the jurists are general deputies [of the 12th Imam]; and based on this *ḥadīth* of Imam al-Ṣādiq who said: 'Look to a man who narrates our *aḥādīth* and knows our rulings, then accept him as a judge, for I have made him a judge over you.'"[116]

---

[115] This means that, when looking at the history of the Friday Prayer and the rules about it in within the Shīʿa Jurisprudence, early scholars did not say that the presence or permission of an immaculate Imam was required for holding this prayer. This idea only appeared later, after the time of Sayyid Murtaḍā (who died in 1044 AD). So, if some later jurists claim there is a consensus saying that an immaculate Imam is required, it doesn't count as a true consensus, because respected early scholars like Shaykh Ṣadūq and Shaykh Mufīd did not agree with this idea or were not included in that agreement. For a consensus to be meaningful in Islamic law, major early scholars need to be part of it, not just later ones. (Tr.)

[116] *Wasāʾil al-Shīʿa*, 5th Edition, Vol. 18, Pg. 98, Section 11, from the Chapters on the Qualities of a Judge. The Arabic text of this is as follows:

If someone says that the meaning of this *ḥadīth* is permission for adjudicating among people only and not [establishing and leading] *Ṣalāt al-Jumuʿah*, then we reply that the meaning of permission is an Imam's appointment in general. Therefore, it will include the disputed matter [of the permissibility of *Ṣalāt al-Jumuʿah*]. Thus, the consensus does not include the claim.[117]

Second Argument: Established Practice

Just as the Noble Prophet of Islam ﷺ and the caliphs after him appointed judges, they also appointed the leaders for *Ṣalāt al-Jumuʿah*. This practice indicates that the leadership of *Ṣalāt al-Jumuʿah*, like passing judgements [in matters of dispute within a Muslim society], requires appointment [from the Noble Prophet ﷺ, or one of his successors]. During the Period of Occultation of the final Imam عجل الله تعالى فرجه الشريف, such appointment is not possible, and [obviously] appointing oneself as the *imam* for *Ṣalāt al-Jumuʿah* is like appointing oneself as a judge, which is not permissible!

Since the leadership of *Ṣalāt al-Jumuʿah* is one of the functions of an immaculate Imam, and consequently, following a prayer leader who has taken the immaculate Imam's place without [his explicit] permission is in fact, following a usurper; due to this, both establishing and attending *Ṣalāt al-Jumuʿah* is forbidden *(ḥarām)*.

أُنْظُرُوا إِلَى رَجُلٍ قَدْ رَوَى حَدِيثَنَا وَعَرَفَ أَحْكَامَنَا فَارْضَوْا بِهِ حَاكِمًا فَإِنِّي قَدْ جَعَلْتُهُ عَلَيْكُمْ حَاكِمًا.

[117] *Risālah fī Ṣalāt al-Jumuʿah*, Pg. 46.

The late Āyatullāh Sayyid Muḥammad Ḥusayn Burūjerdī ؒ said: "Among the narrations about *Ṣalāt al-Jumuʿah*, it is necessary to mention a historical point as an attached indicator. The summary of this point is that, without a doubt, during the time of the Prophet ﷺ, and during the times of the caliphs and rulers, whether Umayyads or ʿAbbāsids, even during the time of the Commander of the Faithful, Imam ʿAlī ibn Abī Ṭālib ؑ, and Imam Ḥasan al-Mujtabā ؑ, they themselves either led *Ṣalāt al-Jumuʿah,* or appointed someone else to do so.

The Noble Prophet of Islam ﷺ and the Commander of the Faithful, Imam ʿAlī ؑ, themselves appointed and dismissed *Ṣalāt al-Jumuʿah imams* in all Islamic lands, and no one saw anyone holding *Ṣalāt al-Jumuʿah* by their own choice or without permission. This method was known among all Muslims, especially among the companions of the Imams ؑ, and the narrations of the Imams ؑ were conveyed to those who witnessed this method.

This process continued until the Ṣafavid government [of Iran]. Therefore, the practice of the Prophet of Islam ﷺ, the caliphs, and the Muslim rulers from the Prophet's ﷺ time until now is that holding *Ṣalāt al-Jumuʿah* is among the office of the Muslim caliphate, and this is conclusive evidence for the necessity of a ruler's, or just, immaculate Imam's permission for establishing and holding the Friday prayer."[118]

The author of *Al-Muʿtabar* says: "Just as it is not valid for anyone to appoint themselves as a judge, it is not valid to

---

[118] Burūjerdī, Āyatullāh Sayyid Muḥammad Ḥusayn, *Al-Badr al-Zāhir fī Ṣalāt al-Jumuʿah wa al-Musāfir*, Dār al-Ḥikmah, Qum, 1st Edition, 1378, Pg. 6.

appoint oneself as the *imam* of *Ṣalāt al-Jumuʿah.* This is not an analogy, but rather, it is a case of: 'Argument by continuous practice throughout the ages and opposing it is contrary to the consensus [of the Shīʿa Jurists].'"[119]

Shaykh Ṭūsī ﵀, in his book, *Al-Khilāf,* also considers this condition a matter of consensus: "It is known that this is the consensus among the people of the ages."[120]

Reflection

From this second argument, reflect on the following points:

1. From the established practice [of the Shīʿa communities throughout the eras], the condition is not understood, but the immaculate Imams' right of priority is understood. The essence of *Ṣalāt al-Jumuʿah* does not depend on the presence of an immaculate Imam.

2. The issue of *Ṣalāt al-Jumuʿah* was a pressing issue for the Shīʿas and all Muslims. So then, why did the immaculate Imams not prohibit holding *Ṣalāt al-Jumuʿah*? On the contrary, we have many narrations that the Imams encouraged participation in *Ṣalāt al-Jumuʿah.*[121]

If the presence of an immaculate Imam was a condition for holding *Ṣalāt al-Jumuʿah,* then he [the immaculate Imam]

---

[119] Muḥaqqiq Ḥillī, Jaʿfar ibn Muḥammad, *Al-Muʿtabar,* Muʾassasa Sayyid al-Shuhadāʾ, Qum, 1364 SH, Vol. 1, Pp. 271 and 297. The Arabic text of this is as follows:

إِسْتِدْلَالٌ بِالْعَمَلِ الْمُسْتَمِرِّ فِي الْأَعْصَارِ، فَمُخَالَفَتُهُ فَرقُ الْإِجْمَاعِ.

[120] Shaykh Ṭūsī, *Al-Khilāf,* Muʾassasa al-Nashr al-Islāmī, Jāmiʿa Mudarrisīn Qum, New Edition, 1414 AH, Vol. 1, Pg. 627, Issue 397.

[121] Shaykh Ḥurr ʿĀmilī, *Wasāʾil al-Shīʿa,* Vol. 5, from the Chapters on Friday Prayer, Ḥadīth 1.

would have certainly addressed it and explicitly stated it, but there are no narrations where any immaculate Imam explicitly prohibited it.[122]

3. Proving this continuous practice for all times and places is difficult. We saw that some great jurists considered *Ṣalāt al-Jumuʿah* a Definite *(Wājib al-Taʿyīnī)* or Optional Obligation *(Wājib al-Taʾkhyīrī)*, even though they were not appointed by an immaculate Imam ﷺ in this regard.[123]

Historians have written that in Shīʿa-dominated cities like Baghdād (in Iraq), Qum, Kāshān, Varāmīn, (cities in Iran), and the various cities of Syria and Ṭabaristān, *Ṣalāt al-Jumuʿah* was always held. Yāqūt al-Ḥamawī in *Muʿjam al-Buldān* wrote: "In the year 329 AH, the Shīʿas would gather in the *Masjid* of Baghdād and hold *Ṣalāt al-Jumuʿah*. Because the Shīʿas would vilify the companions (engage in the act of *sabb*) in this *Masjid*, Raḍī Billāh arrested them and imprisoned them, then he destroyed that *Masjid*. Some Shīʿas informed the *Amīr al-Umarāʾ* (the Leader of Leaders) of Baghdād, and he rebuilt the *Masjid*, and *Ṣalāt al-Jumuʿah* was held there until the year 450 AH, after which it was discontinued."[124]

Abūl Faraj ʿAbdul Raḥmān ibn ʿAlī ibn al-Jawzī in *Al-Muntaẓam fī Tārīkh al-Mulūk wa al-Umam* wrote that: "Abū Bakr al-Khaṭīb said: 'I prayed *Ṣalāt al-Jumuʿah* in Baghdād, and at that time, *Ṣalāt al-Jumuʿah* was held in

---

[122] Raḍānejād, ʿIzz al-Dīn, *Ṣalāt al-Jumuʿah*, Muʾassasa Imam al-Ṣādiq ﷺ, Qum, 1st Edition, 1415 AH, Pg. 178.
[123] Baḥrānī, Shaykh Muḥammad Yūsuf, *Al-Ḥadāʾiq al-Nāḍirah*, Muʾassasa al-Nashr al-Islāmī, Jāmiʿa Mudarrisīn Qum, undated, Vol. 9, Pg. 429.
[124] *Muʿjam al-Buldān*, Vol. 1, Pp. 362–363.

several places in Baghdād, such as Masjid al-Madīna, Masjid al-Raṣṣāfa, Masjid Dār al-Khilāfa, Masjid Burātha, Masjid Quṭīʿa Umm Jaʿfar, and Masjid Ḥadība.'"[125]

Shihāb al-Dīn Tuwārīkhī Shāfiʿī al-Rāzī wrote two books in the year 555 AH and said that the Shīʿas do not establish *Ṣalāt al-Jumuʿah.* In response to these two books, the great preacher, ʿAbdul Jalīl ibn Abī Ḥusayn al-Qazwīnī al-Rāzī wrote a book in Persian called *Al-Naqḍ.* In this, he wrote: "By the praise and grace of Allah, in all Shīʿa cities, this Prayer *(Ṣalāt al-Jumuʿah)* has been established and is being practiced with the sermons and conditions for establishment being met (such as an *imam* to lead it, in congregation, etc.), and all of the other conditions (are also being fulfilled). [This is being done] in the two congregational *masājid* in Qum, and two congregational *masājid* in Sāveh, and one congregational *masjid* in Kāshān, and the congregational *masjid* in Varāmīn, and in all the lands of Syria, and in our region of Māzandarān, and denying this is the height of ignorance."[126]

Therefore, in Shīʿa-populated cities, *Ṣalāt al-Jumuʿah* was held, and in certain cities, there were *masājid* referred to as the *Jāmiʿ Masjid* (or Congregational Mosque) for holding *Ṣalāt al-Jumuʿah.*

For example, Māziyār ibn Qārin in Bārfurūsh, who lived in the city of Bābul built a *masjid* in the year 160 AH and called it *Jāmiʿ* [and it was used to perform *Ṣalāt al-Jumuʿah*].[127]

---

[125] *Al-Muntaẓam fī Tārīkh al-Mulūk wa al-Umam,* Vol. 7, Pg. 238.
[126] *Al-Naqḍ,* Pg. 395.
[127] Ibid.

Therefore, these historical documents indicate that although the Shīʿas lived under a great deal of oppression and fear, wherever and whenever they could, they would establish *Ṣalāt al-Jumuʿah*.

Thus, the statement of the late Āyatullāh Burūjerdī, that the situation of not holding *Ṣalāt al-Jumuʿah* by the Shīʿas continued until the Safavid Era is questionable.

Third Argument: Opposition to Consensus (Ijmāʿ)

If we do not consider the holding of *Ṣalāt al-Jumuʿah* as being forbidden *(ḥarām)*, it implies that we consider it to be an Individual Obligation *(Wājib al-ʿAynī)* to establish and take part in, because this is understood from reviewing the Quran and *Sunnah*; whereas [we know that] there is a consensus [amongst the Shīʿa jurists] that *Ṣalāt al-Jumuʿah* is not an Individual Obligation *(Wājib al-ʿAynī)*.

If *Ṣalāt al-Jumuʿah* is an Individual Obligation *(Wājib al-ʿAynī)*, then performing *Ṣalāt al-Ẓuhr* would not be permissible, but no one accepts the impermissibility of performing *Ṣalāt al-Ẓuhr* on Friday. Therefore, this group of Shīʿa jurists do not accept that *Ṣalāt al-Jumuʿah* is an Individual Obligation *(Wājib al-ʿAynī)*. As a result, holding *Ṣalāt al-Jumuʿah* is forbidden, because there is only one obligation on Friday, not two, and if *Ṣalāt al-Jumuʿah* is obligatory, then *Ṣalāt al-Ẓuhr* would not be permissible to perform.[128]

---

[128] Muḥaqqiq Karakī, *Risālah fī Ṣalāt al-Jumuʿah*; *Dawāzda Risālah Fiqhī*, Rasūl Jaʿfariyān, Anṣāriyān Publications, Qum, 1st Edition, Pg. 117.

Response

First: There is no rational or religious necessity between *Ṣalāt al-Jumuʿah* not being an Individual Obligation *(Wājib al-ʿAynī)*, and being forbidden because many jurists denied that *Ṣalāt al-Jumuʿah* was prohibited to perform; while at the same time, they did not accept that *Ṣalāt al-Jumuʿah* was an Individual Obligation *(Wājib al-ʿAynī)*. Rather, they issued a verdict *(fatwa)* that *Ṣalāt al-Jumuʿah* was an Optional Obligation *(Wājib al-Ta'khyīrī)*.

Second: The evidence derived from the Quran and *Sunnah* is not explicit *(naṣṣ)* concerning its individual obligation *(Wājib al-ʿAynī)* but rather has an apparent meaning *(zuhūr)* of it being an individual obligation *(Wājib al-ʿAynī)* by way of necessity *(iqtidhā)*. However, we possess evidence that contradicts this apparent meaning, which will be explained in its proper place. That evidence will act as a preventative factor, and therefore it is not necessary for us to uphold the view of an individual obligation *(Wājib al-ʿAynī)*.

Fourth Argument: The Dilemma Between Obligation and Prohibition

First: Here, the matter is between obligation *(wājib)* and prohibition *(ḥarām)*, and wherever a matter is between these two things, then common sense rules to avoid it, because the default when it comes to religious responsibilities towards Allah ﷻ is non-obligation, as the juristic maxim states: "People are at ease regarding what they do not know."[129]

---

[129] The Arabic text of this is as follows:

Second: The one who abandons *Ṣalāt al-Jumuʿah*, due to the possibility of it being prohibited to perform during the Period of Occultation of the 12th Imam عجل الله تعالى فرجه الشريف, and the possibility of falling into corruption [as was previously discussed], is excused from this obligation, because avoiding harm is rationally preferred to acquiring benefit [based on the Islamic ruling]. It may be objected that this problem also exists for *Ṣalāt al-Ẓuhr*.

Therefore, in this case, [the ruling on establishing and attending] *Ṣalāt al-Ẓuhr* would also be between obligation and prohibition, and the default is non-obligation and avoidance, so avoidance of *Ṣalāt al-Ẓuhr* would also be necessary, and as a result, both would be forbidden to be performed – meaning *Ṣalāt al-Jumuʿah* and *Ṣalāt al-Ẓuhr*.

On the other hand, at noon on Friday, we are certain that one of these two [either *Ṣalāt al-Jumuʿah* or *Ṣalāt al-Ẓuhr*] is definitely obligatory. If we perform both, then we would be committing a forbidden act [as we need to only do one of the two].

So, what should be done?

The answer is that we should look at what is preferable *(marjīḥāt)* so that we avoid committing a forbidden act.

When we look for what is preferable, we will find that *Ṣalāt al-Ẓuhr* is preferable because: If we perform *Ṣalāt al-Ẓuhr*, then there will be neither usurpation of an office (of the position of an *imam* of *Ṣalāt al-Jumuʿah* – which is reserved for the immaculate 12th Imam of the Time عجل الله تعالى فرجه الشريف), nor slander [against the authority of the 12th Imam of the Time عجل الله تعالى فرجه الشريف, and

---

أَلنَّاسُ فِي سَعَةٍ مَا لَا يَعْلَمُونَ.

his leading or appointing someone to lead *Ṣalāt al-Jumuʿah*]. Since one of the arguments for the prohibition of *Ṣalāt al-Jumuʿah* is that the leadership of *Ṣalāt al-Jumuʿah* is a function exclusive to an immaculate Imam, and occupying this office without his permission is usurpation of the function of a Divinely-appointed Imam, and we are not certain of having his permission to take charge of this act.

If someone says that the command to strive *(jihād)*, the command to attend *Ṣalāt al-Jumuʿah,* and the permission to hold *Ṣalāt al-Jumuʿah* is understood from the narrations,[130] then we also accept that in these narrations, permission to establish *Ṣalāt al-Jumuʿah* is mentioned, just as Shaykh al-Mufīd in *Al-Muqniʿ* states that: "Zurāra ibn Aʿyun and ʿAbdul Malik ibn Aʿyun abandoned *Ṣalāt al-Jumuʿah* out of fear of lack of permission, but the Imam gave them permission to attend *Ṣalāt al-Jumuʿah.* However, granting permission at any time must be issued by the Imam of the time, because permission is among the rulings related to the *wilāyah* of the Imam, not the rulings of Prophethood [meaning that the permission of the *Walī* at that time is required]. Therefore, during the occultation of Imam al-Zamān, his permission is necessary, which does not currently exist; or there must be a general text from one of the Imams that says you can perform *Ṣalāt al-Jumuʿah* at any time [with or without the Imam of that Time being accessible], and such a text is not available. Even if an immaculate Imam gave permission to one or two people, this does not mean that everyone is permitted [to use this

[130] *Wasāʾil al-Shīʿa*, Vol. 5, Chapters on Friday Prayer, Ḥadīth 1 and 2.

permission and establish *Ṣalāt al-Jumuʿah* for all time to come]."[131]

Reflection

There is no incompatibility concerning obligation *(wujūb)* or prohibition *(ḥurmat)* between *Ṣalāt al-Ẓuhr* and *Ṣalāt al-Jumuʿah.* Incompatibility would only exist if the explicit text *(naṣṣ)* were absent, if the text were ambiguous *(ijmāl),* or if there were a conflict *(taṣāduf)* in the texts. However, in this case, all three are absent, because the Quran and *Sunnah* have clearly stated (with the loudest voice and most emphatically) that the Friday prayer is obligatory. The only difference lies in which of these two *forms (Ṣalāt al-Ẓuhr* and *Ṣalāt al-Jumuʿah)* the obligation *(wājib)* will be fulfilled by.[132]

Fifth Argument: The Likelihood of Corruption in the Texts

Holding *Ṣalāt al-Jumuʿah* without an immaculate Imam's permission, or without the immaculate Imam himself leading it will be a place of corruption, sedition, and conflict, because gatherings are often places of dispute, and the wisdom of *Ṣalāt al-Jumuʿah* is to eliminate the cause of dispute and sedition.

Removing disputes is not possible without the ruler's or his deputy's judgement, because the ruler has power, and

---

131 Najafī, Muhammad Ḥasan, *Jawāhir al-Kalām*, Dār Iḥyāʾ al-Turāth al-ʿArabī, Beirut, 7th Edition, 1981, Vol. 1, Pg. 181.

132 Namāzī, ʿAbdul Nabī, *Risālah fī Wujūb Ṣalāt al-Jumuʿah*, Muʾassasa Ismāʿīliyān, Qum, 1st Edition, 1413 AH.

people either follow him out of fear of punishment, or out of the right of his authority. As it relates to the leadership of *Ṣalāt al-Jumuʿah*, justice *(ʿadālah)* is a condition, and an Imam's permission ensures this condition [for the one who is delivering the two sermons and leading the *ṣalāt*]. Therefore, for the leadership of *Ṣalāt al-Jumuʿah*, a just Imam, or his permission is a condition.

Response

First: If in obeying Allah ﷻ and implementing Divine laws and limits, we refrain from performing acts of worship and Divine rituals out of the possibility that disputes and conflict may arise [within the society], the entire system will be disrupted, and at the very least, the ruling of gatherings for daily obligations, the Prayer for Rain *(Ṣalāt al-Istisqāʾ)*, the Prayer for Natural Occurrences such as eclipses *(Ṣalāt al-Āyāt)*, and Prayer for the Deceased *(Ṣalāt al-Mayyit)* would all be abandoned.

We accept that in some circumstances with respect to acts of worship towards Allah ﷻ, there may be a problem of dispute [amongst the believers]; however, this does not mean that everywhere *Ṣalāt al-Jumuʿah* is held, disputes should be caused; rather, *Ṣalāt al-Jumuʿah* is generally supposed to cause unity and solidarity among Muslims. Therefore, the argument is narrower than the claim.

Moreover, holding *Ṣalāt al-Jumuʿah* has been permitted, and there are many narrations *(aḥādīth)* indicating this. For example, the narration of Zurāra who says: "I asked Imam al-Bāqir ؑ: 'Upon whom is *Ṣalāt al-Jumuʿah* obligatory?' The Imam ؑ replied: 'Upon (a minimum) of seven Muslims, the first of whom is the *imam*; so, if seven gather and do not fear, then one of them should lead and deliver the sermon.'"[133]

ʿAbdullāh ibn Bukayr asked Imam al-Ṣādiq ﷺ about a group of Muslims who live in villages and there is no one to establish *Ṣalāt al-Jumuʿah* in that region – can they perform *Ṣalāt al-Ẓuhr* in congregation on Friday? The Imam said: "Yes, if they do not fear."[134]

Second: The author of *Al-Ḥadāʾiq* says: "Even with the presence of a just and immaculate Imam, disputes and conflicts still existed. During the government of the Commander of the Faithful, ʿAlī ﷺ, disputes among Muslims were greater than during the time of the other caliphs. Therefore, the presence of a just and immaculate Imam is not enough to avoid disputes (in other words, the presence of an Imam will not necessarily mean that there will be no disputes or conflicts within the community of believers)."

Third: The mere occurrence of disputes from a religious matter does not indicate that the religious injunction should not be implemented, because the cause of a dispute is the action of the individuals responsible, which has nothing to do with the essence of the religious ruling.

If, just because of the possibility of dispute, a religious ruling is not established, then most rulings would be void,

---

[133] *Wasāʾil al-Shīʿa*, Vol. 5, Section 2, from the Chapters on Friday Prayer, Pg. 8. The Arabic text of this is as follows:

عَلَى سَبْعَةِ نَفَرٍ مِنَ الْمُسْلِمِينَ، أَوَّلُهُمُ الإِمَامُ فَإِذَا اجْتَمَعَ سَبْعَةُ نَفَرٍ وَ لَمْ يَخَافُوا أَمَّهُمْ بَعْضُهُمْ وَخَطَبَهُمْ.

[134] Ibid. The Arabic text of this is as follows:

نَعَمْ إِذَا لَمْ يَخَافُوا.

and there are rulings more important than what we are discussing – namely *Ṣalāt al-Jumuʿah.* Thus, as the saying goes: "Indeed, not even a stick was brought for Islam, nor did a pillar stand firm for it."[135 & 136]

Sixth Argument: The Narrations

The narrations regarding *Ṣalāt al-Jumuʿah* can be divided into three categories:

1. The first category are narrations that generally indicate the obligation of *Ṣalāt al-Jumuʿah;* and after the conditions for holding *Ṣalāt al-Jumuʿah* are met, the obligation to strive towards this *Ṣalāt* is understood from them. Although the generality of these narrations may create the impression that *Ṣalāt al-Jumuʿah* is always an Individual Obligation *(Wājib al-ʿAynī)*, even during the Era of Occultation of the 12th Imam عجل الله تعالى فرجه الشريف.
2. The second category are narrations that state the condition of the Imam or his deputy for the obligation of *Ṣalāt al-Jumuʿah and* consider holding *Ṣalāt al-Jumuʿah* among the duties and offices of an

---

[135] *Al-Ḥadāʾiq al-Nāḍirah*, Vol. 9, Pg. 428. The Arabic text of this is as follows:

بَلْ مَا أَحْضَرَ لِلْإِسْلَامِ عُودٌ وَلَا اسْتَقَامَ لَهُ عَمُودٌ.

[136] This is a metaphorical expression. It means that nothing at all was contributed or done for the sake of Islam – neither something as small as a stick, nor something as significant as a pillar. In other words, no efforts – big or small – was made to support Islam – it stands on its own without the need of people to prop it up in any way whatsoever. (Tr.)

immaculate Imam [to either himself directly implement, or to appoint someone to preside over *Ṣalāt al-Jumuʿah*].

3. The third category are narrations from which it is understood that the immaculate Imams gave the Shīʿa permission to hold *Ṣalāt al-Jumuʿah* during the Era of Occultation of the 12th Imam ﷺ, and upon this permission, the permissibility or obligation of holding *Ṣalāt al-Jumuʿah* is established.

These three categories of narrations are the source of disagreement among the *Imāmīyyah* jurists.

Therefore, those jurists who consider *Ṣalāt al-Jumuʿah* forbidden *(ḥarām)* during the Era of Occultation of Imam al-Mahdī ﷺ say: "The leadership of *Ṣalāt al-Jumuʿah* is among the special responsibilities of the immaculate Imam, and without his permission, *Ṣalāt al-Jumuʿah* cannot be held. This is because in the Era of Occultation, we do not have permission [directly from the 12th Imam ﷺ to establish and take part in *Ṣalāt al-Jumuʿah*], so holding *Ṣalāt al-Jumuʿah* is usurpation of the leadership of the immaculate Imam and is not permissible."

They have argued for this claim with narrations, the most important of which is the supplication of Imam al-Sajjād ﷺ for *ʿEid al-Aḍḥā* and the Day of Friday.

In this regard, jurists infer their desired ruling from the following phrases of this *Duʿāʾ*: "O Allah, this position belongs to Your successors, and Your chosen ones, and the places of Your trustees, in the high rank which You have specified for them, but it has been taken from them, and You have decreed that, and Your command cannot be overcome, and Your determined plan cannot be surpassed, as You Will and how You Will, and for what You know best, not accused regarding Your creation, nor regarding Your Will, until Your chosen ones and successors became overpowered, subdued, and deprived, seeing Your ruling changed, Your Book cast aside, Your obligations distorted from the directions of Your legislation, and the traditions of Your Prophet neglected."[137]

Sayyid Ṭayyib Jazāʾirī Lakhnawī says: "The noble words in this supplication are like a text for the mentioned condition. The phrases 'This position belongs to Your successors,' and '...which You have specified for them, and You have decreed that,' are like a text for the condition and specification, and denying it is clear obstinacy."[138]

The late Āyatullāh Sayyid Muḥammad Ḥusayn Burūjerdī ؒ said: "This supplication for the Day of Friday is among the first proofs that the leadership of *Ṣalāt al-Jumuʿah* was also among the usurped offices following the usurpation of the caliphate."[139]

---

[137] *Al-Ṣaḥīfa al-Kāmila al-Sajjādiyya*, Thāmin al-Aʾimmah Press, 2nd Printing, 1385 SH, Supplication 48 for *ʿEid al-Aḍḥā* and the Day of Friday, Pg. 364. The Arabic text of this is as follows:

أَللّٰهُمَّ إِنَّ هٰذَا الْمَقَامَ لِخُلَفَآئِكَ وَأَصْفِيَآئِكَ وَمَوَاضِعَ أُمَنَآئِكَ فِي الدَّرَجَةِ الرَّفِيعَةِ الَّتِي اخْتَصَصْتَهُمْ بِهَا قَدِ ابْتَزُّوهَا، وَأَنْتَ الْمُقَدِّرُ لِذٰلِكَ، لَا يُغَالَبُ أَمْرُكَ، وَلَا يُجَاوَزُ الْمَحْتُومُ مِنْ تَدْبِيرِكَ كَيْفَ شِئْتَ وَأَنَّى شِئْتَ، وَلِمَا أَنْتَ أَعْلَمُ بِهِ غَيْرُ مُتَّهَمٍ عَلَى خَلْقِكَ وَلَا لِإِرَادَتِكَ حَتَّى عَادَ صِفْوَتُكَ وَخُلَفَاؤُكَ مَغْلُوبِينَ مَقْهُورِينَ مُبْتَزِّينَ، يَرَوْنَ حُكْمَكَ مُبَدَّلًا، وَكِتَابَكَ مَنْبُوذًا، وَفَرَائِضَكَ مُحَرَّفَةً عَنْ جِهَاتِ أَشْرَاعِكَ، وَسُنَنَ نَبِيِّكَ مَتْرُوكَةً.

[138] Jazāʾirī, Sayyid Ṭayyib, *Al-Lamʿah al-Sāṭiʿah fī Taḥqīq Ṣalāt al-Jumuʿah al-Jāmiʿah*, Najaf Press, 1374 SH, Pg. 60.

[139] *Al-Badr al-Zāhir*, Dār al-Ḥukm, Qum, 1378 AH, Pg. 25. The Arabic text of this is as follows:

The author of *Jawāhir al-Kalām* says: "There are several points of indication in this supplication for the desired matter, and it is laughable that one would intend both the immaculate Imams and the *Ṣalāt al-Jumuʿah* leaders from this supplication or intend only *'Eid* from the mentioned phrase."[140]

Therefore, the words of these great scholars are clear that this supplication indicates that the leadership of *Ṣalāt al-Jumuʿah* is one of the offices of the immaculate Imams, and without an immaculate Imam's permission, this position cannot be undertaken.

The author of *Al-Ḥadāʾiq* replies: "First: It is possible that what is meant by 'this position' is the supreme Divine caliphate, whose effects will appear on this day, because the great benefits and wisdom will be manifested with the appearance of the state and government of the [immaculate] Imams. When they command and prohibit, those benefits will appear. For this reason, the Imam says: 'Until Your chosen ones became overpowered, subdued, and deprived, seeing Your ruling changed, Your Book cast aside, and Your

---

هٰذَا الدُّعَاءَ فِي يَوْمِ الْجُمُعَةِ مِنْ أَوَّلِ الدَّلَائِلِ عَلَى أَنَّ إِمَامَةَ الْجُمُعَةِ أَيْضًا كَانَتْ مِنَ الْمَنَاصِبِ الْمَغْصُوبَةِ بِتَبَعِ غَصْبِ الْخِلَافَةِ.

140 Najafī, Muhammad Ḥasan, *Jawāhir al-Kalām*, Dār Iḥyāʾ al-Turāth al-ʿArabī, Beirut, 7th Edition, 1981, Vol. 11, Pg. 158. The Arabic text of this is as follows:

فِيهِ مَوَاضِعُ الدَّلَالَةِ عَلَى الْمَطْلُوبِ وَمِنْ مُضْحِكَاتِ الْمَقَامِ تَجَشُّمُ إِرَادَةِ الْأَعَمِّ مِنْهُمْ عَلَيْهِمُ السَّلَامُ وَمِنْ أَئِـمَّةِ الْجَمَاعَةِ مِنَ الدُّعَاءِ الْمَزْبُورِ، لِتَشَجُّمِ إِرَادَةِ خُصُوصِ الْعِيدِ مِنَ الْفَقْرَةِ الْمَزْبُورِ.

obligations distorted from the directions of Your legislation, and the traditions of Your Prophet neglected.'"[141]

Therefore, these are matters related to the supreme caliphate and guardianship [which are designated by Allah ﷻ].

Second: Just as it is possible that the letter *"lām"* in *"li-khulafā'ika"* [لِخُلَفَائِكَ] is in the meaning of 'possession', while it is also possible that it is used in the meaning of 'entitlement'. Therefore, someone being entitled [to something] does not mean that someone else cannot be entitled at the same time. Here, entitlement means qualification, and being qualified does not prove exclusivity [for that thing or person].

The late Dawānī says: "Exclusivity does not mean restriction, but a special connection is sufficient, like saying 'The saddle is for the horse.' Therefore, there is a difference between [for example, the phrase] *'Al-ḥamdu lillāh'* [All praise belongs to Allah], and *'Lillāh al-ḥamd'* [To Allah belongs the praise]; as well, there is a difference between *'Al-amru lillāh'* [The command and decision is for Allah], and *'Lillāhi al-amr'* [For Allah alone is the command and decision]. Thus, 'This position is for Your successors,' is like the phrase that states *'Al-ḥamdu lillāh,'* and 'The saddle is for the horse' [meaning it is exclusive to the immaculate Imam عليه السلام].

In any case, even if we do not accept the possibilities mentioned by the late Baḥrānī, at least they cause a sense of ambiguity in the narration, and as a result, this supplication cannot be used as evidence for the claim.

---

[141] *Al-Ḥadā'iq al-Nāḍirah*, Vol. 9, Pg. 443.

The late author of *Al-Ḥadāʾiq* further said: "This office of *Imamate* and caliphate is exclusive to the pure, immaculate Imams, and others [their friends and supporters], and the enemies of the Ahlul Bayt ﷺ do not have this right to claim this position. This exclusivity does not negate those who acknowledge the guardianship and imamate of the Ahlul Bayt ﷺ, because the guardianship of the jurists is subordinate to the guardianship of the Ahlul Bayt ﷺ, and they are subordinate to the guardianship and office of imamate."[142]

Therefore, we have no indisputable evidence for the prohibition of *Ṣalāt al-Jumuʿah* during the Era of Occultation – and Allah knows best.

Thus, *Ṣalāt al-Jumuʿah* during the Era of Occultation is not forbidden *(ḥarām)*, but rather, it is permissible. Now, this permissibility includes it being under one of several possibilities: obligation *(wājib)*, recommended *(mustaḥabb)*, disliked or reprehensible *(makrūh)*, and permissible *(mubāḥ)*. Since *Ṣalāt al-Jumuʿah* is an act of worship and worship is inherently preferred, it cannot be compatible with mere permissibility *(mubāḥ)* or being disliked *(makrūh)*. Therefore, this act of worship must either be obligatory *(wājib)* or recommended *(mustaḥabb)*.

Among the jurists, no one has considered that *Ṣalāt al-Jumuʿah* is merely recommended, so logic dictates that it is obligatory.

Moreover, all major Islamic Schools accept the obligation of the Friday Prayer, because the Quran, the *Sunnah*, and consensus indicate this ruling; and in fact, its obligation is

[142] *Al-Ḥadāʾiq al-Nāḍirah*, Vol. 9, Pg. 443.

among the necessities of the true religion of Islam, and obligation is of two types: Definite Obligation *(Wājib al-Taʿyīnī)* and Optional Obligation *(Wājib al-Taʾkhyīrī).*

As this chapter concludes an in-depth examination of the juristic dimensions of *Ṣalāt al-Jumuʿah*, it is essential to recognize that the legal debates and scholarly analyses are meant to serve as a gateway to deeper spiritual realities. The discussion on obligation and permissibility lays the groundwork for understanding the profound place Friday occupies in the Islamic tradition. Yet, the soul of the Jumuʿah experience rests not only in fulfilling legal duties, but in embracing the immense mercy, unity, and spiritual opportunity inherent in this weekly congregation.

Friday is much more than a ritual assembly; it is a Divinely chosen time that combines worship, communal bonding, reflection, and spiritual renewal. From the creation of Prophet Ādam ﷺ to the return and establishment of *Ṣalāt al-Jumuʿah* at the blessed hands of Imam al-Ḥujjah ibn al-Ḥasan عجل الله تعالى فرجه الشريف and from that day until the end of this world – the promise of the final gathering, this day marks pivotal moments in sacred history. The Quran and *Sunnah* both elevate its stature, urging believers to pause their worldly affairs, hasten to collective remembrance, and seek nearness to Allah ﷻ through prayer, supplication, and acts of devotion.

As we transition into the final section of this manual, our journey will now turn from the domain of legal reasoning to the spiritual dimensions of Friday. We will explore not only the subtle wisdom embedded in the traditions of Prophet Muḥammad ﷺ and the immaculate family ﷺ for this day, but also the recommended prayers, supplications, and visitation rites that nurture the heart and character.

Friday serves as a sanctuary in the rhythm of the week, a time to renew one's covenant with the Divine and to reinvigorate the bonds of community. The blessings and transformative potential found in its special acts – when performed with mindfulness and sincerity – ensure that the legacy of Jumuʿah extends beyond jurisprudence, giving nourishment and purpose to souls across generations.

Last Word: Reviving the Spirit of Ṣalāt al-Jumuʿah

1. Reflecting on the Importance of Ṣalāt al-Jumuʿah

Ṣalāt al-Jumuʿah is a unique institution in Islam, offering a weekly pause for spiritual reflection and rejuvenation. It is a practice that connects, and brings together Muslims who live, work, and worship in the same vicinity, emphasizing the communal nature of acts of worship in Islam.

Unlike the daily prayers, which can be performed individually or in congregation, *Ṣalāt al-Jumuʿah* is inherently communal, reminding us about our collective identity as a nation *(ummah)*. By commanding us to leave behind worldly distractions and prioritize this special gathering, Allah ﷻ emphasizes its central role in our spiritual and collective lives. This practice may be optional for us in our current era, meaning during the occultation of the 12th Imam عجّل الله تعالى فرجه الشريف, the rightful representative of Prophet Muḥammad ﷺ; however, we must realize that in its core, it is an obligation to perform when certain conditions are met – and this gives us hope and allows us to earnestly pray for the speedy advent of Imam al-Mahdī ﷻ.

The direct command of the Quran to attend *Ṣalāt al-Jumuʿah* (Chapter 62, Verse 9) highlights the priority it must take over our business, work, and other worldly engagements. Yet, it is not simply the act of attending that matters but doing so with the right intentions and a conscious heart. When we view *Ṣalāt al-Jumuʿah* as more than just a ritual and embrace it as an opportunity for deep reflection, then it can transform into a weekly anchor for our faith. It can help bring us back to our true purpose if life and remind us about the Mercy and Guidance of Allah ﷻ in our lives.

Additionally, *Ṣalāt al-Jumuʿah* serves as a bridge between the physical (worldly) and the non-physical (spiritual). Muslims who might have been consumed by the week's challenges are given a chance to renew their focus in life and turn towards Allah ﷻ. This alignment not only benefits their individual spirituality but also ensures that they approach the coming week with a clearer perspective rooted in Islamic principles. It is, in essence, a recalibration of the soul; and an opportunity for believers to realign their inner compass with the Divine.

2. The Spiritual Impact of Ṣalāt al-Jumuʿah

The spiritual dimension of *Ṣalāt al-Jumuʿah* cannot be overstated. At its core, it is a form of *dhikr* (remembrance of Allah ﷻ) that reorients the heart and mind of a believer. The sermons, as a central component, serve as a Divinely-sanctioned reminder – addressing both timeless spiritual truths, and the pressing concerns of the time.

Delivered in a manner that touches the hearts of the congregation, the sermons elevate the soul and inspire reflection. It is a moment where Divine wisdom meets practical guidance, allowing believers to draw lessons directly applicable to their lives.

The two units of the Friday Prayer which follow the sermons are imbued with special significance. While short in duration, they encapsulate the essence of worship: Humility before Allah ﷻ, gratitude for His countless blessings, and submission to His Divine Will. The physical act of standing shoulder to shoulder with fellow Muslims, bowing, and prostrating together, fosters a sense of spiritual equality and unity, reminding us that before Allah ﷻ, all distinctions of wealth, status, and ethnicity are meaningless.

Beyond the prayer, *Ṣalāt al-Jumuʿah* provides an opportunity to engage in introspection. As we leave the *masjid*, we are encouraged to carry the lessons learned, and the blessings of the prayer into the rest of our week. The spiritual renewal from this *Ṣalāt* is not meant to be confined to Friday; it is meant to ripple into our thoughts, actions, and interactions, ensuring we live our lives with greater awareness of the presence of Allah ﷻ – carrying us into the next week and another day of Friday.

3. Ṣalāt al-Jumuʿah as a Social Catalyst

In addition to its spiritual benefits, *Ṣalāt al-Jumuʿah* serves as a powerful social institution. It is a time when Muslims from all walks of life come together to worship as one. These gathering fosters a sense of community and belonging that strengthens the bonds of brotherhood and sisterhood within the nation *(ummah)*. In a world increasingly marked by individualism and isolation, the social connection fostered by *Ṣalāt al-Jumuʿah* is invaluable.

Historically, the *masājid* have served as centres of community life, and *Ṣalāt al-Jumuʿah* plays a central role in this function. Beyond the prayer itself, the gathering provides an opportunity for announcements, discussions, and addressing communal concerns. Whether raising awareness about societal issues, mobilizing for humanitarian causes, or simply checking in with fellow believers, the Friday Prayer acts as a platform for social cohesion and collective action. It reminds us that Islam is not only about individual spirituality, but also about contributing to the betterment of society.

The social aspect of *Ṣalāt al-Jumuʿah* extends beyond the *masjid* walls. The interactions and conversations that occur before and after the prayer are opportunities to build friendships, share advice, and support one another. For many, it can be a chance to seek guidance, share personal struggles, or celebrate milestones. This sense of interconnectedness reinforces the idea that Muslims are part of a global family, united by their faith and shared values.

4. Addressing Contemporary Challenges

Despite its significance, *Ṣalāt al-Jumuʿah* faces numerous challenges in contemporary times. In some communities, attendance has declined due to competing priorities, such as work or school. For others, the prayer has become a ritual devoid of its deeper meaning, with little effort made to internalize the messages of the sermons. These challenges necessitate a renewed focus on the purpose and spirit of *Ṣalāt al-Jumuʿah* to ensure it remains a vibrant part of Muslim life.

One key challenge is the quality and relevance of the two sermons. In a rapidly changing world, the Friday Prayer leader *(imam)* must address contemporary issues while staying rooted in Islamic teachings. A well-prepared sermon can inspire and energize the congregation, while a poorly delivered one can lead to disengagement. Religious leaders must therefore invest in their own education and public speaking skills to meet the needs of the people in attendance.

Moreover, Muslim communities must promote for accommodations that allow individuals to prioritize *Ṣalāt al-Jumuʿah.* This includes advocating for workplace flexibility, educating employers about the significance of the Friday Prayer, and providing accessible *masājid* for those with limited mobility. By addressing these practical barriers, we can ensure that more Muslims can fulfill this vital obligation without undue hardship.

5. The Role of Youth and Future Generations

The future of *Ṣalāt al-Jumuʿah* in our communities depends on engaging the next generation. It is vital to instill in young Muslims a deep appreciation for the Friday Prayers and its role in their spiritual and communal lives. This begins with creating spaces where youth feel welcomed and valued. The *masājid* must be a place where young people can connect with their faith in ways that resonate with their experiences and challenges.

Educational programs that teach the significance of *Ṣalāt al-Jumuʿah,* coupled with opportunities for active participation, can help bridge the gap between the younger generation and the *masjid.* For instance, encouraging youth to deliver short pre-*Ṣalāt al-Jumuʿah* talks can foster a sense of ownership and responsibility (if time permits). When young Muslims see themselves as active contributors to their communities, they are more likely to remain engaged in the long term.

Parents and educators also play a crucial role in cultivating a love for *Ṣalāt al-Jumuʿah.* By modeling consistent attendance and emphasizing its spiritual and communal benefits, they can inspire young people to prioritize this prayer. Additionally, addressing their questions and concerns with compassion and understanding can help overcome any doubts or apprehensions they may have about this obligation.

6. A Call to Action

As we come to the end of this book, the importance of acting cannot be overstated. *Ṣalāt al-Jumuʿah* is not just an individual act of worship – it is a cornerstone of our collective faith. Let us commit to revitalizing this sacred institution in our personal lives and within our communities. Whether by attending regularly, preparing the centres for the Friday Prayers, or encouraging others to join – every small step contributes to preserving the essence of *Ṣalāt al-Jumuʿah.*

The responsibility to uphold *Ṣalāt al-Jumuʿah* also extends to community leaders, *imams,* and educators. They must strive to make the Friday Prayers accessible, engaging, and meaningful for everyone. *Imams* who are delivering the sermons should do so sincerely and with an open heart; and by addressing the spiritual and practical needs of the congregation, they can inspire a deeper connection to this vital practice.

Finally, to the readers: Let this book serve as a reminder, and a call to action. Reflect on your own relationship with *Ṣalāt al-Jumuʿah* and consider how you can deepen your commitment to this weekly act of worship. Through consistent effort and sincere intention, we can ensure that *Ṣalāt al-Jumuʿah* remains a source of guidance, inspiration, and unity for generations to come.

The Soul's Journey on Fridays

As this book on *Ṣalāt al-Jumuʿah* concludes, it is only fitting to end by reflecting on the spiritual treasures that adorn this sacred day. *Ṣalāt al-Jumuʿah* is far more than an act of communal worship, it is a weekly milestone on our journey to Allah ﷻ, enriched by opportunities for personal supplication, connection, and devotion.

In the final section of this book, we offer a collection of beautiful supplications, visitations, and acts of spiritual devotions recommended for Fridays. There are many other highly recommended acts of worship, supplications, and prayers to perform on Friday such as the *ghusl* for Jumuʿah, recitation of *Duʿāʾ al-Nudbah*, etc.; however, for brevity, we have not included them all. Refer to more detailed books on devotions including *Mafātīḥ al-Jinān* of the late Shaykh ʿAbbās al-Qummī.

These practices – deeply rooted in the Quran and the traditions of Prophet Muḥammad ﷺ and his Divinely-appointed successors, the Imams of the Ahlul Bayt عليهم السلام – serve as invaluable tools to nurture our relationship with Allah ﷻ and improve our spiritual and mental well-being.

1. Duas and Ziyārat: Anchoring the Soul in Devotion

The supplications and visitations recommended for the day of Friday are unparalleled in their ability to foster a profound sense of connection to the Creator and His chosen representatives.

These acts of devotion help believers align their hearts with Divine Mercy and Guidance. By reciting these, believers bridge the temporal and spiritual realms, forging a bond with Allah ﷻ and His appointed representatives.

On a practical level, these devotional acts encourage mindfulness and focus. As a person recites, reflects, and internalizes the meanings of these supplications, the heart becomes more attuned to Divine realities. This practice not only cleanses the soul but also reinforces a sense of hope and purpose. The act of addressing the 12th Imam عجل الله تعالى فرجه الشريف, particularly, reminds us about our role in preparing for his eventual reappearance. It is a call to action, urging us to refine ourselves, our communities, and our world in anticipation of the ultimate justice that he will establish.

2. The Mental Health Benefits of Spiritual Connection

In a time marked by increasing stress, anxiety, and a sense of disconnection, the spiritual practices associated with the day of Friday offer profound mental health benefits. Supplications and devotions provide an anchor in the chaos of modern life, offering solace and clarity amidst uncertainty. When we turn to Allah ﷻ in supplication *(duʿāʾ)*, we not only seek His assistance, but also release our burdens into His care. This act of surrender and trusting the Will and infinite Wisdom of Allah ﷻ, can alleviate the mental strain of trying to control outcomes beyond our capacity.

Similarly, engaging with the visitations *(ziyārāt)* connects us to a broader narrative of Divine Mercy and Guidance. It reminds us that our struggles are not isolated, but part of a larger, Divinely ordained journey towards perfection. Knowing that we are under the watchful care of Allah ﷻ, the intercession of the final Prophet ﷺ, and the support of the 12 immaculate Imams عليهم السلام brings a sense of reassurance and resilience. This connection can alleviate feelings of loneliness and despair, replacing them with a sense of belonging to the nation *(ummah)*, and the Ahlul Bayt's spiritual lineage.

Incorporating these practices into one's weekly routine on the day of Friday can serve as a powerful form of mental health care. By dedicating time to reflect on one's purpose and calling upon the infinite Mercy and Grace of Allah ﷻ, a believer can foster a sense of inner peace and balance that is otherwise hard to achieve in today's fast-paced and chaotic world.

3. Importance of Connection to the Ahlul Bayt عليهم السلام

Central to the Friday devotional acts is the relationship between a believer and the Ahlul Bayt عليهم السلام, especially the awaited saviour of humanity, Imam al-Mahdī عجل الله تعالى فرجه الشريف.

The Imams are not only guides, but also spiritual mediators who help us draw closer to Allah ﷻ. Their teachings and examples illuminate the path of righteousness, making them an indispensable part of our spiritual journey.

The emphasis on visitations *(ziyārāt)* and supplications *(duʿās)* dedicated to the Imams ﷺ is a reminder of their enduring presence in our lives – even during the Era of Occultation.

The 12th Imam ﷺ represents hope for humanity – a promise of justice, equity, and the fulfillment of the Divine Plan of Allah ﷻ. Engaging with the *ziyārah* that is specific for the day of Friday in which we address our 12th Imam ﷺ will strengthen our bond with him and remind us about our responsibilities in his absence. Each *duʿāʾ* and *ziyārah* directed towards him renews our allegiance and prepares us spiritually to be among those who will support his mission upon his reappearance.

This connection to the Ahlul Bayt ﷺ is not merely an intellectual exercise, but a transformative one. By contemplating their sacrifices, virtues, and unwavering devotion to Allah ﷻ, we are inspired to embody their teachings in our own lives. Their example teaches us patience, resilience, and the value of striving for truth and justice in every facet of life.

4. Friday as a Gateway to the Mercy of Allah ﷻ

Ṣalāt al-Jumuʿah, combined with the other recommended devotional acts for the day of Friday, positions this day of the week as one of immense spiritual potential. It is a weekly opportunity to rejuvenate our connection to Allah ﷻ, recalibrate our priorities, and draw strength from the Divine. Whether through personal actions, such as the major ablution *(ghusl)*, or recommended supplications and visitations; communal prayers; or reflecting on the lives of the Ahlul Bayt ﷺ – Friday becomes a gateway to the immense Mercy and Blessings of Allah ﷻ.

The acts of devotion outlined in this book offer a roadmap for how to fully utilize the spiritual opportunities of this sacred day. They are not obligations, but gifts – tools for enhancing our spiritual well-being and fostering a sense of inner peace. For those seeking to deepen their connection to Allah ﷻ, the Prophet ﷺ, and the 12 Imams ﷺ, these practices provide a tangible and transformative way forward.

5. A Call to Action: Reclaiming the Blessings of Friday

As we conclude this journey about *Ṣalāt al-Jumuʿah*, let us commit to reclaiming the full blessings *(barakāt)* of the day of Friday. This involves not only attending the Friday Prayers, but also immersing ourselves in the supplementary acts of devotion that enrich the day. By reciting the supplications *(duʿās)*, performing the visitations *(ziyārāt)*, and connecting with the 12th Imam عجل الله تعالى فرجه الشريف, we can transform Fridays into a source of spiritual strength that sustains us until the following Friday.

The significance of this day lies not just in its rituals, but in the mindset that it fosters. It is a day of renewal, reflection, and hope – a reminder of our ultimate purpose and destination. Let us strive to make every Friday a step closer to Allah ﷻ, a day that heals our hearts, strengthens our spirits, and prepares us for the challenges ahead.

Duʿāʾ after Ṣalāt al-ʿAṣr[143]

بِسْمِ ٱللّٰهِ ٱلرَّحْمٰنِ ٱلرَّحِيمِ

In the Name of Allah, the All-Compassionate, the All-Merciful.

أَسْتَغْفِرُ ٱللّٰهَ ٱلَّذِي لَا إِلٰهَ إِلَّا هُوَ،

I seek the forgiveness of Allah, the One, whom there is no god except for Him,

أَلْحَيُّ ٱلْقَيُّومُ،

The Ever-Living, the Self-Subsisting,

أَلرَّحْمٰنُ ٱلرَّحِيمُ،

The All-Compassionate, the All-Merciful,

---

143 This supplication is recommended to be recited every day after *Ṣalāt al-ʿAṣr*. We include it here to provide a comprehensive package of supplications for Friday.

ذُو ٱلْـجَلاَلِ وَٱلْإِكْرَامِ،

The One Who possesses all Majesty and Honour.

وَ أَسْأَلُهُ أَنْ يَتُوبَ عَلَيَّ،

And I ask Him to turn back towards me (after I have sinned and repented to Him),

تَوْبَةَ عَبْدٍ ذَلِيلٍ، خَاضِعٍ، فَقِيرٍ، بَائِسٍ، مِسْكِينٍ، مُسْتَكِينٍ، مُسْتَجِيرٍ،

the repentance of a slave who is: submissive, humble, poor, miserable, despondent, dejected, seeking refuge (with Him),

لَا يَـمْلِكُ لِنَفْسِهِ نَفْعًا وَلَا ضَرًّا،

(a slave who does) not control for oneself any benefit, nor harm,

وَلَا مَوْتًا وَلَا حَيَاةً وَلَا نُشُورًا.

and does not control (one's own) death, nor life, nor raising to life.

أَللّٰهُمَّ إِنِّي أَعُوذُ بِكَ مِنْ نَفْسٍ لَا تَشْـبَعُ،

O Allah, I seek protection with You from the soul that is unsatisfied (with what it has been given),

وَمِنْ قَلْبٍ لَا يَـخْشَعُ،

and (I seek protection with You) from a heart that does not have reverence (of You),

وَمِنْ عِلْمٍ لَا يَنْفَعُ،

and (I seek protection with You) from (that) knowledge, which is of no benefit,

وَمِنْ صَلَاةٍ لَا تُرْفَعُ،

and (I seek protection with You) from that prayer which does not ascend (to the Heavens, and thus is not accepted),

وَمِنْ دُعَآءٍ لَا يُسْمَعُ.

and (I seek protection with You) from any supplication that I recite, but it is unanswered.

أَللّٰهُمَّ إِنِّي أَسْأَلُكَ ٱلْيُسْرَ بَعْدَ ٱلْعُسْرِ،

O Allah, indeed, I ask You to grant me ease after difficulty,

وَٱلْفَرَجَ بَعْدَ ٱلْكَرْبِ،

and (I ask You) for relief after grief,

وَٱلرَّخَآءَ بَعْدَ ٱلشِّدَّةِ.

and (I ask You) for comfort after distress.

أَللّٰهُمَّ مَا بِنَا مِنْ نِعْمَةٍ فَمِنْكَ.

O Allah! There is no bounty which reaches us, except that it is from You.

لَا إِلٰهَ إِلَّا أَنْتَ، أَسْتَغْفِرُكَ وَأَتُوبُ إِلَيْكَ.

There is no god except You, I seek forgiveness from You (for my sins), and I turn back towards You.

Supplication (Duʿāʾ) for Friday

بِسْمِ اللهِ ٱلرَّحْمٰنِ ٱلرَّحِيمِ

In the Name of Allah, the All-Compassionate, the All-Merciful.

أَللّٰهُمَّ صَلِّ عَلىٰ مُحَمَّدٍ وَّآلِ مُحَمَّدٍ.

O Allah, send Your blessings on Muḥammad and the family of Muḥammad.

أَلْحَمْدُ لِلّٰهِ ٱلْأَوَّلِ قَبْلَ ٱلْإِنْشَآءِ وَٱلْإِحْيَآءِ،

All Praise is for Allah, the First, before the beginning and the creation of life,

وَٱلْآخِرِ بَعْدَ فَنَآءِ ٱلْأَشْيَآءِ.

and the Last, after the perishing of all things.

أَلْعَلِيمِ ٱلَّذِي لَّا يَنْسىٰ مَنْ ذَكَرَهُ،

The All-Knowing who does not forget one who remembers Him,

وَلَا يَنْقُصُ مَنْ شَكَرَهُ،

and does not reduce (the blessings of) one who thanks Him,

وَلَا يَـخِيبُ مَنْ دَعَاهُ،

and does not disappoint the one who supplicates to Him,

وَلَا يَقْطَعُ رَجَآءَ مَنْ رَجَاهُ.

and does not cut off the hopes of one who places hope in Him.

أَللّٰهُمَّ إِنِّي أُشْهِدُكَ وَكَفىٰ بِكَ شَهِيدًا،

O Allah, indeed, I call You to witness, and You are enough as a witness,

وَأُشْهِدُ جَمِيعَ مَلآئِكَتِكَ وَسُكَّانَ سَمٰوَاتِكَ وَحَمَلَةَ عَرْشِكَ،

and I call to witness all Your angels, and the dwellers of Your heavens, and the bearers of Your Throne,

وَمَنْ بَعَثْتَ مِنْ أَنْبِيَآئِكَ وَرُسُلِكَ،

and those whom You have appointed from among Your Prophets and Your Messengers,

وَأَنْشَأْتَ مِنْ أَصْنَافِ خَلْقِكَ.

and the various kinds of creatures that You have created.

أَنِّي أَشْهَدُ أَنَّكَ أَنْتَ ٱللهُ لَا إِلٰـهَ إِلَّا أَنْتَ،

That I bear witness that You are Allah, there is no god except You (alone),

وَحْدَكَ لَا شَرِيكَ لَكَ وَلَا عَدِيلَ،

and that You are One, have no partner and no associate,

وَلَا خُلْفَ لِقَوْلِكَ وَلَا تَبْدِيلَ.

and Your Word is not contradicted, nor does it change.

وَأَنَّ مُحَمَّدًا صَلَّى ٱللهُ عَلَيْهِ وَآلِهِ،

And I bear witness that Muḥammad, blessings of Allah be upon him and his family,

عَبْدُكَ وَرَسُولُكَ.

is Your servant and Your Messenger.

أَدَّى مَا حَمَّلْتَهُ إِلَىٰ ٱلْعِبَادِ،

He delivered to (Your) servants what You obliged him with,

وَجَاهَدَ فِي ٱللهِ عَزَّ وَجَلَّ حَقَّ ٱلْجِهَادِ،

and he struggled in the Way of Allah, Glorious and Exalted, as it was due,

وَأَنَّهُ بَشَّرَ بِمَا هُوَ حَقٌّ مِنَ ٱلثَّوَابِ،

and he gave the good news of the truth of the reward,

وَأَنْذَرَ بِمَا هُوَ صِدْقٌ مِنَ ٱلْعِقَابِ.

and he warned what was true about the punishment.

أَللّٰهُمَّ ثَبِّتْنِي عَلَىٰ دِينِكَ مَا أَحْيَيْتَنِي،

O Allah, make me firm in Your religion so long as You keep me alive,

وَلَا تُزِغْ قَلْبِي بَعْدَ إِذْ هَدَيْتَنِي،

and do not let my heart deviate after You have guided me,

وَهَبْ لِي مِنْ لَدُنْكَ رَحْمَةً إِنَّكَ أَنْتَ ٱلْوَهَّابُ.

and give me mercy from You, surely, You are the Bountiful Giver.

صَلِّ عَلَىٰ مُحَمَّدٍ وَّعَلَىٰ آلِ مُحَمَّدٍ،

Blessings be upon Muḥammad and upon the family of Muḥammad,

وَٱجْعَلْنِي مِنْ أَتْبَاعِهِ وَشِيعَتِهِ،

and place me among his followers and his Shīʿa,

وَاحْشُرْنِي فِي زُمْرَتِهِ،

and resurrect me in his company,

وَوَفِّقْنِي لِأَدَآءِ فَرْضِ ٱلْجُمُعَاتِ،

and give me the success of carrying out the duties of (the Day of) Friday,

وَمَا أَوْجَبْتَ عَلَيَّ فِيهَا مِنَ ٱلطَّاعَاتِ،

and (carrying out) the acts of obedience that You have made obligatory upon me in it,

وَقَسَمْتَ لِأَهْلِهَا مِنَ ٱلْعَطَآءِ فِي يَوْمِ ٱلْجَزَآءِ.

and (receiving) the favours that You have allotted for its people on the Day of Recompense.

إِنَّكَ أَنْتَ ٱلْعَزِيزُ ٱلْحَكِيمُ.

Surely, You are the All-Mighty, the All-Wise.

Prostration (Sajdah) of Thanks

Once we finish our daily prayers, we should go into the state of prostration *(sajdah)* so that we can thank Allah ﷻ for all that He has given and blessed us with.

Although in *sajdah*, we can thank Allah ﷻ in any language we want, and supplicate to Him saying anything that comes to our heart, it has been recommended to recite the following supplication three times: first with the forehead on the *turbah;*[144] then with the right cheek on the *turbah*; followed

---

[144] A *turbah*, also known as *mohr* in Persian and other languages and also known as a *sajdahgah*, is a small piece of clay or soil – often molded into a tablet – used during the prostration (*sajdah*) in daily prayers and all other prayers such as *Ṣalāt al-ʿEid.* Its primary purpose is to symbolize humility before Allah ﷻ by placing one's forehead on a natural element of the earth, as was the practice of Prophet Muḥammad ﷺ and his family.

The most recommended *turbah* is one that is made from the dirt of Karbalāʾ, the site of the martyrdom of Imam Ḥusayn ؑ, due to its deep spiritual and historical significance. However, using dirt from any location is valid, and the essential requirement is that the material must be natural earth or something that grows from it (but is not edible or wearable).

by the left cheek on the *turbah;* and lastly with the forehead again on the *turbah.*

Recite 3 Times:

شُكْرًا لِلّٰهِ

(All) Thanks is due to Allah.

Shīʿa Jurisprudence, based on the teachings of Imam Jaʿfar al-Ṣādiq ﷺ and other Imams ﷺ, stipulates that prostration **must** be performed on pure earth or what naturally grows from it, provided it is not something commonly eaten or worn.

If a *turbah* is not available, then Shīʿa Jurisprudence allows for several alternatives, following a specific order of preference:

1. **Natural Earth or Soil:** Any clean, pure soil or earth can be used.
2. **Unprocessed Stone or Natural Materials:** Stones such as limestone, gypsum, or unpolished marble are acceptable. One may also use unpainted, untreated wood, or leaves from trees that are not edible or wearable.
3. **Paper:** Paper made from natural materials (wood pulp, grass, cotton, flax) is acceptable, as it originates from permissible items.
4. **Other Surfaces (in Order of Precedence):** If none of the above are available, then one may use tar or asphalt.

If none of these even are available, then as a last resort, prostration can be performed on one's own clothing, or the back of the hand, although this is **only** permissible when no other suitable material is available.

Note: The *turbah* is not considered essential in itself; rather, it is a practical and symbolic means to fulfill the requirement of prostrating on earth or its permissible derivatives. (Tr.)

Then Recite 1 Time:

عَظُمَ ٱلذَّنْبُ مِنْ عَبْدِكَ، فَلْيَحْسُنِ ٱلْعَفْوُ مِنْ عِنْدِكَ.

The sin of Your servant is enormous, so let the splendor of Your Pardon be (even more) very pleasant.

Prostration of Gratitude (Sajdah al-Shukr)[145]

Issue 1474: It is recommended *(mustaḥabb)* for a person to perform the *Sajdah al-Shukr* (Prostration of Gratitude) after completing every prayer – whether it is an obligatory *(wājib)* or recommended *(mustaḥabb)* prayer. Simply prostrating and placing the forehead on the ground with the intention of gratitude is sufficient, even if no specific supplication *(dhikr)* is recited. However, it is better to say *Shukran Lillāh* (Thanks to Allah), *Shukran* (Thanks), or *ʿAfwan* (Forgiveness) either 100 times, three times, or even just once.

It is also preferable to perform two prostrations of gratitude in the following manner:

1. Place the forehead on the ground with the intention of performing the first prostration.
2. Then place the right side of the forehead, or the right cheek – or both – on the ground.
3. Afterward, place the left side of the forehead, or the left cheek – or both – on the ground.
4. Finally, place the forehead on the ground again with the intention of performing the second prostration.

---

145 Extracted from the four-volume *Tawzīḥ al-Masāʾil Jāmiʿ* (Comprehensive Explanation of Issues – Volume 1).

Additionally, it is recommended to perform *Sajdah al-Shukr* anytime a person receives a blessing, or whenever a calamity is averted.

Issue 1475: In *Sajdah al-Shukr,* it is recommended *(mustaḥabb)* for a person to put both arms (from the elbows down to fingertips), one's chest, and stomach right down (such that these touch the ground). After lifting one's head from prostration, a person should wipe their place of prostration with their hand and then pass this hand over their face and the front portion of one's body.

Issue 1476: As a matter of obligatory precaution *(iḥtiyāṭ wājib),* a person should place one's forehead on a *turbah/mohr* (see previous footnote explaining this), or another object upon which it is permissible to prostrate on during *sajdah.* Additionally, as a recommended precaution *(iḥtiyāṭ mustaḥabb),* other parts of the body should be placed on the ground in accordance with how they are positioned during regular prostration in prayer.

It is worth noting that if a person wants to perform *Sajdah al-Shukr,* but one cannot physically prostrate on the ground, they may indicate it by lowering their head and placing their cheek on their palm (Note: The palm includes the fingers), or its back while expressing gratitude to Almighty Allah.

Supplication (Duʿāʾ) for Muslim Unity

Although this supplication is not officially known as the supplication for Muslim Unity, it has developed this name in many centres over the years, so we will retain this name. In actuality, the following supplication has been recommended to be recited every day as a part of the daily supplication regiment after the *ṣalāt* – whether we pray individually *(furādah),* or in congregation *(jamāʿah).*

بِسْمِ ٱللَّهِ ٱلرَّحْمَٰنِ ٱلرَّحِيمِ

In the Name of Allah, the All-Compassionate, the All-Merciful.

لَا إِلَٰهَ إِلَّا ٱللَّهُ، إِلَٰهًا وَاحِدًا وَنَحْنُ لَهُ مُسْلِمُونَ.

There is no god except Allah, the One God, and we are all Muslims who submit only to Him.

لَا إِلٰهَ إِلَّا ٱللّٰهُ، وَلَا نَعْبُدُ إِلَّا إِيَّاهُ،

There is no god except Allah, and we do not worship anyone except Him,

مُخْلِصِينَ لَهُ ٱلدِّينَ،

being sincere to Him in our religion,

وَلَوْ كَرِهَ ٱلْمُشْرِكُونَ.

even though the polytheists may detest this.

لَا إِلٰهَ إِلَّا ٱللّٰهُ، رَبُّنَا وَرَبُّ آبَائِنَا ٱلْأَوَّلِينَ.

There is no god except Allah, He is our Maintainer, and the Lord of our forefathers – those who came before us.

لَا إِلٰهَ إِلَّا ٱللّٰهُ، وَحْدَهُ، وَحْدَهُ، وَحْدَهُ.

There is no god except Allah, He is the One, He is the One, He is the One.

أَنْجَزَ وَعْدَهُ، وَنَصَرَ عَبْدَهُ، وَأَعَزَّ جُنْدَهُ، وَهَزَمَ ٱلْأَحْزَابَ وَحْدَهُ.

He (Allah ﷻ) is the One who made His promise true, and helped His servant, and strengthened His soldiers, and by Himself defeated (all the) opponents.

فَلَهُ ٱلْـمُلْكُ وَلَهُ ٱلْـحَمْدُ، يُـحْيِـي وَيُـمِيتُ، وَيُـمِيتُ

وَيُـحْيِـي.

Then to Him (Allah ﷻ) belongs the Kingdom, and to Him belongs (all) Praise. He brings things to life and causes things to die; and He causes things to die, and He brings them back to life again.

وَهُوَ حَيٌّ لَا يَـمُوتُ، بِيَدِهِ ٱلْـخَيْرُ.

And He (Allah) is the One who was always Living and will never die; in His Hand is (all) goodness.

وَهُوَ عَلَىٰ كُلِّ شَيْءٍ قَدِيرٌ.

And He has Power over all things.

Special Visitation (Ziyārah) for the Day of Friday

Each of the seven days of the week is specially dedicated to one, or more, of the 14 Immaculates *(Maʿṣūmīn)* عليهم السلام. Friday is dedicated solely to the 12th Imam, al-Ḥujjah ibn Ḥasan عجل الله تعالى فرجه الشريف. For this special day, the following visitation is recommended for one to recite to remember him and his Divine mission to establish justice and equality.

بِسْمِ ٱللّٰهِ ٱلرَّحْمٰنِ ٱلرَّحِـــيمِ

In the Name of Allah, the All-Compassionate, the All-Merciful.

أَللّٰهُمَّ صَلِّ عَلىٰ مُحَمَّدٍ وَّآلِ مُحَمَّدٍ.

O Allah, send Your blessings on Muḥammad and the family of Muḥammad.

أَلسَّلَامُ عَلَيْكَ يَا حُجَّةَ ٱللّٰهِ فِي أَرْضِهِ.

Peace be upon you, O Proof of Allah on His Earth.

أَلسَّلَامُ عَلَيْكَ يَا عَيْنَ ٱللّٰهِ فِي خَلْقِهِ.

Peace be upon you, O Eye of Allah among His creatures.

أَلسَّلَامُ عَلَيْكَ يَا نُورَ ٱللّٰهِ ٱلَّذِي يَهْتَدِي بِهِ ٱلْمُهْتَدُونَ،

Peace be upon you, O Light of Allah by which those who are guided find guidance,

وَيُفَرَّجُ بِهِ عَنِ ٱلْمُؤْمِنِينَ.

and by which the believers find ease and consolation.

أَلسَّلَامُ عَلَيْكَ أَيُّهَا ٱلْمُهَذَّبُ ٱلْخَائِفُ.

Peace be upon you, O the Refined, the awe-inspiring.

أَلسَّلَامُ عَلَيْكَ أَيُّهَا ٱلْوَلِيُّ ٱلنَّاصِحُ.

Peace be upon you, O the Beloved Advisor.

أَلسَّلَامُ عَلَيْكَ يَا سَفِينَةَ ٱلنَّجَاةِ.

Peace be upon you, O the Ship of Salvation.

أَلسَّلَامُ عَلَيْكَ يَا عَيْنَ ٱلْحَيَاةِ.

Peace be upon you, O the Source of Life.

ٱلسَّلامُ عَلَيْكَ صَلَّى ٱللّٰهُ عَلَيْكَ،

Peace be upon you, may the blessings of Allah be upon you,

وَعَلىٰ آلِ بَيْتِكَ ٱلطَّيِّبِينَ ٱلطَّاهِرِينَ.

and upon your family the pure, the purified.

ٱلسَّلامُ عَلَيْكَ عَجَّلَ ٱللّٰهُ لَكَ مَا وَعَدَكَ مِنَ ٱلنَّصْرِ وَظُهُورِ ٱلْأَمْرِ.

Peace be upon you; may Allah hasten for you the victory and the manifestation (of your leadership) that He has promised you.

ٱلسَّلامُ عَلَيْكَ يَا مَوْلَايَ،

Peace be upon you, O my master,

أَنَا مَوْلَاكَ عَارِفٌ بِأُوْلَاكَ وَأُخْرَاكَ.

I am your follower; I am aware of your aim and your ultimate purpose.

أَتَقَرَّبُ إِلَىٰ ٱللّٰهِ تَعَالىٰ بِكَ وَبِآلِ بَيْتِكَ،

I seek nearness to Allah, the All-High, through you and your family,

وَأَنْتَظِرُ ظُهُورَكَ وَظُهُورَ ٱلْـحَقِّ عَلىٰ يَدَيْكَ.

and I await your appearance, and the appearance of the truth through you.

وَأَسْأَلُ ٱللّٰهَ أَنْ يُصَلِّيَ عَلىٰ مُحَمَّدٍ وَّآلِ مُحَمَّدٍ،

And I ask Allah to send blessings upon Muḥammad and the family of Muḥammad,

وَأَنْ يَـجْعَلَنِي مِنَ ٱلْمُنْتَظِرِينَ لَكَ،

and place me with those who are waiting for you,

وَٱلتَّابِعِينَ وَٱلنَّاصِرِينَ لَكَ عَلىٰ أَعْدَآئِكَ،

and those who will follow and help you against your enemies,

وَٱلْمُسْتَشْهَدِينَ بَيْنَ يَدَيْكَ فِي جُمْلَةِ أَوْلِيَآئِكَ.

and those who will achieve martyrdom (when fighting) with you along with your special, devoted friends.

يَا مَوْلَايَ يَا صَاحِبَ ٱلزَّمَانِ.

O my master, O Imam of the Time.

صَلَوَاتُ ٱللهِ عَلَيْكَ وَعَلىٰ آلِ بَيْتِكَ.

Blessings of Allah be upon you and upon your family.

هٰذَا يَوْمُ ٱلْـجُمُعَةِ،

This is the Day of Friday,

وَهُوَ يَوْمُكَ ٱلْمُتَوَقَّعُ فِيهِ ظُهُورُكَ،

and it is your day in which your appearance is expected,

وَٱلْفَرَجُ فِيهِ لِلْمُؤْمِنِينَ عَلىٰ يَدَيْكَ،

and the coming of relief for the believers through you,

وَقَتْلُ ٱلْكَافِرِينَ بِسَيْفِكَ.

and the killing of the disbelievers by your sword.

وَأَنَا يَا مَوْلَايَ فِيهِ ضَيْفُكَ وَجَارُكَ،

And I am, O my master, in it (on this day) your guest seeking closeness to you,

وَأَنْتَ يَا مَوْلَايَ كَرِيمٌ مِنْ أَوْلَادِ ٱلْكِرَامِ،

and you, O my master, are generous from the sons of the generous ones,

وَمَأْمُورٌ بِالضِّيَافَةِ وَٱلْإِجَارَةِ.

and those appointed for receiving and protecting.

فَأَضِفْنِي وَأَجِرْنِي،

So, receive me and protect me,

صَلَوَاتُ ٱللهِ عَلَيْكَ،

blessings of Allah be upon you,

وَعَلىٰ أَهْلِ بَيْتِكَ ٱلطَّاهِرِينَ.

and upon your family, the purified ones.

Supplication (Duʿāʾ) for the 12th Imam

بِسْمِ ٱللَّهِ ٱلرَّحْمَٰنِ ٱلرَّحِيمِ

In the Name of Allah, the All-Compassionate, the All-Merciful.

أَللَّهُمَّ كُنْ لِوَلِيِّكَ ٱلْحُجَّةِ بْنِ ٱلْحَسَنِ صَلَوَاتُكَ عَلَيْهِ

وَعَلَىٰ آبَآئِهِ.

O Allah, be for Your deputy, al-Ḥujjah ibn Hasan, may Your blessings be upon him and his ancestors.

فِي هَٰذِهِ ٱلسَّاعَةِ وَفِي كُلِّ سَاعَةٍ:

In this moment, and in every moment (always):

وَلِيًّا وَحَافِظًا وَقَآئِدًا وَنَاصِرًا وَدَلِيلًا وَعَيْنًا،

A Master, and a Protector, and a Guide, and a Helper, and a Proof, and a Guard,

حَتّٰى تُسْكِنَهُ أَرْضَكَ طَوْعًا،

until he resides peacefully on Your Earth,

وَتُـمَتِّعَهُ فِـيهَا طَوِيلًا.

and let him enjoy (his reign) for a long time.

Ziyārat Āle Yāsīn

بِسْمِ ٱللَّهِ ٱلرَّحْمٰنِ ٱلرَّحِـــيمِ

In the Name of Allah, the All-Beneficent, the All-Merciful

أَللَّهُمَّ صَلِّ عَلَىٰ مُحَمَّدٍ وَّ آلِ مُحَمَّدٍ.

O Allah send Your blessings on Muḥammad and the family of Muḥammad.

سَلَامٌ عَلَىٰ آلِ يٰـسٓ.

Peace be upon (the) progeny of Yāsīn.

أَلسَّلَامُ عَلَيْكَ يَا دَاعِيَ ٱللَّهِ وَرَبَّانِـيَّ آيَاتِهِ.

Peace be upon you, O the caller of Allah and place of manifestation of His signs.

أَلسَّلَامُ عَلَيْكَ يَا بَابَ ٱللّٰهِ وَدَيَّانَ دِينِهِ.

Peace be upon you, O the door of Allah and the devout one of His religion.

أَلسَّلَامُ عَلَيْكَ يَا خَلِيفَةَ ٱللّٰهِ وَنَاصِرَ حَقِّهِ.

Peace be upon you, O the vicegerent of Allah and the helper of His truth.

أَلسَّلَامُ عَلَيْكَ يَا حُجَّةَ ٱللّٰهِ وَدَلِيلَ إِرَادَتِهِ.

Peace be upon you, O the proof of Allah and the symbol of His ordinance.

أَلسَّلَامُ عَلَيْكَ يَا تَالِيَ كِتَابِ ٱللّٰهِ وَتَرْجُمَانَهُ.

Peace be upon you, O the reciter of Allah's book and its interpreter.

أَلسَّلَامُ عَلَيْكَ فِي آنَاءِ لَيْلِكَ وَأَطْرَافِ نَهَارِكَ.

Peace be upon you in your night and in your day.

أَلسَّلَامُ عَلَيْكَ يَا بَقِيَّةَ ٱللّٰهِ فِي أَرْضِهِ.

Peace be upon you, O the remnant of Allah on His earth.

أَلسَّلَامُ عَلَيْكَ يَا مِيثَاقَ ٱللهِ ٱلَّذِي أَخَذَهُ وَوَكَّدَهُ.

Peace be upon you, O the covenant of Allah, which He took and affirmed.

أَلسَّلَامُ عَلَيْكَ يَا وَعْدَ ٱللهِ ٱلَّذِي ضَمِنَهُ.

Peace be upon you, O the promise of Allah which He guaranteed.

أَلسَّلَامُ عَلَيْكَ أَيُّهَا ٱلْعَلَمُ ٱلْـمَنْصُوبُ،

Peace by upon you, O the raised flag

وَٱلْعِلْمُ ٱلْـمَصْـبُوبُ،

and the one who is molded with knowledge,

وَٱلْغَوْثُ وَٱلرَّحْمَةُ ٱلْوَاسِعَةُ وَعْدًا غَيْرَ مَكْذُوبٍ.

the help, the far-reaching mercy, and the promise which is not a lie.

أَلسَّلَامُ عَلَيْكَ حِينَ تَقُومُ.

Peace be upon you while you are standing.

أَلسَّلَامُ عَلَيْكَ حِينَ تَقْعُدُ.

Peace be upon you while you are sitting.

أَلسَّلَامُ عَلَيْكَ حِينَ تَقْرَأُ وَتُـبَيِّنُ.

Peace be upon you when you are reading and explaining (the Qurān).

أَلسَّلَامُ عَلَيْكَ حِينَ تُصَلِّي وَتَـقْنُتُ.

Peace be upon you when you are praying and supplicating.

أَلسَّلَامُ عَلَيْكَ حِينَ تَرْكَعُ وَتَسْجُدُ.

Peace be upon you when you are bowing (in *rukū'*) and prostrating (in *sajdah*).

أَلسَّلَامُ عَلَيْكَ حِينَ تُـهَلِّلُ وَتُكَبِّرُ.

Peace be upon you when you are announcing the *tahlīl* (saying: 'There is no god but Allah') and *takbīr* (saying: 'Allah is greater [than can be described]').

أَلسَّلَامُ عَلَيْكَ حِينَ تَحْمَدُ وَتَسْتَغْفِرُ.

Peace be upon you when you are praising (Allah) and seeking forgiveness.

أَلسَّلَامُ عَلَيْكَ حِينَ تُصْبِحُ وَتُـمْسِي.

Peace be upon you when you enter the morning and the evening.

أَلسَّلَامُ عَلَيْكَ فِي ٱللَّيْلِ اِذَا يَغْشىٰ وَٱلنَّهَارِ إِذَا تَجَلَّى.

Peace be upon you in the night when it envelops and the day when it becomes manifest.

أَلسَّلَامُ عَلَيْكَ أَيُّهَا ٱلإِمَامُ ٱلْـمَأْمُونُ.

Peace be upon you, O the protected leader.

أَلسَّلَامُ عَلَيْكَ أَيُّهَا ٱلْـمُقَدَّمُ ٱلْـمَأْمُولُ.

Peace be upon you, O the one whose coming is hoped for.

أَلسَّلَامُ عَلَيْكَ بِجَوَامِعِ ٱلسَّلَامِ.

Peace be upon you by the collections of the salutations.

أُشْهِدُكَ يَا مَوْلَاىَ أَنِّي أَشْهَدُ أَنْ لَا اِلٰهَ إِلَّا ٱللّٰهُ،

I call you as a witness, O my Master, that certainly I testify that there is no god except Allah,

وَحْدَهُ لَا شَرِيكَ لَـهُ.

He is alone, there is no partner with Him.

وَأَنْ مُحَمَّدًا عَبْدُهُ وَرَسُوْلُهُ لَا حَبِيبَ إِلَّا هُوَ وَأَهْلُهُ.

And (I testify) that indeed Muḥammad is His servant and His Apostle; there is no beloved except him and his progeny.

وَأُشْهِدُكَ يَا مَوْلَايَ أَنْ عَلِيًّا أَمِيرَ ٱلْـمُؤْمِنِينَ حُجَّتُهُ،

And I call you as a witness, O my Master, that certainly ʿAlī, the Commander of the Believers is His proof;

وَٱلْـحَسَنَ حُجَّتُهُ،

and Ḥasan is His proof;

وَٱلْـحُسَيْنَ حُجَّتُهُ،

and Ḥusayn is His proof;

وَعَلِيَّ بْنَ ٱلْـحُسَيْنِ حُجَّتُهُ،

and ʿAlī, son of Ḥusayn is His proof;

وَمُحَمَّدَ بْنَ عَلِيٍّ حُجَّتُهُ،

and Muḥammad, son of ʿAlī is His proof;

وَجَعْفَرَ بْنَ مُحَمَّدٍ حُجَّتُهُ،

and Jaʿfar, son of Muḥammad is His proof;

وَمُوسَىٰ بْنَ جَعْفَرٍ حُجَّتُهُ،

and Mūsā, son of Jaʿfar is His proof;

وَعَلِيَّ بْنَ مُوسَىٰ حُجَّتُهُ،

and ʿAlī, son of Mūsā is His proof;

وَمُحَمَّدَ بْنَ عَلِيٍّ حُجَّتُهُ،

and Muḥammad, son of ʿAlī is His proof;

وَعَلِيَّ بْنَ مُحَمَّدٍ حُجَّتُهُ،

and ʿAlī, son of Muḥammad is His proof;

وَٱلْحَسَنَ بْنَ عَلِيٍّ حُجَّتُهُ،

and Ḥasan, son of ʿAlī is His proof;

وَأَشْهَدُ أَنْكَ حُجَّةُ ٱللّٰهِ.

and I testify that indeed you are the proof of Allah.

أَنْتُمُ ٱلأَوَّلُ وَٱلآخِرُ.

You (all) are the first and the last.

وَأَنَّ رَجْعَتَكُمْ حَقٌّ لَا رَيْبَ فِيهَا،

And surely your return is a truth, there is no doubt in it,

يَوْمَ لَا يَنْفَعُ نَفْسًا إِيْـمَانُـهَا لَمْ تَكُنْ آمَنَتْ مِنْ قَبْلُ أَوْ

كَسَبَتْ فِي إِيْـمَانِـهَا خَيْرًا.

(on) the day when (the) belief of none will benefit them who previously did not believe or acquired goodness through their belief.

وَأَنَّ ٱلْـمَوْتَ حَقٌّ،

And indeed death is (an inescapable) truth;

وَأَنَّ نَاكِرًا وَنَكِيرًا حَقٌّ،

and indeed (the questioning of) *Nākir* and *Nakīr* is truth;

وَأَشْهَدُ أَنَّ ٱلنَّشْرَ حَقٌّ،

and I testify that indeed the dispersion (on the Day of Judgement) is a truth;

وَالْبَعْثَ حَقٌّ،

and the resurrection is a truth;

وَأَنَّ ٱلصِّرَاطَ حَقٌّ،

and indeed the (narrow) bridge (over Hell) is a truth;

وَٱلْـمِرْصَادَ حَقٌّ،

and the place of observation is a truth;

وَٱلْـمِيزَانَ حَقٌّ،

and the (measuring) scale is a truth;

وَٱلْحَشْرَ حَقٌّ،

and the gathering (of all human beings) is a truth;

وَٱلْحِسَابَ حَقٌّ،

and the accounting (of deeds) is a truth;

وَٱلْجَـنَّةَ وَٱلنَّارَ حَقٌّ،

and Paradise and Hell is truth;

وَٱلْوَعْدَ وَٱلْوَعِيدَ بِهِمَا حَقٌّ.

and the promise and the threat of both of them are truth.

يَا مَوْلايَ شَقِيَ مَنْ خَالَـفَكُمْ وَسَعِدَ مَنْ أَطَاعَكُمْ.

O my master, one who opposes you (all) is wretched and the one who obeys you (all) is successful.

فَاشْهَدْ عَلىٰ مَا أَشْهَدْتُكَ عَلَيْهِ.

Then testify whatever I made you a witness upon.

وَأَنَا وَلِيٌّ لَكَ بَرِيـءٌ مِنْ عَدُوِّكَ.

And I am a friend of yours, distanced from your enemy.

فَالْحَقُّ مَا رَضِـيتُمُوهُ،

So the truth is whatever you are pleased with,

وَٱلْبَاطِلُ مَا سَخِطْـتُمُوهُ،

and falsehood is whatever you are angry with,

وَٱلْـمَعْرُوفُ مَا أَمَرْتُمْ بِهِ،

and goodness is whatever you have ordered,

وَٱلْـمُنْكَرُ مَا نَـهَـيْتُمْ عَنْهُ.

and evil is whatever you have prohibited.

فَنَفْسِي مُؤْمِنَةٌ بِاللّٰهِ وَحْدَهُ لَا شَرِيكَ لَهُ،

So I am a believer in Allah, the One, He has no partner,

وَبِرَسُولِهِ،

and (I am a believer) in His Messenger,

وَبِأَمِيرِ الْـمُؤْمِنِينَ،

and in the Commander of the Faithful,

وَبِكُمْ يَا مَوْلَايَ أَوَّلِكُمْ وَآخِرِكُمْ.

and in you, O my master, the first among you and the last among you.

وَنُصْرَتِي مُعَدَّةٌ لَكُمْ،

And my help is ready for you,

وَمَوَدَّتِي خَالِصَةٌ لَـكُمْ.

and my love is purely for you.

آمِينَ آمِينَ.

Ameen! Ameen! (Accept! Accept! [whatever I have asked for]).

The following *Du'ā'* should then be recited to complete this *Ziyārat*:

أَللّٰهُمَّ أَنِّي أَسْأَلُكَ أَنْ تُصَلِّيَ عَلىٰ مُحَمَّدٍ نَبِيِّ رَحْمَتِكَ،

O Allah, surely I ask You to send blessings upon Muḥammad - the Prophet of Your mercy,

وَكَلِمَةِ نُورِكَ.

and the Word of Your Light.

وَأَنْ تَـمْلأَ قَلْبِي نُورَ ٱلْيَقِينِ،

To fill my heart with the light of certainty;

وَصَدْرِي نُورَ ٱلإِيـمَانِ،

and my chest with light of faith;

وَفِكْرِي نُورَ ٱلنِّيَّاتِ،

and my thinking with the light of intentions;

وَعَزْمِي نُورَ ٱلْعِلْمِ،

and my determination with the light of knowledge;

وَقُوَّتِي نُورَ ٱلْعَمَلِ،

and my strength with the light of action;

وَلِسَانِي نُورَ ٱلصِّدْقِ،

and my tongue with the light of truthfulness;

وَدِيـنِي نُورَ ٱلْبَصَائِرِ مِنْ عِنْدِكَ،

and my religion with the light of understanding from You;

وَبَصَرِي نُورَ ٱلضِّـيَآءِ،

and my vision with the light of illumination;

وَسَمْعِي نُورَ ٱلْحِكْمَةِ،

and my hearing with the light of wisdom;

وَمَوَدَّتِي نُورَ ٱلْـمُوَالَاةِ لِـمُحَمَّدٍ وَآلِهِ عَلَيْهِمُ السَّلَامُ،

and my love with the light of friendship for Muḥammad and his progeny, peace be upon all of them,

حَتَّىٰ أَلْقَاكَ وَقَدْ وَفَيْتُ بِعَهْدِكَ وَمِيثَاقِكَ.

until I meet You having certainly fulfilled (my duty to) Your promise and Your covenant.

فَتُغَشِّيَنِي رَحْمَتَكَ يَا وَلِيُّ يَا حَمِيدُ.

So You cover me with Your mercy, O Master! O Praiseworthy.

أَللّٰـهُمَّ صَلِّ عَلىٰ مُحَمَّدٍ حُجَّتِكَ فِي أَرْضِكَ،

O Allah, send Your blessings upon Muḥammad, Your proof on Your earth;

وَخَلِيفَتِكَ فِي بِلَادِكَ،

and your vicegerent over Your lands;

وَٱلدَّاعِي إِلىٰ سَبِيلِكَ،

and the caller towards Your way;

وَٱلْقَائِمِ بِقِسْطِكَ،

and the establisher of Your justice;

وَٱلسَّائِرِ بِأَمْرِكَ،

and the one who follows Your command,

وَلِيِّ ٱلْمُؤْمِنِينَ،

and the master of the believers,

وَبَوَارِ ٱلْـكَافِرِينَ،

and the (cause of) ruin of the disbelievers;

وَمُجَلِّي ٱلظُّلْمَةِ،

and the enlightener of the darkness;

وَمُنِيرِ ٱلْحَقِّ وَٱلنَّاطِقِ بِالْحِكْمَةِ وَٱلصِّدْقِ،

and the illuminator of the truth; the speaker with wisdom and truth;

وَكَلِمَتِكَ ٱلتَّآمَّةِ فِي أَرْضِكَ،

and Your complete Word on Your Earth,

ٱلْـمُرْتَقِبِ ٱلْخَآئِفِ وَٱلْوَلِيِّ ٱلنَّاصِحِ،

the anxious anticipator and the counselling master;

سَـفِينَةِ ٱلنَّجَاةِ،

the ship of salvation;

وَعَلَمِ ٱلْـهُدىٰ،

and the flag of guidance;

وَنُورِ أَبْصَارِ ٱلْوَرىٰ،

and the light of the sight of humanity;

وَخَيْرِ مَنْ تَقَمَّصَ وَٱرْتَدىٰ،

and the best of he who was attired and was clothed;

وَمُجَلِّي ٱلْعَمىٰ،

and the illuminator of the blind;

ٱلَّذِي يَمْلَاءُ ٱلأَرْضَ عَدْلًا وَقِسْطًا،

the one who will fill the earth with justice and equity,

كَمَا مُلِئَتْ ظُلْمًا وَجَوْرًا.

just as it was filled with injustice and oppression.

إِنَّكَ عَلىٰ كُلِّ شَيْءٍ قَدِيرٌ.

Surely You are Powerful over all things.

أَللّٰهُمَّ صَلِّ عَلىٰ وَلِيِّكَ وَٱبْنِ أَوْلِيَائِكَ،

O Allah, send Your blessings upon Your close friend and son of Your close friends,

أَلَّذِينَ فَرَضْتَ طَاعَتَهُمْ،

those whom You have ordered (us) to obey,

وَأَوْجَبْتَ حَقَّهُمْ،

and whom You made (the observation of) their rights compulsory;

وَأَذْهَبْتَ عَنْهُمُ ٱلرِّجْسَ وَطَهَّرْتَـهُمْ تَطْهِيرًا.

and You removed from them all uncleanliness and purified them with a thorough purification.

أَللّٰـهُمَّ ٱنْصُرْهُ وَٱنْـتَصِرْ بِهِ لِدِيـنِكَ،

O Allah, help him and come to the aid of Your religion through him,

وَٱنْصُرْ بِهِ أَوْلِيَائَكَ وَ أَوْلِيَائَهُ،

and help Your close friends – (those who are) his friends,

وَشِيعَتَهُ وَأَنْصَارَهُ وَٱجْعَلْنَا مِنْهُمْ.

and his followers and his helpers, and place us among them.

أَللّـٰهُمَّ أَعِذْهُ مِنْ شَرِّ كُلِّ بَاغٍ وَطَاغٍ وَمِنْ شَرِّ جَمِيعِ خَلْقِكَ،

O Allah, protect him from the evil of every tyrant and despot, and from the evil of all Your creatures;

وَٱحْفَظْهُ مِنْ بَيْنَ يَدَيْهِ وَمِنْ خَلْفِهِ وَعَنْ يَـمِيـنِهِ وَعَنْ شِـمَالِهِ،

and grant him protection from his front, his back, his right and his left;

وَٱحْرُسْهُ وَٱمْنَعْهُ مِنْ أَنْ يُوصَلَ إِلَيْهِ بِسُوءٍ.

and protect him, and prevent the reaching of any evil towards him.

وَٱحْفَظْ فِيهِ رَسُولَكَ وَآلَ رَسُولِكَ،

And protect Your Prophet and the family of Your Prophet through him,

وَأَظْهِرْ بِهِ ٱلْعَدْلَ وَأَيِّدْهُ بِالنَّصْرِ،

and make justice manifest through him; support him by victory;

وَٱنْصُرْ نَاصِرِيهِ وَٱخْذُلْ خَاذِلِيهِ،

and aid his helpers and abandon his deserters;

وَٱقْصِمْ قَاصِمِيهِ وَٱقْصِمْ بِهِ جَبَابِرَةَ ٱلْكُفْرِ.

and crush his enemies and break up the forces of disbelief through him.

وَٱقْتُلْ بِهِ ٱلْكُفَّارَ وَٱلْمُنَافِقِينَ وَجَمِيعَ ٱلْمُلْحِدِينَ

حَيْثُ كَانُوا،

And through him, kill the disbelievers and the hypocrites and all the infidels wherever they be,

مِنْ مَشَارِقِ ٱلأَرْضِ وَمَغَارِبِهَا،

in the east of the earth and its west,

بَرِّهَا وَبَحْرِهَا.

and its land and its sea.

وَٱمْلأْ بِهِ ٱلأَرْضَ عَدْلاً،

Fill the Earth with justice through him,

وَأَظْهِرْ بِهِ دِينَ نَبِيِّكَ صَلَّى ٱللّٰهُ عَلَيْهِ وَآلِهِ.

and manifest the religion of Your Prophet, blessings be upon him and his progeny (through him).

وَٱجْعَلْنِي ٱللّٰهُمَّ مِنْ أَنْصَارِهِ وَأَعْوَانِهِ وَأَتْبَاعِهِ وَشِيعَتِهِ،

And place me, O Allah, among his helpers and his aides and his followers and his partisans,

وَأَرِنِي فِي آلِ مُحَمَّدٍ عَلَيْهِمُ السَّلاَمُ مَا يَأْمُلُونَ،

and show me in the progeny of Muḥammad, peace be upon them, whatever they are hoping for,

وَفِي عَدُوِّهِمْ مَا يَحْذَرُونَ،

and in their enemies whatever they (the enemies) are afraid of,

إِلٰهَ ٱلْحَقِّ آمِينَ.

O Lord of the Truth, Āmīn (Accept).

يَا ذَا ٱلْجَلاَلِ وَٱلإِكْرَامِ يَا أَرْحَمَ ٱلرَّاحِمِينَ.

O the Possessor of Splendour and Honour! O the Most Merciful One of those who show mercy!

Comprehensive Visitation (Ziyārah)

After completing our daily prayers *(ṣalāt)*, and supplications *(duʿās)* previously noted, and before we leave the prayer mat, we should send our greetings upon the emissaries sent by Allah ﷿ for our guidance.

Keeping in daily touch with these honoured personalities which Allah ﷿ has chosen through the following supplication/visitation is one way to remember them.

بِسْمِ ٱللَّهِ ٱلرَّحْمَٰنِ ٱلرَّحِيمِ

In the Name of Allah, the All-Compassionate, the All-Merciful.

أَللّٰهُمَّ أَنْتَ ٱلسَّلَامُ،

O Allah! Truly You are Peace,

وَمِنْكَ ٱلسَّلَامُ،

and from You comes Peace,

وَلَكَ ٱلسَّلَامُ،

and for You is Peace,

وَإِلَيْكَ يَعُودُ ٱلسَّلَامُ.

and back to You returns Peace.

سُبْحَانَ رَبِّكَ رَبِّ ٱلْعِزَّةِ عَمَّا يَصِفُونَ،

Glory be to your Lord, the Lord of Greatness, from that which they attribute (to You),

وَسَلَامٌ عَلَىٰ ٱلْمُرْسَلِينَ،

and peace be upon those who have been sent (as Messengers),

وَٱلْحَمْدُ لِلَّهِ رَبِّ ٱلْعَالَمِينَ.

and all praise belongs to Allah, Lord of the Worlds.

أَلسَّلَامُ عَلَيْكَ أَيُّهَا ٱلنَّبِيُّ وَرَحْمَةُ ٱللَّهِ وَبَرَكَاتُهُ.

Peace be upon you, O (the final) Prophet, and may the Mercy of Allah and His blessings (be upon you).

أَلسَّلَامُ عَلَىٰ ٱلْأَئِمَّةِ ٱلْهَادِينَ ٱلْمَهْدِيِّينَ.

Peace be upon the guiding and guided leaders.

أَلسَّلَامُ عَلىٰ جَمِيعِ أَنْبِيَاءِ ٱللهِ وَرُسُلِهِ وَمَلآئِكَتِهِ.

Peace be upon all of the Prophets of Allah, and His Messengers, and His Angels.

أَلسَّلَامُ عَلَيْنَا وَعَلىٰ عِبَادِ ٱللهِ ٱلصَّالِحِينَ.

Peace be upon us, and upon all of the righteous servants of Allah.

أَلسَّلَامُ عَلىٰ عَلِيٍّ أَمِيرِ ٱلْمُؤْمِنِينَ.

Peace be upon ʿAlī, the Commander of the Faithful *[Amīr al-Muʾminīn].*

أَلسَّلَامُ عَلىٰ ٱلْحَسَنِ وَٱلْحُسَيْنِ سَيِّدَيْ شَبَابِ أَهْلِ ٱلْجَنَّةِ أَجْمَعِينَ.

Peace be upon Ḥasan and Ḥusayn, the Leaders of all the Youth of Paradise.

أَلسَّلَامُ عَلىٰ عَلِيِّ بْنِ ٱلْحُسَيْنِ زَيْنِ ٱلْعَابِدِينَ.

Peace be upon ʿAlī, son of Ḥusayn, the Ornament of the Worshippers *[Zayn al-ʿĀbidīn].*

أَلسَّلَامُ عَلَىٰ مُـحَمَّدِ بْنِ عَلِيٍّ بَاقِرِ عِلْمِ ٱلنَّبِيِّـينَ.

Peace be upon Muḥammad, son of ʿAlī, the Splitter of Knowledge of the Prophets *[Bāqir al-ʿUlūm].*

أَلسَّلَامُ عَلَىٰ جَعْفَرِ بْنِ مُـحَمَّدٍ ٱلصَّادِقِ.

Peace be upon Jaʿfar, son of Muhammad, the Truthful One *[al-Ṣādiq].*

أَلسَّلَامُ عَلَىٰ مُوسَىٰ بْنِ جَعْفَرٍ ٱلْكَاظِمِ.

Peace be upon Mūsā, son of Jaʿfar, the One who Suppresses his Anger *[al-Kāẓim].*

أَلسَّلَامُ عَلَىٰ عَلِيِّ بْنِ مُوسَى ٱلرِّضَا.

Peace be upon ʿAlī, son of Mūsā, the Pleased One *[al-Riḍā].*

أَلسَّلَامُ عَلَىٰ مُـحَمَّدِ بْنِ عَلِيٍّ ٱلْـجَوَادِ.

Peace be upon Muḥammad, son of ʿAlī, the Generous One *[al-Jawād].*

أَلسَّلَامُ عَلَىٰ عَلِيِّ بْنِ مُـحَمَّدٍ ٱلْـهَادِي.

Peace be upon ʿAlī, son of Muḥammad, the Spiritual Guide *[al-Hādī].*

أَلسَّلَامُ عَلَىٰ ٱلْـحَسَنِ بْنِ عَلِيٍّ، ٱلزَّكِيِّ ٱلْعَسْكَرِيِّ.

Peace be upon Ḥasan, son of ʿAlī, the Purified One *[al-Zakī]*, the One [who lived under surveillance] in a Military Camp *[al-ʿAskarī]*.

أَلسَّلَامُ عَلَىٰ ٱلْـحُجَّةِ بْنِ ٱلْـحَسَنِ ٱلْقَائِمِ ٱلْـمَهْدِيِّ.

Peace be upon al-Ḥujjah, son of Ḥasan, the One who will Rise Up *[al-Qāʾim]*, the Guided One *[al-Mahdī]*.

صَلَوَاتُ ٱللّٰهِ عَلَيْهِمْ أَجْـمَعِينَ.

May the blessings of Allah be upon all of them.

Supplication (Duʿāʾ) Taught by Imam al-Mahdī عجل الله تعالى فرجه الشريف

This brief, yet powerful, and meaningful supplication has been taught to us directly by Imam al-Mahdī عجل الله تعالى فرجه الشريف. It is unique in that in his own words, the final and awaited saviour of humanity is teaching us not only a supplication to make to Allah عز وجل, but more importantly, some of the most important traits we must try to instill within ourselves; and qualities which various people in our Muslim society need to strive to attain.

Not only does this supplication focus on ourselves, but it expands to praying for so many others, such as our religious scholars; the students; those who listen to lectures; the sick; the deceased; the seniors; the youth; the women; the rich; the poor; those struggling in the Way of Allah عز وجل; the wrongfully imprisoned; the political leaders; the citizens of the countries; and last, but not least, those who are embarking on *Ḥajj*, *ʿUmrah*, and *Ziyārāt* to the scared Shrines.

What a beautiful supplication that our awaited master has taught us in which we not only think about ourselves and our needs, but we are also concerned about every other segment of our Muslim society and are instructed to pray for the betterment of one another!

بِسْمِ ٱللَّهِ ٱلرَّحْمَٰنِ ٱلرَّحِيمِ

In the Name of Allah, the All-Compassionate, the All-Merciful.

أَللّٰهُمَّ ارْزُقْنَا تَوْفِيقَ ٱلطَّاعَةِ،

O Allah, grant us the good fortune of being obedient (to You),

وَبُعْدَ ٱلْمَعْصِيَةِ،

and (keep us) away from disobedience,

وَصِدْقَ ٱلنِّيَّةِ،

and (let us be) sincere in our intentions,

وَعِرْفَانَ ٱلْحُرْمَةِ،

and (provide us with) the understanding of what is revered,

وَأَكْرِمْنَا بِالْهُدٰى وَٱلْإِسْتِقَامَةِ،

and honour us with guidance and determination,

وَسَدِّدْ أَلْسِنَتَنَا بِالصَّوَابِ وَٱلْحِكْمَةِ،

and direct our tongues to what is right and wise,

وَٱمْلَأْ قُلُوبَنَا بِالْعِلْمِ وَٱلْمَعْرِفَةِ،

and fill our hearts with knowledge and cognizance,

وَطَهِّرْ بُطُونَنَا مِنَ ٱلْحَرَامِ وَٱلشُّبْهَةِ،

and purify our stomachs from the forbidden and doubtful (food and drink),

وَٱكْفُفْ أَيْدِيَنَا عَنِ ٱلظُّلْمِ وَٱلسَّرِقَةِ،

and prevent our hands from oppression and theft,

وَٱغْضُضْ أَبْصَارَنَا عَنِ ٱلْفُجُورِ وَٱلْخِيَانَةِ،

and (help us to be able to) lower our gaze (out of modesty) from immorality and treachery,

وَٱسْدُدْ أَسْمَاعَنَا عَنِ ٱللَّغْوِ وَٱلْغِيبَةِ،

and protect our ears from listening to foolish, worthless talk and backbiting,

وَتَفَضَّلْ عَلىٰ عُلَمَائِنَا بِالزُّهْدِ وَٱلنَّصِيحَةِ،

and bless our religious scholars with piety, and the ability to offer sincere advice,

وَعَلىٰ ٱلْمُتَعَلِّمِينَ بِالْجُهْدِ وَٱلرَّغْبَةِ،

and (bless) the students with the (ability to) struggle and desire to learn,

وَعَلىٰ ٱلْمُسْتَمِعِينَ بِالْإِتِّبَاعِ وَٱلْمَوْعِظَةِ،

and (bless) those who listen (to religious teachings) with the desire to follow them,

وَعَلىٰ مَرْضىٰ ٱلْمُسْلِمِينَ بِالشِّفَاءِ وَٱلرَّاحَةِ،

and (grant) the Muslims who are suffering from illnesses, with cure and ease,

وَعَلىٰ مَوْتَاهُمْ بِالرَّأْفَةِ وَٱلرَّحْمَةِ،

and (bless) their deceased ones with kindness and mercy,

وَعَلىٰ مَشَايِخِنَا بِالْوَقَارِ وَٱلسَّكِينَةِ،

and (grant) our seniors' dignity and peace of mind (tranquillity in the heart),

وَعَلىٰ ٱلشَّبَابِ بِالْإِنَابَةِ وَٱلتَّوْبَةِ،

and (grant) the youth remorse (from their sins) and repentance (guidance to turn back to Allah and repent),

وَعَلىٰ ٱلنِّسَاءِ بِالْحَيَاءِ وَٱلْعِفَّةِ،

and (bestow upon) the women modesty and chastity,

وَعَلىٰ ٱلْأَغْنِيَاءِ بِالتَّوَاضُعِ وَٱلسَّعَةِ،

and (allow) the rich (to deal) with humility and (have) generosity,

وَعَلىٰ ٱلْفُقَرَاءِ بِالصَّبْرِ وَٱلْقَنَاعَةِ،

and (bless) the poor with patience and contentment,

وَعَلىٰ ٱلْغُزَاةِ بِالنَّصْرِ وَٱلْغَلَبَةِ،

and (give) those fighting in Your way assistance and victory,

وَعَلىٰ ٱلْأُسَرَاءِ بِالْخَلَاصِ وَٱلرَّاحَةِ،

and (bless) the imprisoned ones (prisoners) with freedom (salvation) and ease,

وَعَلىٰ ٱلْأُمَرَاءِ بِٱلْعَدْلِ وَٱلشَّفَقَةِ،

and (instill) the rulers with justice and kindness,

وَعَلَىٰ ٱلرَّعِيَّةِ بِالْإِنْصَافِ وَحُسْنِ ٱلسِّيرَةِ،

and (enable) the ruled ones (subjects) to receive just (fair) treatment and good character,

وَبَارِكْ لِلْحُجَّاجِ وَٱلزُّوَّارِ فِي ٱلزَّادِ وَٱلنَّفَقَةِ،

and bless those who have gone to *Ḥajj* and *Ziyārat* with adequate (and increased) support,

وَٱقْضِ مَا أَوْجَبْتَ عَلَيْهِمْ مِنَ ٱلْحَجِّ وَٱلْعُمْرَةِ.

and help them complete what is obligatory upon them in *Ḥajj* and *ʿUmrah.*

بِفَضْلِكَ وَرَحْمَتِكَ يَا أَرْحَمَ ٱلرَّاحِمِينَ.

With Your Grace and Your Mercy, O the Most Merciful One of those who show mercy!

اللهم صل على محمد وآل محمد وعجل فرجهم

O Allah! Send Your blessings upon Muḥammad and the family of Muḥammad and hasten their relief [through the advent of the 12th Imam]!

Other Publications Available[1]

1. *A Land Most Goodly: The Story of Yemen in the Quran and in the Times of Prophet Muḥammad and Imam ʿAlī ibn Abī Ṭālib,* by Jaffer Ladak
2. *A Star Amongst the Stars: The Life and Times of the Great Companion: Jabir ibn Abdullah al-Ansari,* by Jaffer Ladak*
3. *Alif, Baa, Taa of Kerbala,* by Saleem Bhimji and Arifa Hudda
4. *Arbāʿīn of Imam Ḥusayn,* compiled and translated by Saleem Bhimji
5. *Daily Devotions,* compiled and translated by Saleem Bhimji*
6. *Deficient? A Review of Sermon 80 from Nahj al-Balāgha,* by Āyatullāh al-ʿUẓmā Shaykh Nāṣir Makārim Shīrāzī and translated by Saleem Bhimji
7. *Exegesis of the 29th Juz of the Quran a Translation of Tafsīr Nemunah,* by Āyatullāh al-ʿUẓmā Shaykh Nāṣir Makārim

[1] The following is a list of all the original writings and translations from the Islamic Publishing House. As many of these titles are out of stock, we are slowly re-releasing all our works via Print-on-Demand through various online services. You can find all the titles with a "*" after the name at **https://mybook.to/pH0x**. If you cannot find any of the above titles online, feel free to email us at **iph@iph.ca**.

Shīrāzī and translated by Saleem Bhimji*

8. *Foundations of Islamic Unity* a translation of *Al-Fuṣūl al-Muhimmah fī Ta'līf al-Ummah,* by ʿAbd al-Ḥusayn Sharaf al-Dīn al-Mūsawī al-ʿĀmilī and translated by Batool Ispahany*
9. *Fountain of Paradise: Fāṭima az-Zahrā' in the Noble Quran,* by Āyatullāh al-ʿUẓmā Shaykh Nāṣir Makārim Shīrāzī, compiled and translated by Saleem Bhimji*
10. *God and god of Science,* by Syed Hasan Raza Jafri*
11. *House of Sorrows,* by Shaykh ʿAbbās al-Qummī and translated by Aejaz Ali Turab Husayn Husayni*
12. *Iʿtikāf: The Spiritual Retreat – The Philosophy, Spiritual Mysteries and Practical Rulings,* compiled and translated by Saleem Bhimji*
13. *Inspirational Insights,* by Mohammed Khaku
14. *Islam and Religious Pluralism,* by Āyatullāh Murtaḍā Muṭahharī and translated by Sayyid Sulayman Ali Hasan
15. *Journey to Eternity – A Handbook of Supplications for the Soul,* compiled and translated by Saleem Bhimji and Arifa Hudda*
16. *Living The Quran Through The Living Quran: Sūrah al-Fātiḥa (1),* by Shaykh Muḥsin Qarā'atī, translated by Saleem Bhimji*
17. *Living The Quran Through The Living Quran: Sūrah Yāsīn (36),* by Shaykh Muḥsin Qarā'atī, translated by Saleem Bhimji*
18. *Living The Quran Through The Living Quran: Sūrah Qāf (50),* by Shaykh Muḥsin Qarā'atī, translated by Saleem Bhimji*
19. *Living The Quran Through The Living Quran: Sūrah al-*

Najm (53), by Shaykh Muḥsin Qarāʾatī, translated by Saleem Bhimji*

20. *Living The Quran Through The Living Quran: Sūrah al-Wāqiʿah (56),* by Shaykh Muḥsin Qarāʾatī, translated by Saleem Bhimji*
21. *Living The Quran Through The Living Quran: Sūrah al-Mujādilah (58),* by Shaykh Muḥsin Qarāʾatī, translated by Saleem Bhimji*
22. *Love and Hate for Allah's Sake,* by Mujtaba Saburi, translated by Saleem Bhimji*
23. *Love for the Family,* compiled and translated by Yasin T. Al-Jibouri, Saleem Bhimji, and others*
24. *Moral Management,* by Abbas Rahimi, translated by Saleem Bhimji*
25. *Morals of the Masumeen,* by Arifa Hudda
26. *Prayers of the Final Prophet – A Collection of Supplications of Prophet Muḥammad,* by ʿAllāmah Sayyid Muḥammad Ḥusayn Ṭabāʾṭabāʾī, translated by Tahir Ridha-Jaffer*
27. *Propaganda and Piety: The Umayyad Rewriting of Syria [From Historical Syria to Apocalyptic Syria],* written by Shaykh Rasul Jafariyan, translated by Saleem Bhimji*
28. *Prospering Through a Cost of Living Crisis,* by Jaffer Ladak*
29. *Ramaḍān Reflections,* compiled by A Group of Muslim Scholars, translated by Saleem Bhimji*
30. *Ṣalāt al-Āyāt,* by Saleem Bhimji
31. *Ṣalāt al-Ghufaylah: Salvation through Patience & Perseverance,* written by Saleem Bhimji*
32. *Secrets of the Ḥajj,* by Āyatullāh al-ʿUẓmā Shaykh Ḥusayn Mazāherī, translated by Saleem Bhimji

33. *Sunan an-Nabī,* by ʿAllāmah Sayyid Muḥammad Ḥusayn Ṭabāʾṭabāʾī, translated by Tahir Ridha-Jaffer
34. *Tears from Heaven's Flowers: An Anthology of English Poetry about the Ahlulbayt,* by Abrahim al-Zubeidi*
35. *The Day the Germs Caused Fitnah,* by Umm Maryam*
36. *The Firmest Armament: Commentary on Āyatul Kursī (The Verse of the Throne),* by Sayyid Nasrullah Burujerdi, translated by Saleem Bhimji*
37. *The Last Luminary and Ways to Delve into the Light,* by Sayyid Muhammad Ridha Husayni Mutlaq, translated by Saleem Bhimji*
38. *The Muslim Legal Will Booklet,* by Saleem Bhimji*
39. *The Pure Life,* by Āyatullāh al-ʿUẓmā as-Sayyid Muḥammad Taqī al-Modarresī, translated by Jaffer Ladak with commentary by Dr. Zainali Panjwani and Jaffer Ladak*
40. *The Third Testimony: Imam ʿAlī in the Adhān,* compiled and translated by Saleem Bhimji*
41. *The Torch of Perpetual Guidance – A Brief Commentary on Ziyārat al-ʿĀshūrāʾ,* by ʿAbbās Azizi, translated by Saleem Bhimji
42. *The Tragedy of Kerbalāʾ,* as narrated by Imam ʿAlī ibn al-Ḥusayn al-Sajjād عليه السلام, recorded by Shaykh al-Ṣadūq, translated by ʿAbdul Zahrāʾ ʿAbdul Ḥusayn*
43. *The Truth Revealed: Volume 1,* by Hamid bin Shabbir, translated by Mir Baqir Alikhan, Syed Hamid Rizvi, and Kaniz Fatima Alikhan
44. *The Truth Revealed: Volume 2,* by Hamid bin Shabbir, translated by Mir Baqir Alikhan, Syed Hamid Rizvi, and Kaniz Fatima Alikhan*

45. *The Truth Revealed: Volume 3,* by Hamid bin Shabbir, translated by Mir Baqir Alikhan, Syed Hamid Rizvi, and Kaniz Fatima Alikhan

46. *Weapon of the Believer,* by ʿAllāmah Muḥammad Bāqir Majlisī, translated by Saleem Bhimji*

47. *Weekly Spiritual Ascent: Ṣalāt al-Jumuʿah: Philosophy, Practice, and Personal Piety,* compiled and translated by Saleem Bhimji*

Other Translations[2]

1. *40 Aḥādīth: Completion of Islam – Ghadīr,* by Mahmud Sharifi ⁺
2. *40 Aḥādīth: Qurʾan,* by Sayyid Majid Adili, translated by Arifa Hudda and Saleem Bhimji ⁺
3. *40 Aḥādīth: The Saviour of Humanity – The 12th Imam in the Eyes of the Ahl al-Bayt,* by Nasir Karimi ⁺

---

[2] The following are other translations by Saleem Bhimji available from various publishers:

- Books with a "⁺" are published by The World Federation of KSIMC – **www.world-federation.org**
- Books with a "⁺⁺" are published by Islamic Humanitarian Service (IHS) – **www.al-haqq.net**
- Books with a "⁺⁺⁺" are published by the Islamic Publishing House (IPH), but are currently out of print – **www.iph.ca**
- Books with a "⁺⁺⁺⁺"have been published by various overseas publishers.
- Books with a "⁺⁺⁺⁺⁺" are published by Al-Kisa Foundation – **www.alkisfoundation.org**

4. *40 Aḥādīth: The Spiritual Journey – Ḥajj,* by Mahmud Mahdipur •
5. *A Biography of the Marjaʿ Taqlid of the Shiʿa World: Āyatullāh al-ʿUẓmā Sayyid ʿAlī al-Ḥusaynī Sīstānī* ••••
6. *A Code of Ethics for Muslim Men and Women,* by Sayyid Masʿud Maʿsumi, translated by Arifa Hudda and Saleem Bhimji ••
7. *A Mother's Prayer,* compiled and translated by Saleem Bhimji and Arifa Hudda •• & •••
8. *A Summary of the Rulings of Ṣalātul Jamāʿat,* according to the edicts of Āyatullāh al-ʿUẓmā Sayyid ʿAlī al-Ḥusaynī Sīstānī ••
9. *Ethical Discourses: Volume 1,* by Āyatullāh al-ʿUẓmā Shaykh Nāṣir Makārim Shīrāzī •••
10. *Ethical Discourses: Volume 2,* by Āyatullāh al-ʿUẓmā Shaykh Nāṣir Makārim Shīrāzī •••
11. *Ethical Discourses: Volume 3,* by Āyatullāh al-ʿUẓmā Shaykh Nāṣir Makārim Shīrāzī •••
12. *Guiding the Youth of the New Generation,* by Āyatullāh Murtaḍā Muṭahharī ••
13. *History Behind Masjid Jamkarān along with Selected Supplications to the 12th Imam* ••
14. *Introduction to Islam* ••
15. *Introduction to the Science of Tafsīr of the Quran,* by Shaykh Jaʿfar Subḥānī ••
16. *Islamic Edicts on Family Planning,* by the UNFPA with the Ministry of Health of the Islamic Republic of Iran ••••
17. *Istikhāra: Seeking the Best from Allah,* by Muḥammad Bāqir Ḥayderī ••

18. *Khums: The Islamic Tax,* by Āyatullāh al-ʿUẓmā Shaykh Nāṣir Makārim Shīrāzī (unpublished)
19. *Meʿrāj: The Night Ascension,* by Mullah Muḥammad Faydh al-Kāshānī **
20. *Message of the Quran: A Translation of Payām-e-Quran – Volume 1 – A Thematic Exegesis of the Noble Quran,* by Āyatullāh al-ʿUẓmā Shaykh Nāṣir Makārim Shīrāzī *
21. *Method of Ṣalāt,* by Muḥammad Qādhī ****
22. *On the Shore of Contemplation: Authority of the Jurist (Wilāyatul Faqīh)* – compiled by the office of Shaykh Jaʿfar Subḥānī ***
23. *Rules Relating to the Deceased: Condensed Version,* according to the edicts of Āyatullāh al-ʿUẓmā Sayyid ʿAlī al-Ḥusaynī Sīstānī **
24. *Rules Relating to the Deceased: Philosophy and Aḥkām,* according to the edicts of Āyatullāh al-ʿUẓmā Sayyid ʿAlī al-Ḥusaynī Sīstānī **
25. *Simplified Islamic Laws for Youth and Young Adults,* according to the edicts of Āyatullāh al-ʿUẓmā Sayyid ʿAlī al-Ḥusaynī Sīstānī **
26. *Simplified Islamic Laws for Youth and Young Adults,* according to the edicts of the late Āyatullāh al-ʿUẓmā Shaykh Luṭfullāh Ṣāfī Gulpāygānī ****
27. *The Clear Guidance: The Quran – Volume 1 of...* *****
28. *The Clear Guidance: The Quran – Volume 2 of...* *****
29. *The Islamic Moral System: A Commentary of Sūrah al-Ḥujurāt,* by Shaykh Jaʿfar Subḥānī * & **
30. *The Light of the Family of the Prophet: A Colouring Book with Ḥadīth for Young Muslim Children* **

31. *The Tasbīḥ of Fāṭima al-Zahrā'*, by 'Abbas Azizi and translated by Arifa Hudda and Saleem Bhimji **

32. *Ziyārah: History, Philosophy and Etiquette* ***

Upcoming Publications by the IPH

1. *Between Two Worlds: Navigating the Practical Laws of Burial in Islam* according to the edicts of Āyatullāh al-'Uẓmā Sayyid 'Alī al-Ḥusaynī Sīstānī, translated by Saleem Bhimji
2. *Blessed Desires: Islamic Perspectives on Sexuality and the Soul*, by 'Alī Ḥoseinzādeh, translated by Saleem Bhimji
3. *Faith on the Move: Praying while Travelling*, according to the edicts of Āyatullāh al-'Uẓmā Sayyid 'Alī al-Ḥusaynī Sīstānī, translated by Saleem Bhimji
4. *Guided By Faith: The Islamic Management Model*, by 'Abbās Raḥīmī, translated by Saleem Bhimji
5. *Knocking on Heaven's Doors*, compiled with translations by Saleem Bhimji
6. *Morals of the Masumeen (Third Edition)*, written by Arifa Hudda
7. *Planting for Paradise: 40 Ḥadīth on Farming and the Eternal Rewards of Stewardship of the Earth*, translated by Saleem Bhimji
8. *Ramaḍān Devotions: A Collection of Supplications for the Nights of Qadr*, compiled with translations by Saleem Bhimji
9. *Sacred Remembrance: Understanding the Exclusive Significance of the Arba'īn of Imam al-Ḥusayn* ﷺ, by the late Āyatullāh al-Sayyid Muḥammad Muḥsin Ḥusaynī Ṭehrānī, translated by Saleem Bhimji

10. *Secrets of the Ḥajj – Second Edition [25th Anniversary Edition]*, by Āyatullāh al-ʿUẓmā Shaykh Ḥusayn Mazāherī, translated by Saleem Bhimji
11. *Shadows of Dissent*, by Āyatullāh Nāṣir Makārim Shīrāzī, translated by Saleem Bhimji and a Group of Translators
12. *Supplication for the People of the Frontiers*, by Shaykh Ḥusayn Anṣāriān, translated by Saleem Bhimji
13. *The Arbaʿīn: A look into the Ziyārat of Arbaʿīn*, by Saleem Bhimji
14. *The Comprehensive Book of Marriage and Divorce Formulas*, by Saleem Bhimji
15. *The Ninth Day: The Complete Collection of Supplications for the Day of ʿArafah*, compiled and translated by Saleem Bhimji
16. *The Young Muslims Daily Devotions Manuals – Volumes I and II*, compiled and translated by Saleem Bhimji
17. *Victor Not Victim: A Biography of Lady Zaynab binte ʿAlī and two hundred Short Stories*, researched and written by Saleem Bhimji

The commentary of the following chapter of the Quran will also be released in the future under our, *Living The Quran Through The Living Quran*, series:

1. Sūrah al-Ṣaff (61)

Supporting Our Projects

عَنْ أَبِي عَبْدِ اللهِ عَنْ آبَائِهِ عليهم السلام: قَالَ جَآءَ رَجُلٌ إِلَىٰ رَسُولِ اللهِ ﷺ فَقَالَ: يَا رَسُولَ اللهِ مَا الْعِلْمُ؟ قَالَ أَلْإِنْصَاتُ. قَالَ ثُمَّ مَهْ؟ قَالَ أَلْإِسْتِمَاعُ. قَالَ ثُمَّ مَهْ؟ قَالَ أَلْحِفْظُ. قَالَ ثُمَّ مَهْ؟ قَالَ أَلْعَمَلُ بِهِ. قَالَ ثُمَّ مَهْ يَا رَسُولَ اللهِ؟ قَالَ: نَشْرُهُ.

Abū ʿAbdillāh [Imam Jaʿfar ibn Muḥammad al-Ṣādiq عليه السلام] narrates from his ancestors عليهم السلام who said the following: "A man once came to the Messenger of Allah ﷺ and said: 'O Messenger of Allah, what is knowledge?' The Prophet replied: **'It is silence.'** The man then asked: 'Then what?' The Prophet said: **'It is listening.'** The man asked again: 'Then what?' The Prophet replied: **'Then it is remembering.'** The man asked: 'Then what?' The Prophet said: **'Then it is to practice (according to what one has learned).'** The man then asked: 'Then what O Messenger of Allah?' The Prophet replied: **'Then it is to disseminate (what one has learned to others).'**"[148]

Established in early 2001, gaining inspiration from the above *ḥadīth* from Prophet Muḥammad ﷺ, the *Islamic Publishing House* (IPH) is North America's premier publisher of high-quality Islamic literature for Muslims of all ages. Our mission is to ensure that the authentic teachings of Islam in all aspects of life as imparted by Prophet Muḥammad ﷺ and his

[148] *Al-Kāfī*, Vol. 1, Pg. 48, Tradition 4.

immaculate family, the Ahlul Bayt, are made available for everyone – in a clear and easy to understand language.

Over the past 25 years, we have been blessed to publish close to **50** full-length books which have been distributed throughout the world in print and digital format. In addition, we have released multiple ePubs and translated hundreds of articles – all thanks to the blessings of Allah, the grace of the Prophet ﷺ, and his Ahlul Bayt, and the continued support from donors all over the world.

Our publications and video content (found on YouTube under the name **Islamic Publishing House**) are all supported by generous individuals for whom we are extremely grateful.

As we continue to produce English publications and original video content, we invite those who have a passion for the spread of the teachings of Islam as preserved by the family of the Prophet Muḥammad ﷺ – namely the Ahlul Bayt to assist us in promoting these teachings.

If you would like to donate to any of our ongoing projects, including our many upcoming book publications, video content, or articles, you can contribute in the following ways:

Within Canada: Send an e-transfer to **iph@iph.ca**

International: Send your transfer via PayPal to **saleem1176@rogers.com**

For more information, go to: **www.iph.ca**
Contact us at: **iph@iph.ca**

www.ingramcontent.com/pod-product-compliance
Lightning Source LLC
LaVergne TN
LVHW051824080426
835512LV00018B/2718
9781927930533